JOB/
SECURITY

LABOR AND TECHNOLOGY
Winifred R. Poster, series editor

Madison Van Oort, *Worn Out: How Retailers Surveil and Exploit Workers in the Digital Age and How Workers Are Fighting Back*

Sofya Aptekar, *The Green Card Soldier: Between Model Immigrant and Security Threat*

Margaret Jack, *Media Ruins: Cambodian Postwar Media Reconstruction and the Geopolitics of Technology*

Coleen Carrigan, *Cracking the Bro Code*

Danny Goodwin and Edward Schwarzschild, *Job/Security: A Composite Portrait of the Expanding American Security Industry*

JOB/
SECURITY

A COMPOSITE PORTRAIT OF THE EXPANDING AMERICAN SECURITY INDUSTRY

DANNY GOODWIN AND EDWARD SCHWARZSCHILD

foreword and afterword by Winifred R. Poster

The MIT Press
Cambridge, Massachusetts
London, England

The MIT Press would like to thank the anonymous peer reviewers who provided comments on drafts of this book. The generous work of academic experts is essential for establishing the authority and quality of our publications. We acknowledge with gratitude the contributions of these otherwise uncredited readers.

This book was set in Arnhem Pro and Interstate by The MIT Press. Printed and bound in the United States of America.

Library of Congress Cataloging-in-Publication Data

Names: Goodwin, Danny, author. | Schwarzschild, Edward, 1964– author.
Title: Job/security : a composite portrait of the expanding American security industry / Danny Goodwin and Edward Schwarzschild ; foreword and afterword by Winifred R. Poster.
Description: Cambridge, Massachusetts : The MIT Press, [2024] | Includes bibliographical references.
Identifiers: LCCN 2023045631 | ISBN 9780262048699 (hardcover)
Subjects: LCSH: Security sector—United States. | Internal security—United States. | Law enforcement—United States. | Private security services—United States.
Classification: LCC HV6419 .G66 2024 | DDC 363.2—dc23/eng/20240207
LC record available at https://lccn.loc.gov/2023045631

10   9   8   7   6   5   4   3   2   1

For our families

And nothing disrupts dehumanization more quickly than inviting someone over, looking into their eyes, hearing their voice, and listening . . .
—Sarah Schulman, *Conflict Is Not Abuse*

CONTENTS

FOREWORD

Security in the world of work has become a catchall for many different types of activities and social functions. Security can mean protecting the physical safety of an individual or their property (as security guards do). It can mean patrolling a municipality and its geographic space (as police do). It can mean protecting transport spaces like airports (as Transportation Security Administration [TSA] staff do). It can be the work of defending a nation and its interests at home or abroad (through military, intelligence, or border patrol jobs). Or alternatively, security can involve responding to an area during, before, and after a disaster (as in emergency management). Especially in recent times, it can involve protecting things that are seemingly nonmaterial—like data and digital networks (as in cybersecurity).

Security is a proliferating enterprise undertaken by state, private sector, and civil society organizations alike. Scores of new jobs are being created to perform these activities, and old jobs are transforming to incorporate security tasks and functions. Yet there has been very little accounting of what these jobs encompass, what the range of their tasks involve, and what they mean to the people involved. This book sets out to fill this gap and create a multifaceted portrait of the labor of security.

Danny Goodwin and Edward Schwarzschild have undertaken a critical and one-of-a-kind endeavor to catalog the experience of being a security worker in the context of US society. They come to this not as typical writers on the topic, that is, as labor scholars, political scientists, or military analysts. Rather, they come to it from a different place—as people who are concerned about what the industry is doing to society, and as people who are making meaning out of this process through narrative and artistic expression. Notably, they also come to it as individuals who have been affected by the encroaching security state. As I elaborate below, the work of security has diffused throughout society—even to realms where it is not expected. For these authors, this has meant that security labor has entered their homes. Both authors have fathers who have worked for this industry in one capacity or another. Schwarzschild even interfaced with security work briefly himself, in the form of a short stint as a TSA worker.

Their special talents are combined to produce a highly original documentation and interpretation of security work as a phenomenon. We are able to see the *words* that security workers use to describe their jobs, *photographs* of how such workers present themselves, *images* of the sites where workers do their jobs as well as at home, and *artistic renderings* of what security does to landscapes. While there have been compelling books on individual security jobs (e.g., police, security guards, border patrol, cybersecurity), few books have attempted to bridge the range and complexity of what security might involve, nor to present it in such a creative and humanistic way, with such a diverse set of sources.

A KALEIDOSCOPE OF WORDS AND IMAGES

This book explores security by crossing research traditions of social science, biography, humanities, art, and design. With heterogeneous methods, the authors have assembled interviews, on-site observations, photography, and art. The amount of care and thoughtfulness that has gone into decisions about each of these sources cannot be understated. In addition, Goodwin and Schwarzschild have done much of the research for this project *together* (rather than just dividing it up). They traveled to locations where security functions and administrations are happening. Moreover, they were especially sensitive in honoring requests of the workers, meeting them (even during the pandemic) at the places where those individuals wanted to be photographed. This has brought us a rare glimpse into the worlds of the interviewees, and what their stories tell about the experience and impact of the work.

For the interviews, as a first major source of material, Goodwin and Schwarzschild were careful in selecting a range of perspectives from inside this vast field. The interviews include both women and men, many different ethnic-racial and religious backgrounds, and a variety of geographic locales throughout the United States. We see a diversity of job titles, departments, and types of organizations. The authors have also included workers who have left the job. As you'll see, this is key to capturing a spectrum of viewpoints, especially from those who don't agree with what they are doing at work. The list of interviewees also includes people who are not workers themselves, but experts providing insightful analyses of the issue.

Doing a pathbreaking project of this kind comes with unique benefits and as well as compromises. On one hand, it means we get rare access to people like high-level administrators in Homeland Security, intelligence officers, and secret service personnel—some of whom we don't get to hear from very often. (No doubt, Schwarzschild's personal history in security work helped encourage the interviewees to talk so freely.)

On the other hand, researching these kinds of personnel means working within the constraints of the broader systems in which they are employed—including the secrecy of the jobs themselves. Indeed, given the extensive "securing" of information in this work, the authors encountered barriers regarding what interviewees are able to say. Sometimes this is due to formal policies of employers and organizations. In other cases, this happens more informally, as workers place restraints on themselves. They do this out of a fear that divulging too much might compromise future job prospects or their reputations in the field. In turn, some of the interviews were self-censored or reworked to remove sensitive material. I mention this not to diminish the impact of the content, but instead to remind us that there is, as usual, always more to the story.

In terms of presenting interviews to readers, the authors chose to place the interviews in the text as *transcripts*. These transcripts were carefully edited for length and clarity (in consultation with the interviewees), but remain free from the typical academic repackaging some of us are used to. I have to admit this idea was new for me. As a qualitative interviewer myself, I was not accustomed to showing interviews in their original form, without more critical analysis. Yet, interestingly, it is a strategy that shifts some of the analytical and ethical responsibility to the reader. It implicitly asks readers to make sense out of the content and draw meaning from it on their own. This was done intentionally, with reasons discussed further below.

Quickly I came to see how, through this method, we get different and valuable kinds of insights. We hear about security labor from the workers' own mouths. We get their whole stories, not just snippets. We learn about their backgrounds, family dynamics, and their daily routines. We see the full length of their careers. This gives an added bonus of hearing not just about the positions they are in now, but the many security jobs they've done along the way. Especially refreshing is that we get viewpoints of both *enforcers* and *targets* of security regimes (even though they are, for the most part, security workers themselves). This nuanced approach provides a glimpse into the inherent complexities of security work.

The artwork, as a complement to the interview material, enables us to connect with the visuals of security. Three sets of "portfolios" dispersed throughout the book present the complexities of how we can both understand and question the dynamics of security. In "Simulations," we see the literal theater of security, and places where military personnel practice their invasive maneuvers with hired actors on elaborate sets. This underscores how the work of security—at least in its training stage—can involve acting and performance.

In "Border Stories," we see landscapes of security in border zones. These include border cities, parks, and the border wall between the United States and Mexico. In "Constructions," we see Goodwin's ingenious exercise in uncovering the omissions of surveillance; we see his exploration of who and what gets protected by being left out of the data markers in satellite images from Google Earth. Making the invisible visible, he recreates these places and sites through tabletop-sized models, which are themselves partially made of Google Earth printouts.

THE MANY SIDES OF JOB SECURITY

The title of the book, *Job/Security*, is a play on words urging us to think about hidden complexities in this phenomenon. On face value, the term refers to a *job* with the designation of security. This is important to start with, because at the core, security happens in the context of labor. While there are many dynamics involved with the work (as described below), they are all woven through the core relationship of employment.

With *security*, the title also indicates the importance of the substance of the work. Surveillance is often the major activity that people are doing in these jobs. The authors are concerned about this, and therefore they pose a critical question in this book: What does it mean that workers are increasingly being asked to monitor and enforce surveillance systems on their own community members?

Quite ironically, the job is also about secrecy. Many of the tasks involve intelligence gathering, while at the same time, that intelligence is not to be repeated or discussed. Instead, workers are meant to withhold information about their jobs from anyone outside the organization. One could argue that few occupations require such contradictory behaviors from their workers. Accordingly, Goodwin and Schwarzschild are "deeply interested in gathering stories that explore the challenges and consequences ordinary humans face when living their lives while holding so much secret."

This leads to a third possible meaning of the book title, regarding the relation of the job to security more broadly. Who exactly is becoming more secure from these jobs? In practice, doing security often means servicing the surveillance agendas of elite institutions like the state, defense contractors, tech companies, and other organizations. It's possible this work may also benefit the public residing within the state's borders. However, as the cases here highlight, this is not always true. In fact, one might ask if this job is making certain groups of people "less secure" and more subject to harmful interventions in their lives, families, and communities.

In all these ways, security is a job with profound internal contradictions. It is a site where multiple, interwoven systems of power become entangled. Capitalism and bureaucracy may disempower these individuals as workers, yet such workers may also be disempowering the public while enacting practices of systemic racism and anti-immigrant bias. In this sense, this book draws attention to the harm being done both *to workers* but also *by workers* with regard to other groups in society. Power dynamics in this job are further complicated by the unusual amount of authority that this industry bestows upon its employees. Even those of lowest status—like frontline border patrol workers—may be making vital decisions over other people's lives through small decisions they make on the job.

On an ethical level, then, this book offers a different kind of experience for the reader. A person's empathy may shift—from the worker, to the people being surveilled, and to society as a whole. There is no unitary or preset modality for interpreting material in this book.

In fact, this book will ask the reader to do many things at the same time. To question why security has developed as an industry (both inside and outside the state), and whom it protects. To ask what role workers play in that system, and under what conditions they become enactors of its principles. To examine the motivations of workers in terms of why they participate, as well as what they gain and lose. To see impacts on individuals as a result of being an employee in this industry. To see impacts on larger communities, especially vulnerable groups like immigrants, people of color, women, and children. In short, this project will ask the reader to focus on both individuals as well as the institutions in which they work, and to recognize how each is an equal part of the larger story.

IMPLICATIONS: PROFESSIONAL, ACADEMIC, AND PERSONAL

Several kinds of audiences will appreciate the material in this book. Insiders to the security profession may find this to be a true-to-life account of the work, and a uniquely in-depth and illuminating resource. We have been told by security professionals that this is an original collection and unlike most offerings in the literature. While other books may describe accounts of working on the job (or "in the field," as security folks say), few offer a comprehensive picture of the different types of work, or package them in such a well-designed and thoughtful way.

Professionals on the other side of security may find useful material here as well. Legal experts, policymakers, social justice activists, and people in nonprofit organizations may find this book valuable for challenging institutions of surveillance. Those working toward information privacy, transparency in algorithms and government, and curbs on overpolicing and immigrant abuse have much to learn from these stories too. The collection not only sheds new light on workings of the security state, but includes input from those who have devoted careers to resisting and unraveling it.

Academics gain an archival resource on security workers to use in further study. Goodwin and Schwarzschild are both professors themselves, so readers can be assured that scholarly methods were employed when collecting and presenting the cases. Interviewees were selected carefully for representativeness in the range of security work. Respondents were asked similar sets of questions, addressing a common set of overall themes (e.g., how they ended up in the job, what are day-to-day experiences, what are effects on family life). This kind of standardization was applied to the photographs as well. Portraits were taken in a deliberately leveling manner, using black-and-white images, for instance, so that no one individual should be seen as more important than others despite their positions in the official hierarchy. Thus, while the raw material is presented for readers to view, there was much behind-the-scenes care that went into preparing readers for that experience.

With these scholarly aids, we can then devote our attention to the cornucopia of fascinating reveals about what goes on in these jobs. To me, the implications span a wide range of academic disciplines and public debates, and it was hard to narrow down just a couple of the most important themes. In the afterword I offer an analysis of what struck me about the images and words: how they illuminate discussions about labor; what they invoke for critical security studies and the encroaching security society; how they underscore the growing trends of technology and surveillance; what the crucial underpinnings of gender, masculinity, racialization, and transnationalism are; what impacts on individuals, family life, and communities there are; and what all this suggests for strategies of resistance.

The implications of this book may be personal as well. It will undoubtedly yield an array of reactions for readers. One may feel surprise, as historic events in US security are told in new ways and by people who were there at the time. One may feel shock in reading about the violence that workers have enacted as part of their jobs. Some may feel the need for patience, especially when reading about the minutiae of security work, as it includes some professional jargon meant for insiders (which would, of course, be the case for most of our jobs). But I guarantee that, if you're like me, this book will send you alternatively into nodding acknowledgment, outrage at abusive systems, pride at employees working hard in service for their communities, and awe at the ingenuity and courage of individuals to speak out for justice.

SETTING UP A CONVERSATION

The aim of this book, as Goodwin and Schwarzschild described to me, is to create a set of conversations. These may be metaphorical or literal. For instance, what if the experts presented here could talk to each other, especially those who have diametrically opposing viewpoints on a particular policy? If they were to read each other's pieces, what insights could they gain? And in the process, could they withhold judgment (at least temporarily) and be open to new ideas? Might state officials understand how their border policies generate moral injury for the frontline workers who have to carry them out day-to-day? More importantly, could those officials recognize how such policies in fact engineer the deaths of migrants who are crossing the border? Alternatively, might a frontline agent come to understand wider power systems at hand, in the sense that the rules workers are enforcing come not just from an immediate superior, but in fact from the highest levels of government? In this way, the content here helps us imagine what kinds of dialogues might be possible between the experts themselves, even though they may not be happening often enough in practice.

Another aim is to draw the general public into these conversations. This book challenges the idea that security discussions should be limited to elite circles of government, defense industries, and corporations. A regular person does not typically get the opportunity to hear what insiders in the security regime are saying to each other. But what if they could? What kinds of action would that inspire?

Goodwin and Schwarzschild's vision for an upcoming art installation gives a tangible example of what this could look like. Several pairs of vertical screens will face each other, showing actors reading the interviews from the book. As exhibit-goers walk between the screens and hear the voices talking over each other, it may be difficult to understand given all the noise. However, if a person steps closer to one side, and then the other, the volume changes so they can hear what the speakers are saying. This scenario urges us to take a moment to listen, and then find the humanity within an otherwise dehumanizing situation.

Ultimately, we hope that this book prompts a reflection on our shared responsibility for an industry that is rapidly expanding. The securitized society is being built in our name (i.e., for "public safety"), even if without our input or consent. But is it possible that this is also happening through our indirect participation as consumers and citizens? Or through our lack of effort in obstructing it? Starting with this volume, perhaps we can become better informed and equipped to address such issues, and to consider pathways for a more fair society.

Winifred R. Poster

BEGINNINGS: SECURITY IN THE FATHERLAND

EDWARD SCHWARZSCHILD

MY FATHER WAS born in 1937. While in high school, he made an eight-year commitment to the Air Force Reserves that lasted from 1954 to 1962, one weekend per month, two weeks every summer. When he enlisted, he'd hoped to become a pilot, but he had lousy eyesight. In one of the handful of stories he tells about that time in his life, he managed to memorize some eye charts and pass a few tests, but then a doctor put up a newer eye chart and shot down his flying career. My father became a radio operator and a paratrooper instead.

There were other stories: about teaching hand-to-hand combat in Guatemala and parachuting into Lebanon and training soldiers to fight at the Bay of Pigs and floating in a raft for days after a mishap off the coast of northern California.

What child wouldn't ask his father to fill out such tantalizing tales? As I grew older, I pushed repeatedly for more information. My father said he was sworn to silence. He said it was all classified material. And yet, though he refused to share any additional details about exactly what he did, he couldn't resist mentioning the secret missions again and again.

These days, my father is deep into his eighties. Short and squat, he shuffles slowly down the long hallways of his retirement community. Outside, he still often stops in the middle of a conversation to gaze up into the sky at a passing jet, as if he expects to see one of his fellow ex-paratroopers floating down for a visit. He jokes that he was much taller before the 250 jumps from 12,000 feet compacted his body into its current size.

Another story: He was forced to lace up other guys' shoes in his squadron. "I still don't like to lace shoes up," he said, "because it brings back terrible memories of all these guys making me lace their shoes. They called me Jew-boy. There were a lot more of them than there were of me. Some fights I won and some I lost. Eventually, it just became easier to lace their shoes."

And another: "There was a fire at a records center in St. Louis, in 1973, I think. The service records of everyone with last names starting with a letter from N to Z were destroyed. That's why I don't get any VA benefits."

I grew up fascinated by my father's mysteriously incomplete narratives. Were they true? Were they exaggerations? Were they fantasies? Were they all of the above? These persistent questions about what was real and what was imagined probably helped push me toward storytelling. I became a fiction writer, an English professor, a director of a creative writing program. Here's a story I tell: One night, more than forty-five years ago, when I was eleven or twelve, my father invited me into his den and said, "I want to show you a few things. I think you're ready."

I can't recall anything out of the ordinary that prompted this invitation. I can't tell you what changed. I don't know what made him decide I was, suddenly, "ready."

He closed the door and told me there was no such thing as a fair fight. He told me you could kill someone if you hit them hard enough in the right way on the bridge of their nose. He told me the throat was a good place to punch a person. Then he unlocked his gun cabinet.

There'd been guns in the house my whole life, but I'd never seen my father hold one in his hands. A few antique revolvers were displayed in a sealed, glass-covered case above the desk. There were rifles in the gun cabinet, but, until now, I'd never seen that cabinet unlocked, let alone opened.

The first thing my father removed from the cabinet was a small manual filled with illustrated instructions about what to do if someone attacks you with a knife, if someone tries to choke you, if someone attacks you with two knives. I paid attention as my father explained a few basic moves—always step away from a punch, always keep your guard up and your head down. I tried to picture myself in hand-to-hand combat with an enemy of some sort, but I couldn't get that image to come into focus. Instead, I saw myself as I was—a scrawny, nerdy boy who carried around paperback science fiction books so I could avoid talking to people.

My father reached into the cabinet again and this time he pulled out a rifle.

"One day," he said, "it might be up to you to save the family."

He showed me where he kept the key to the cabinet and where he stored the boxes of ammunition. He showed me how to load a clip and how to push a clip into the gun. "If someone ever breaks into the house while you're here," he said, "let them take whatever they want. The telephone is your first and best weapon. But you should know about these weapons, too."

Was this his way of finally sharing more information about the work he'd done for the Air Force Reserves? Was he trying to teach me how to feel more safe and secure in this troubled world?

I don't know what he was thinking, but I didn't feel safer or more secure. I didn't want to touch the gun. I felt no desire to hold it in my hands. I wanted to see my father lock it back up in the cabinet where it belonged.

"Look," he said. "Watch what I'm doing."

In August 2001, I moved to Upstate New York to teach at the University at Albany, State University of New York. During that first semester, as we all reeled from 9/11, I met a new colleague, the photographer Danny Goodwin. Though Goodwin grew up in Dallas and I grew up outside Philadelphia, we shared similar fatherlands. Goodwin has a father with his own security-related secrets:

> My dad was an engineer. Growing up, I knew he did important stuff, but we didn't really know exactly what. As I got older, I realized he couldn't tell us exactly what because he was working on a lot of the most secret projects in the military-industrial complex at the time. He was working on some of the night vision systems, for instance. He didn't know that the CIA was his client because that's kind of how it works, but that was his start in the world of Black programs.

In part because of the secrets that shaped his childhood, Goodwin has spent the last twenty-plus years working on what he describes as "photographic projects that relate, by turns directly and obliquely, to the US intelligence community and attendant issues including surveillance, secrecy, and violence." He explains that his work "is as much an ongoing interrogation of photographic veracity as it is a critique of escalating authoritarian power in America and the world."

Goodwin and I also discovered that we shared a deep admiration for the book *Let Us Now Praise Famous Men* (1941), the genre-bending collaboration between the writer James Agee and the photographer Walker Evans. Those two artists' flawed, original, beautiful attempt to capture on the page the lives of a handful of Alabama tenant farming families left a mark on both of us. We were particularly drawn to the hybrid nature of their multimedia documentary practice, the way they worked across various disciplines in order to illuminate in compelling detail lives that had previously been invisible. Agee and Evans strove "to recognize the stature of a portion of unimagined existence, and to contrive techniques proper to its recording, communication, analysis, and defense." They saw their work as "an independent inquiry into certain normal predicaments of human divinity."[1]

In the years that followed 9/11, Goodwin and I talked a great deal about the exponential growth of the security industry and the potential societal ramifications of such growth. Because of our upbringings, we couldn't help wondering how many more families would be warped by security-related secrecy, how many children would never know what really happened when their parents went off to work, how many parents wouldn't be allowed to share the whole story of their work lives with the ones they loved. We weren't convinced that the security industry needed or deserved our "defense," and we didn't see an immediate connection between security labor and "human divinity," but we began to imagine creating a documentary project together. It would be an Agee/Evans-inflected composite portrait of the contemporary security industry that could reveal its effects on individuals and families across the United States.

Throughout our years of work on this project, Goodwin and I have drawn upon our upbringings, our research, and our wide-ranging conversations with people in and around the Department of Homeland Security. Still, there is no doubt that when it comes to the world of security labor, we remain outsiders looking in. Goodwin is a photographer and I am a fiction writer. As a result, this is not a work of traditional scholarship, though we hope it will be, among other things, a vital addition to the growing field of Security Studies.

Even my most direct, immersive experience—for a few months in 2012, I trained to become one of the TSA's Transportation Security Officers (TSO) at Albany International Airport—left me with more questions than answers about the daily lives, ethical standards, moral judgments, working conditions, and unique struggles of security workers.

Here's a story I tell about that period in my life: Day after day, early morning shift after early morning shift, I kept trying to feel in charge at the checkpoint. I found that, in some ways, my time as a writer and English professor provided good training for many of the duties of a TSO. Years of assessing students' essays meant I could check documents at a good clip. Thanks to a specialization in film studies, I had spent a good deal of time examining images on screen, searching for unusual, hidden, crucial details—fine practice for working the X-ray machine. And my first teaching position, right out of graduate school, had taken me to a small women's college in central Virginia, where I learned a certain genteel politeness—politeness that served me well as I searched through bags while harried passengers stood by, scowling and impatient.

No part of my teaching experience, however, prepared me to perform pat-downs. Back at that southern women's college, I had learned that the only really acceptable form of student/faculty physical contact was a high-five. Now, every morning, as part of my job, I was supposed to run my hands up and down the legs, torsos, and arms of my fellow citizens. I was supposed to do this in such a way that no one would feel groped.

My fellow rookies and I practiced on each other first, patting each other down multiple times. There was nervous, lighthearted banter. Our cheerful instructors offered guidance. They said the procedure was clinical. Exert the same pressure you use to spread peanut butter on a sandwich. Say clearly what you're going to do and then do it. We'd grow numb to it before long, they assured us.

As we practiced, a few lines from Bob Dylan's song "George Jackson" kept running through my mind. Dylan sings about how it can seem as if the "whole world" is nothing but "one big prison yard" in which we serve as either prisoners or guards.

How could I put my hands on someone else like this? And yet, was there a better way to keep our airplanes safe?

Walt Whitman's poem "A Song for Occupations" offered this: *Neither a servant nor master I / I will be even with you and you shall be even with me.*

But how could I perform pat-downs in such a way that they would foster both security and compassion? I remembered *Newjack*, Ted Conover's book about the year he worked as a corrections officer in the notorious maximum-security prison Sing Sing. Day after day, he had had to do much more than the TSA's standard pat-down, and he voiced his worries about the consequences of his actions, about how the job might lead him to lose touch with his compassion, with his better self: "'Leave it at the gate,' you hear time and again in corrections. Leave all the stress and bullshit at work; don't bring it home to your family. This was good in theory. In reality, though, I was like my friend who had worked the pumps at a service station: even after she got home and took a shower, you could still smell the gasoline on her hands. Prison got into your skin, or under it. If you stayed long enough, some of it probably seeped into your soul."

I didn't think I would be able to work a full year at the checkpoint, but I wanted to stay at the job long enough to understand it better. I hoped my soul—as well as the souls of all the passengers I encountered—wouldn't be stained. I knew airport checkpoints were disturbing, dehumanizing, and frightening places for many people. And these days, more than ever, it becomes almost impossible to pass through an airport without thinking about how many people are detained on their way. How many have their property confiscated. How many feel violated. How many are forced to leave and forbidden to return. But, back then, I tried to reassure myself: Albany's checkpoint was a bright, airy, high-ceilinged space. I hadn't witnessed any inappropriate behavior. Technically, as TSOs, we weren't even allowed to detain people—that was police work.

My professorial intellectualizing didn't help much the first time I had to shadow a TSO named Lance, a hard-working bodybuilder so thick with muscle that he had to walk through the scanner sideways. He showed devotion to all the rules, held at least one other security job, and went to night school. When he wasn't working or studying, he was watching cop shows, preparing himself for the latest threats. In other words, he was a true believer with big aspirations in the security field. Only a fool would have tried to get in his way. When he watched me perform a pat-down, I flubbed my lines and forgot to check the passenger's feet. Lance was not impressed. "That being-nice stuff," he said, "you have to let that go."

The next time I was paired with Lance, he focused harder on my pat-down technique. Again, he was not impressed. "Have you been practicing your verbiage at home?" he asked.

"Not really."

"It's a yes or no question," he said.

I felt like a student woefully unprepared for class. "No," I admitted.

He shook his freshly shaved head and went over to speak to the supervisor. When he returned, he led me off to the side of the checkpoint and told me to practice a pat-down on him. A few of the other officers and officers-in-training glanced our way. I noticed a handful of passengers watching, too.

"Do the whole script," Lance said.

"Can you see your belongings," I began, "or would you like me to bring them over here?"

"You need to enunciate better," Lance said.

"I'm going to use my hands to pat down the clothed areas of your body. I'll use the backs of my hands on the sensitive areas, the buttocks and the zipper line. I'll be clearing your collar and your waistline with two fingers. And I'll be clearing each inner thigh, sliding up until I reach resistance."

"Say it like you believe it," Lance said. "You need to do pat-downs like they mean what they're supposed to mean. Every pat-down is done to make sure the person in front of you is not a risk, right?"

I nodded and went on, nervous, wondering if my job was on the line. "Do you have any internal or external medical devices? Do you have any painful or tender areas on your body? Do you have absolutely everything out of your pockets?"

"This is your house," Lance said.

"A private screening is available if you'd prefer. You can request one at any time."

"Go ahead," he told me.

So I did what I said I was going to do and, as was the case with every pat-down, eventually I was down on the dull brown airport carpet, on my knees. I cleared Lance's big feet, then his legs, and I went up until I met resistance.

"That's better," Lance said. "Remember, if you're not doing a pat-down properly, then you're doing it improperly, and isn't your whole Mr. Nice Guy thing about not doing anything improper?"

When I stood up, the rest of the checkpoint was still humming along as usual. Was I being hazed? Humbled? Embarrassed? Schooled? All of the above, of course.

Later in the shift, while we were working the bag-search position, a young woman lost the backing to her earring. She seemed willing to let it go, but I knelt on the carpet again and managed to find it, a small speck of silver amid the brown strands studded with dust. The woman beamed at us as she reattached the earring. "My day is going to be much better now," she said.

That pleased me, and it pleased me even more when Lance, smiling, looked my way and said: "You got a hawk-eye or something?"

Just forever seeking the approval of my father, or father-figure of the moment, I could have said. Security. Homeland. Fatherland. That night, at home, while my family slept, I made sure to study my verbiage.

When I share that story—and others—about my months at the checkpoint, and when I talk about the novel I wrote that drew upon my brief time in the TSA, I sense that people are surprised, maybe even disappointed. They expect to hear tales of corrupt, inept, mean-spirited TSOs screwing in family restrooms, smuggling drugs, stealing laptops, tormenting the elderly, and harassing Muslims, all while failing one critical Homeland Security test after another.

Long after I stopped working at the checkpoint, I continued to closely follow coverage of the TSA in the news, and it seems clear to me that far too many officers abuse their power. Toddlers are patted down. Cancer survivors are forced to remove their prosthetic breasts. The list goes on and on, impossible to overlook. In short, the TSA seems frequently to offer evidence that the large-scale infrastructure of security is inescapably exploitative and dehumanizing. I certainly have no desire to be an apologist, for the TSA or for any of the other areas of the Department of Homeland Security covered in this book.

At the same time, a mantra I heard throughout my training helped me navigate my months on the job: "If you've been to one airport, you've been to one airport." While I can't speak for what happens at other airports, or what might happen in the future, I can tell you what I experienced and observed during my time at Albany International. It's not a particularly sexy or edgy reveal. I saw a diverse group of men and women of all ages who sought TSA employment because it offered a combination that seems scarce these days: entry-level positions with real health benefits, job security, and the possibility of career development. For all its supposed faults, employment in the TSA is an opportunity for thousands of people who want to help keep their finances and/or nation secure. Some were more skeptical about the mission than others, and some were more crass in their conduct than others, but everyone I saw performed the job they had been trained to do as best they could.

I've held other entry-level jobs over the course of my life: kennel cleaner, dishwasher, waiter, gardener, gravedigger, office temp, lab assistant. Working as a TSO-in-training was as challenging as any other work I've done, including writing and teaching. At the checkpoint, we were often urged to practice focused attention, hour after hour, shift after shift, and it could get exhausting. We rotated from station to station, repeating our scripts, studying documents and images, searching bags—and we were supposed to perform each task as if our lives and the lives of everyone around us were continuously at stake.

By the end of 2013, I had finished a draft of my TSA-based novel and Goodwin and I had been discussing our security-related documentary project for almost a decade. Then, in January of 2014, the governor of New York announced that UAlbany, our very own workplace, would house the nation's first College of Emergency Preparedness, Homeland Security and Cybersecurity (CEHC). UAlbany's website went on to boast that CEHC "is the very first standalone college dedicated to the topics of emergency preparedness, Homeland Security, and cybersecurity, and provides highly comprehensive academic programming for undergraduate and graduate students to prepare them to meet the challenges and risks that we face today."[2]

Predictably, there were debates about resources on and off campus. How would the creation of this brand-new college affect the finances and enrollments of the colleges already at the university? Would ethical questions arise about how CEHC fit or didn't fit within the mission of the university? What does it mean, for example, for a state university to have its own drone lab? Like many other people on and off campus, Goodwin and I wrestled with such questions. We also realized that we'd been granted access to the very world we'd been trying to describe. Our nascent documentary project suddenly began to seem at once unavoidable and more essential than ever.

We began to take candid photographs and conduct frank, in-depth interviews with people working at all levels of Homeland Security. We spoke with EMTs and firemen; we spoke with people who'd worked for the CIA, Secret Service, Border Patrol, Marine Corps, Army, Navy, Air Force, TSA, and more. We spoke with dozens of men and women at all career levels (from former agency chiefs to new hires), with a diverse array of backgrounds. We also spoke with people who have criticized and/or suffered at the hands of our surveillance-filled nation. Our goal then—and now—is to make the invisible aspects of security labor visible. We want to create a work of art as well as, essentially, an interdisciplinary archive of first-person storytelling for citizens, noncitizens, students, teachers, potential employees, critics, scholars, and others—for anyone, really, who is seeking to better understand this expanding American growth industry. We see our book as an inherently crossover/hybrid project that offers an accessible introduction to this particular part of our world and lives, and we hope that these personal, heartfelt interviews and portraits will reach the broadest audience possible.

The earliest interviews included here took place in 2016 and the most recent took place in 2022. We have sought to compile as broad and diverse a collection of interviews as possible while also keeping the interviews substantial, usually between 2,500 and 5,000 words, so that readers can get to know each individual. The interviews have been lightly edited for clarity. Each interviewee was given the opportunity to review their interview.

Though each interview followed its own course, we were guided by several interconnected, overarching questions: How does security labor affect individuals' abilities to create and maintain family and domestic structures? What are the challenges and consequences of holding a job so closely related to secrecy and privacy? How does performing security labor shape individuals' perceptions of security? Does the work itself make the workers feel more secure or less secure? What does the existence and expansion of this particular workforce mean for our society as a whole?

Fifty years ago, in his groundbreaking oral history *Working* (1972), Studs Terkel didn't ask precisely these questions, but he did note in a general way the proliferation of security-related labor in the United States. "As some occupations become obsolete," he wrote, "others come into being. More people are being paid to watch other people than ever before." Terkel could not have anticipated the post-9/11 exponential expansion of the global security workforce, but the subtitle he gave to *Working*—"People Talk about What They Do All Day and How They Feel about What They Do"—offered additional inspiration and direction for this project. Terkel described how "improvisation and chance played their roles" when it came to the people he wound up interviewing: "A tip from an acquaintance. A friend of a friend telling me of a friend or non-friend. A face, vaguely familiar, on the morning bus." His book is almost 600 pages long, and yet he was aware of many "omissions": "Whom to visit? Whom to pass by? In talking to the washroom attendant, would I be remiss in neglecting the elevator operator? . . . In visiting the Chicago bookbinder, I missed the old Massachusetts basket weaver."[3]

We did not have to choose among bookbinders, basket weavers, washroom attendants, and elevator operators, but we remain cognizant of how incomplete this project is. The Department of Homeland Security alone currently employs more than 260,000 people.[4] And, of course, security labor is practiced in many other realms outside the DHS. According to a 2022 article in *The New Yorker*, "The number of Americans who possess a security clearance has swelled to more than five million, because classification has swathed in secrecy so many functions of defense and intelligence work."[5]

These numbers continue to grow. In such a context, this collection of eighteen interviews is obviously only a beginning. We arranged the interviews so that they begin with several branches of the military, then move to the Border Patrol, then to the CIA and Secret Service, and then to various sectors of emergency management. While these broad categories are both unofficial and porous, they remain useful and help structure our composite portrait of this expanding enterprise. In addition to interviews with the laborers themselves, we have also included interviews with writers, artists, and activists who have devoted their careers to trying to understand the costs and benefits of security labor. We hope that reading these interviews in order gives you the opportunity to experience a wide range of voices in this crucial, unfolding conversation.

We have tried to remain as neutral as possible throughout the making of this book, allowing the interviewees to speak uninterrupted from their various standpoints. We've been guided in this decision by these words from the writer and activist Sarah Schulman: "nothing disrupts dehumanization more quickly than inviting someone over, looking into their eyes, hearing their voice, and listening."[6] We want our readers to hear and listen and attend to as many sides of this developing story as possible. To give just one example, we include not only the voice of Carla Provost, former chief of the Border Patrol, who celebrates the hard work and sacrifice of Border Patrol officers, but also the voice of Francisco Cantú, who worked several years for the Border Patrol, resigned, and wrote a memoir about how he remains haunted by the recurrent violence and injustice he witnessed on the job. We believe we all share the responsibility of coming to terms with what security labor means to us as individuals and as a society. It is only becoming more and more true that this kind of work touches us all and we all have a clear stake in talking it over with each other. For better or worse, Homeland Security isn't going away anytime soon.

At this point, we feel our work is far from done. We want this book to serve as the first volume of a much larger project. We are already planning an online database and we are in the initial phases of collaborating on an even broader project about security labor globally that will lead to a scholarly symposium and an edited volume of essays about security labor around the world. We have also been working on a *Job/Security*-related museum exhibition that is scheduled to open in the fall of 2024. A central intention for all of these interconnected projects is to inspire others to conduct their own interviews and, ultimately, to help build an online archive of words and images so that this composite portrait of security labor can continue to deepen and expand for years to come.

In other words, there is much, much more to learn. As Colonel James Vizzard put it near the end of his interview: "If you want to know what the costs are for families and family life, you've got to get it from all sides. Maybe you should talk to my sons, or my wife. Because I don't know what I don't know, and I don't know what they don't tell me."

As this composite portrait grows, moving from person to person, family to family, community to community, and, soon, nation to nation, we'll all hopefully be able to see more clearly what "job/security" offers and what "job/security" costs all around the world.

After working on this project for several years, I convinced my father to sit for a formal interview. I should have known better, but I couldn't help hoping he would, at last, decide to open up about the military past that clearly meant so much to him. Sitting out in my backyard with the tape recorder running, he paused several times to gaze up at the airplanes flying by. And, once again, he refused to flesh out any of his old stories. He talked once more about lacing other guys' shoes, the classified nature of the work he did, the fire in St. Louis.

Ultimately, it might be inaccurate to call my father's vague, unsupported incident reports about his brief military career *stories*. Whatever they were, they contained few specific details, no real characters, no rising or falling action, no beginnings, middles, or ends. Probably better to call them prompts. Hints and guesses. Mysterious, haunting fragments. Inspirations for a storyteller, which is what I remain, asking questions, trying to sort out what is true and what is fiction in a narrative about the fatherland I see everywhere around me. These days, now a father myself, I still seek to understand what my father's service actually entailed as well as what it cost him and our family. That desire to understand the service and its consequences—to understand, as well, the stories, fragments, hints, and guesses we share about the entire experience—pervades this project.

Of course, I'll never understand it all.

During one of my father's recent visits to Albany, he took a look at the sneakers my young son was wearing. They happened to be untied. My father knelt down, laced the sneakers tighter, and showed his grandson how to tie them better. "This is called a paratrooper's knot," he said. "It won't come untied."

Was he, as he focused on my son's shoes, remembering the long ago fights back when he was forced to lace the shoes of the other men in his squadron? How many fights had there been? Had there been any fights at all? Once again, I searched his face for answers, for some revelatory sense of sorrow or upset, but I couldn't be sure one way or the other. I watched him stand up and muss my son's hair.

I don't think I'll ever arrive at the definitive truth about my father's time in the Air Force Reserves. I did, however, finally do an internet search for "records center" + "fire" + "St. Louis." A split second after typing those words, I found myself looking at the website of the US National Archives. The first line of the entry that comes up is: "On July 12, 1973, a disastrous fire at the National Personnel Records Center (NPRC) destroyed approximately 16–18 million Official Military Personnel Files (OMPF)."[7]

That simple research reminded me that there are plenty of examples of real truth that can be discovered, even about my frequently mysterious father. The definitive truth might be too lofty a goal when it comes to him and his work experience, but if we do enough research, talk with enough people, listen carefully to what they have to say, maybe we can move ever closer to a complete story about the expanding world of security labor.

LEARNING TO SEE SECURITY

DANNY GOODWIN

OVER THE SEVEN years that Edward Schwarzschild and I have worked on this book, we have encountered a range of reactions from friends, family, and colleagues when we've told them we're working on a project about security. Everyone has a security-related story to share, but many people diplomatically question our qualifications, expertise, and access, revealing one of the essential paradoxes of Security (with a capital S): whereas there is a clear inside/outside to the enterprise, security work nonetheless impacts us all. And the enterprise is nothing short of a growth industry in this country. Yet, when the term comes up, we often assume that we agree on its definition. But we probably don't, depending on our experience/identity/job/background. One of the earliest organizing questions we sought to answer in undertaking this project was "security by and for whom?" Furthermore, how do we visualize such a nebulous, creeping expansion of this global workforce? The stories and images in this book do not presume to offer answers, but they will pose and re-pose these critical questions about security labor.

Further, the varied approaches I have taken to see and show the security industry with a camera echo the approaches we have taken with the interviews. As we work to construct a composite portrait, we want readers to be aware of both what is on the page and what is missing from the page. For instance, we did not include every interview we conducted. We lightly edited all of the interviews we have included. We imagine doing many more interviews in the future. Similarly, the individual portraits are frank photographs made in open collaboration with the subjects. The images of simulation areas are as highly contrived and staged as the uncanny areas themselves. And the studio constructions are an exercise to visualize the barely visible world of the security industry, which grows increasingly omnipresent.

In other words, the photographs in this volume fall roughly into three categories that, although distinct, inform and are informed by each other:

- Black-and-white portraits of interview subjects and landscape studies
- Color photographs of emergency simulation and security training facilities
- Color photographs of tabletop, paper models of sites visited as well as sites we were not able or permitted to photograph.

Most of the portraits, interspersed among the interviews, were made immediately following the subject's interview, although several required follow-up sessions (especially with those folks interviewed over Zoom during the zenith of the COVID-19 pandemic). In each case, I invited the subject to select a location or environment that was meaningful to or otherwise comfortable for them. The extremely shallow depth of focus renders the subject's face very clearly but leaves the surroundings quite blurred. This is not unlike what happens in our vision when listening intently to someone speaking to us. Although the portraits offer little in the way of setting for the viewer, it was my hope that the subject would at least be a bit more at ease.

The uncanny images of the sites and spaces associated with the New York State Preparedness Training Center in Oriskany, New York, on the site of the former Griffiss Air Force Base, offer a glimpse of one of the working models of emergency resilience and anti-terrorist training. On the day we were finally permitted access to the facility to make these photographs, law enforcement from across New York State had assembled for the annual "Excelsior Challenge" competition (even though we requested access when no people might wander into the frame). Our handler suggested that Ed and I should have ribbons attached to our ankles to designate us as "out of play" for the live-fire active-shooter and other simulations that would take place that day. As "straight" images of real structures in the real world that are not what they appear to be, these images fit squarely between the earnest, sincere portraits and the slippery, disorienting models, exhibiting aspects of both.

Finally, the photographs of oddly constructed paper models may seem to be visual non sequiturs, but they in fact hew more closely to the kind of studio practice I've been pursuing for years, that is, images that essentially turn the lens back upon itself, photographs that are as much about photography as they are about the subject depicted. The thread that connects this practice to the shadowy worlds of spycraft and national security has much to do with the misguided expectations we impose on the medium to represent reality or, dare I say, truth. I maintain a nuanced sensitivity to the shifting and contingent contemporary definitions of the *Real*. Although we encounter countless examples everyday of uses of photography that should make us wary of believing what we see (e.g., AI/CGI, "Deep Fakes"), the urge to look *through* the frame of a photograph at the moment depicted on the other side, rather than looking *at* and *reading* the two-dimensional representation, remains as strong as ever.

In 1993, I created the *CIA Museum*.[1] Escape and evasion devices developed by CIA's Office of Technical Services were reproduced as props, based on descriptions obtained from open-source documents, and photographed in the manner of cosmetics or other consumer goods. This work was an extended impersonation that sought to lend visual and poetic form to some of the more troubling aspects of the Agency's endeavors from the 1960s to the 1990s. In the early 2000s, I became preoccupied with a rather paranoid curiosity regarding what the surveillance I was likely under would look like.[2] In a ham-fisted attempt to visualize it, I constructed numerous models of my home and work locations and photographed them as if from the sky. Simultaneously, I launched handmade wireless video cameras, tethered to nine-foot-diameter latex weather balloons, to capture actual aerial footage that traced my comings and goings. By 2003, I obtained the home addresses of several high-ranking members of the George W. Bush cabinet and made miniature models of their homes.[3] Wireless video cameras, suspended beneath helium-filled Mylar balloons in neutral buoyancy, sent feeds to a bank of monitors in an adjacent room in the galleries in which this work was exhibited, simulating twenty-four-hour surveillance of the Masters of War. A few years later, I was again constructing models, this time of unexploded ordnance or Improvised Explosive Devices that failed to or were prevented from detonating, based on descriptions of the devices.[4] Each of these projects was an attempt to leverage the visually plausible to advance the logically impossible: none of these simulations held up under scrutiny, which was part of the point.

For this book, hundreds of images of sites of interest, culled from Google Earth Ground View were printed and reassembled (mostly incorrectly) into three-dimensional models and then re-photographed with a large-format camera. As such, the most well-articulated aspects of the resulting images are the fissures and ruptures. The $4'' \times 5''$ camera captures, in unforgivingly high resolution, the low resolution and painterly areas of the crude texture-mapping, contrasted with the sharp edges of the paper model's seams. In some cases, even the virtual proxy for a location is invisible—off-limits to Google Earth due, ostensibly, to its national-security sensitivity. In those cases, the spaces are visualized largely through signs and symbols: the familiar gray checkerboard pattern, for example, of a transparent layer in Photoshop (which is now a more apt signifier of empty space than actual empty space) represents more than a passive, benign background—it is part of our new, weird grammar of visualizing the invisible. Hand-constructed environments and objects, in this work, impersonate their virtual counterparts and reveal the circular logic that too often undergirds the current popular fascination with virtual- and augmented-reality, 3D printing, and related imaging technologies. Further, sourcing the paper-thin veneer of images from Google Earth is more than an aesthetic choice; there's also a conceptual conceit: In-Q-Tel, CIA's venture capital arm, invested heavily in the startup Keyhole, the precursor to Google Earth.[5]

Having worked for over two decades on photographic projects that relate, by turns directly and obliquely, to the US intelligence community and attendant issues including surveillance, secrecy, and violence, these images bring me full circle back to my earliest obsessions to ask: What do we mean when we speak of security, and what, if anything, can we know with certainty?

1

HOMELAND SECURITY AND THE MILITARY

When I was a kid, my family would go to Newport, Rhode Island, for vacation and we would visit the Navy base up there. I can remember being on the beach in Newport, and you could see the Navy ships coming and going from the base.

When I was in seventh, eighth, and ninth grade, I was involved in the Navy's Sea Cadet program, which was a Navy program for kids. Even at a young age, I knew I was going to join the Navy. I just knew that's what I was going to do. I never thought about going to college. I didn't think about getting a job anywhere. I literally graduated high school on the 28th of June, and on the 30th of June, I was in the Navy.

When I first joined the Navy, I didn't know anything about Navy SEALs.[1] I didn't know any of that stuff existed. I really wasn't sure what I wanted to do when I joined the Navy, so I enlisted in the Navy and went into the Fireman Apprenticeship Program.

The recruiter sold it to me as, "Hey, when you go to boot camp you'll go to a three-week-long school, then you'll go to a ship. When you get to that ship, you'll get to work in all these different areas, and then when you find one you like, that's what you get to do for the rest of the time you're in the Navy." I was like, "Sign me up. That sounds great."

So, off to boot camp I went. After boot camp graduation, I received orders to my first ship. I checked on board, and was sent straight to the boiler room, or the fire room where the boiler was. It was the worst job in the Navy. It was the absolute worst job in the Navy. That's how I started my Navy career. My very first work day on board that ship was a twelve-hour-long day. I spent the entire day working inside the boiler with a steel brush scrubbing things called the down tubes. It was not what I expected.

When I came out of the boiler, I was dirty, filthy, and covered in soot. The next day I went to my boss and I said, "Chief, I don't think I want to be a boiler tech. I want to go work somewhere else." He looked me square in the eyes, laughed in my face, and said, "You're not going anywhere."

That right there planted a motivational seed.

The type of ship I was on had Navy deep sea divers stationed onboard.[2] I would see these guys wearing their Underwater Demolition Team shorts, blue and gold T-shirts, and diving on the ships. I'm like, "That's the job I want to do in the Navy."

Long story short, I went back to the dive locker—that's where the divers worked—and talked to them about becoming a diver. I spent my first year in the Navy onboard that ship working in the fire room as a boiler tech until I finally received orders to attend Second Class Dive School in Little Creek, Virginia.

It's while I was attending Second Class Dive School that I got introduced to what Navy SEALs were. I saw these guys rappelling out of helicopters and doing all this really fun-looking stuff, and I'm like, "That's what I want to do."

After I graduated Second Class Dive School, I went back to the same ship. This time, I was working back in the dive locker as a Navy diver. Shortly after returning to the ship, I went to the master diver, who was my boss, and I said, "Hey, I don't want to be a diver anymore, I want to be a Navy SEAL." He basically gave me the same response as my previous boss, except he was like, "You're going to be a diver. We just sent you to dive school, so you're going to be a diver."

So, I was a Navy deep sea diver for three of my first four years in the Navy and spent that whole time applying for orders to attend SEAL training, or what's better known as BUD/S (Basic Underwater Demolitions/SEALS). I submitted several "packages," or requests for orders, to BUD/S training. At that time, to get orders to BUD/S you had to submit a package to the SEAL detailer which included your ASVAB test scores, a copy of a dive physical, and your SEAL physical fitness test scores along with a copy of your evaluations.[3] Although I met all the requirements for SEAL training, I kept getting denied orders to BUD/S because I'd just gone through Second Class Dive school, and the diving detailer would not release me from being a second class diver.

While I was a diver, I was stationed in Norfolk, Virginia, and, at the time, the enlisted detailers were all located in Washington, DC. So, after the third or fourth time of having my request for BUD/S training denied, I put on my dress whites and I hand-delivered my "package" to BUD/S to the SEAL detailer in DC. Finally, the diving detailer agreed to release me as a Navy diver. He said, "Okay. We'll give you your orders to BUD/S, but when you don't make it through BUD/S training, you're not going to come back and be a diver. You're going back to the fire room as a boiler tech."

Again, that was serious motivation for me to make it through BUD/S training.

There was never a doubt in my mind about making it through SEAL training. I just knew I was going to make it. No matter what happens, I'm going to make it through training. All you have to do in BUD/S is not quit. You just get up every day and do the training. That was my mindset.

The guys with the loudest mouths, the guys with the biggest attitudes, were usually the first ones to quit.

It was the quiet guys who made it through. You really can't say who's going to make it and who's not going to make it. You just don't know. It's completely internal and it is ultimately up to that individual if they succeed or fail.

I actually enjoyed BUD/S. It was fun and I liked it.

I was in BUD/S class 187, and of the 120 or so of us that started training, only eight of us, out of the original 120, graduated without getting rolled back. There were a total of eighteen graduates in my BUD/S class. I graduated as the class honor man, or the number-one student in the class. After graduation, I received orders to SEAL Team TWO and spent the rest of my career in the SEAL teams.

During my deployments, I performed the job both as a SEAL Operator and as a SEAL Leader. The deployments I did earlier in my career, I was more of an operator. As an operator, your focus is more on assaulting targets, kicking doors, the stuff that makes you want to be a SEAL. As my career progressed, and I continued to get promoted, I deployed in more of a leadership position. My last combat deployment to Iraq in '08, I was deployed in a leadership position as a SEAL Task Unit Senior Enlisted Advisor. I had a 235-person task unit working underneath me. We did some really good stuff, and, leadership-wise, it was a challenging but also a rewarding deployment. Nobody got seriously hurt or injured and everybody came home. It was just a good deployment overall.

My deployment to Afghanistan in '05 was a really great deployment as an operator because, at that time, all eyes were focused on Iraq, and Afghanistan was just this thing over here. No one was paying too much attention to what was going on in Afghanistan, so we weren't micro-managed on the battlefield, and we could go out and do what we needed to do.

FIGURE 1.1
Dan Izzo, Johnstown, New York, 2023.

In Afghanistan, you really felt like you made a difference. You felt like you were there for a purpose, a cause, and we were saving lives.

I completed thirteen deployments during my career. Basically, I deployed once every twelve to eighteen months over my career. Most of my deployments lasted between six and eight months, with some lasting as long as ten months.

As I mentioned earlier, my final deployment to Iraq was challenging for me as a leader. I don't want to go too deep into this, but basically, a majority of the guys I had working for me in '08 were the same guys who were in Iraq two years before when things were really bad.[4] And, unfortunately for them, they lost a couple of guys in their platoon. So, when they went back in '08, they were expecting the operational tempo to be the same as it was when they were deployed there in '06. But the environment on the battlefield had completely changed; operationally, it was not the same as it was in in '04, '05, or '06. During the '08 deployment, the guys were not operating as much and the ops they were doing were not the same ones they had done on their previous deployments. So, I had a group of operators who were not doing much "operating." Does that make sense? These guys are war fighters and they wanted to go back over there and "get some." It was very challenging as a leader to keep those guys focused and motivated.

Being in the SEAL teams is a lifestyle, not a job. You don't wake up in the morning, go to work, and come home at the end of the day. You wake up in the morning, you go to work, and you come home three months later. It's a lifestyle, and you have to understand that and accept that, and that's pretty much what I did. I was consistently doing a pre-deployment workup or training cycle to deploy, and then I would deploy. That's just how it was.

My wife and I met when she was in the Navy; we were both stationed on the same ship in Norfolk. She did her four years and got out. When we met, she was seventeen and I was nineteen years old and we've been together ever since.

We made a conscious decision not to have children due to my job. First, because of the inherent dangers that come with the job and, second, because my wife was like, "I'm not going to be a single parent." That was a choice we both made. So, later on in my career, by the time we got to a point where we were like, "All right, maybe we should think about having kids," we were both in our forties. I was like, "Do you really want to have a baby at forty years old?" So we ended up exploring the option of adoption and adopted our daughter. We did an international adoption, adopting our daughter from Latvia. She's been part of our family for a couple years now.

I have no regrets about the career choices I've made. In 2014, I had to decide whether to stay in or get out of the Navy. At that time, we were right in the middle of the adoption process and the Navy wanted me to go to Afghanistan for one year. I was like, "Not doing it."[5]

That was finally the point where I decided I've got to put my family ahead of the teams. For basically twenty-two years, I was in a cycle where I was either getting ready to deploy, or deployed. Getting ready to deploy, or deployed. During those training cycles, you're away from your family for nine to ten months out of the year and it was like that back to back to back.

The last major deployment I did was in '08 to Iraq. When I came back from that deployment, I received orders to what is called "shore duty," which is a non-operational, non-deployable billet. It took me about eight months of being non-operational to start being "normal" again. While I was on shore duty, I had a lot of time to look back at the last twenty-two years of my life and I realized that, "Holy crap. I can't believe some of the stuff I did."

I looked back at what I had done, and I was like, "I can't believe I did this, I did that." After I had time to reflect on my past deployments, the reality of the situations I put myself in started to hit home. At that point, I knew I could never go back to being that person I was. I couldn't turn that switch on again and regain that operational mindset you need to have to be successful on the battlefield.

It was as if I had passed through a doorway and then it was like, "I don't think I can get back to being that guy who's going to be deployed ten months out of the year." And that was fine with me. I was completely okay with it. No regrets, no looking back. It was a good decision I made. I'm glad I made it.

I had a great career. I don't know how many people you could ask, "If you could do it all over again would you do it the same way?" My answer would be, "Exactly the same way." It's just one of those things.

FIGURE 1.2
Ed interviewing Dan, Albany, New York, 2016.

I had this friend of mine who was the epitome of a SEAL operator. If you were to put the word Navy SEAL operator in the dictionary his picture would show up. He was the real deal, the kind of guy you want as a SEAL operator. He was physically fit, very well educated, and an overall great leader. He was that guy, but when you peel the layers back, he had a son who was in prison and a daughter who was working at a strip club. His kids didn't even talk to him, and he came out and told me that one day. He was like, "Dude, my family life sucks."

It's really hard to maintain your family life in the SEAL teams. There is an incredible work imbalance. I think the decision to not have kids and the fact that my wife is a very independent person significantly contributed to our staying together. My wife is just a very special person to be able to deal with me and my career choice. She's very independent; she can take care of her own.

For twenty-two-plus years, I was never home longer than two weeks, never. The short time that I was home, or in between training trips, if I were home longer than five or six days, my wife would be like, "Hey, you rearranged where I put the salt. You drank all the milk." She was like, "Isn't it time for you to go? Don't you have a trip to go on?"

That was one of those things that you don't think about. When I finished deploying after all those years, it took some adjustment for both of us to learn to live together.

My wife and I are the exceptions. One platoon I was in, when we returned for deployment, I think everybody in the platoon ended up getting a divorce except for me and maybe one other guy. The divorce rate in the SEAL teams is extremely high.

When you're in a SEAL platoon you will spend more time with the guys in the platoon than with your own family. You know everything about those guys; you can recognize someone from across the room just by their shadow. When I was home, I dedicated that time to being with my wife, whereas a lot of guys would be home, and then they'd still be out at the bars with the boys hooting and hollering all night. That doesn't go over very well. There's a lot of guys out there who retire after twenty-plus years in the teams and their family lives are a mess.

Dan Izzo is a retired Navy SEAL master chief petty officer who served twenty-eight years on active duty. He completed over a dozen deployments during his military career, earning two Bronze Star Medals, three Combat Action Awards, and numerous other personnel medals and campaign awards.

EYAL PRESS

As a child I think I had two very different images of security—of people in uniforms—in my mind. And it was kind of black and white.

One was the Israeli soldier which to me was this noble figure. It was what people in my family had done and I figured they were in the right. And the other sort of image of a uniformed officer was a Nazi. And that's because one side of my family are Holocaust survivors, including my mother.

And so, even though we never talked about that, that was always in my mind. The image in my mind was not even of the malevolent and malicious Nazi. It was more the one who follows the orders, who just carries out the orders because that's what you're supposed to do.

I knew that was all part of my family history. But I also felt like I was given this incredible privilege of being removed from the conflicts and traumatic events that other generations of my family lived through.

FIGURE 1.3
Eyal Press, Bryant Park, New York City, 2022.

I never took a single course on Nazi Germany in college. I avoided it. I felt like I already knew it. Same with the Israeli-Palestinian conflict. I didn't really study it. It was just sort of part of my biography.

I never thought I would write about this stuff. The security realm isn't something that I have ever consciously thought, "Oh, I'm drawn to that." But what does and has drawn me are the inner conflicts that a person experiences in a situation where they're told to do something that in the normal walk of life wouldn't be legitimate.

That's very much a soldier's reality, right? Killing is not sanctioned in society but in the context of war it is.

My father served in the Israeli Army. My grandfather served in the Jewish Brigade of the British Army and then in the Haganah when Israel became a country. I don't know that they thought about these issues very much because there was such a sense of pride and patriotism through that first thirty, forty years of Israeli's existence that it was like the more you did, the higher your social prestige was.

By the time I was growing up, that was changing. And I grew up here (in the United States), so I was an outsider to that whole experience. But I had cousins exactly my age who were being drafted into the Israeli Army. This was literally right at the beginning of the first Intifada when Palestinians were starting to protest, organize, and sometimes throw stones and basically tell these soldiers to get out of their neighborhoods.[6]

I would talk to my cousins about, you know, what are you going to do if you're there? There started to be this thing called "selective refusal" or "being a refusenik" and I wrote about that in my book *Beautiful Souls*.[7]

I think that in the security realm the stakes are so high. If you make the wrong decision, an innocent person can die. If you don't make that decision, you might put yourself or someone else at risk. And then there's the whole issue—which really interests me—of what does society expect of people in security?

On the one hand, I think there is an expectation of "Be a little bit brutal," you know, as Cheney put it after 9/11. There's going to be some things going on in the dark side. And we don't want to ask too many questions about that.

On the other hand, when a scandal is exposed, there are often expressions of shock and "Oh, how could you do this?" That doublespeak is something that comes up in my book *Dirty Work* and I think it's very central to security in so many realms. Not just in the military. Not just in a case like Abu Ghraib where it was very obvious that America had kind of taken the gloves off.[8]

I think that phrase—"take the gloves off"—was even used in congressional testimony. And then when we saw the pictures of what taking the gloves off means, everyone was like "Oh, this is horrible. This is barbaric." And then a few low-ranking people were held accountable.

But not just in the military realm. Also in prisons. One of the most powerful passages of Everett Hughes' essay from the '60s on "dirty work" is really the starting point of my book. Hughes is imagining a prison guard. And he describes the person as someone who may have a penchant for brutality.[9]

And then a story appears in the newspaper and it turns out this person was involved in it. Hughes then shifts to the perspective of the security guard and the guard looks at the higher-ups in society and the good people and he says, "Well, what do you really want from me? You really want me to be nice or do you want me to be a little bit brutal?"

That's what I heard from the prison guards I interviewed in Florida. They all basically said, "What does society want from us? They invest very little in terms of resources, rehabilitation services, even adequate staffing in these massive prisons. How do they think we're going to enforce order in these places?" As one of them told me, you learn very quickly the way you do that is through brutality and fear.

And so, I'm interested in the hypocrisy of how as a society we scapegoat security personnel when it's convenient for us. And then, at the same time, we quietly signal to them that actually the rough treatment they mete out is acceptable and may be even desirable. We can also say that of border guards. That's why I wrote about border guards as well.

One thing that has always surprised me is the thoughtfulness of the people I've interviewed who work in security professions—and I think that's probably my own class bias and my own assumptions.

To give you a very recent example, there's a Black corrections officer in *Dirty Work* who goes under a pseudonym. And I talked to him a bunch of times. Quite a lot, actually. And I didn't really know how he'd feel about the book because, you know, sometimes I would spell out very clearly what the book's about. And then other times, I'd just kind of frame it in a general way. Like, "Oh, it's about people who do the hardest, most thankless jobs in our society." And he was into that. And in the book I'm obviously providing a kind of interpretive lens. I'm telling these people whose lives are involved in these professions, "This is how society sees you. This is your place in the social order and it's not a good one."

There's a lot of privilege that goes with that. Just to hear someone's story and put their life in some kind of rubric like that.

I was a little unsure how this guy would react to the book. But I figured he'll never ask me. You know? I'll just never hear about it. And then, the other day, I'm sitting there and I see a text message. I don't recognize that number, but it's vaguely familiar. It's someone in Florida.

So I click on it and it's this guy. And he says, "Hey, I read your book cover to cover. I want to thank you. I really was blown away by it. And I'm really happy that my story's in there. And anytime you want to come down to Florida . . ."

There's that surprise element, right? What an assumption I'd made about him. And he didn't just read the stuff on his own life in the book. He read the whole thing. And it really interested him.

I've been asked about the prison guards who don't ever claim to have any qualms about what they're doing. They think this is a good job. They're proud of what they do. They flash their badge and all the rest.

What I think of is when I was given a tour of a jail in Colorado. There's one section of the book that's in Colorado, the prison section. That's where I interviewed the most prison guards. I spent a week talking to all these guards.

I went around with the warden of this jail. And I asked him that exact question. And he said, "You know, those are the guys I worry about." He was talking about suicide and guys just losing it. And he said, "Those are the guys I worry about. The guys who tell me, Nah, I have no problem with that. I'll go down there. I'll bust that guy's ass. Don't you worry about it. I'll take care of it. And act as though there's just this hard shell."

I think that that hard shell can also be interpreted as an adjustment to the work and it's not a natural condition. Some of the guards who spoke to the psychiatrist I met in that area of Colorado would talk about that. They'd say, "I had to wear band-aids on everything. I put band-aids over everything to get through this job. The problem is I can't take them off when I leave work. So that's how I am at home and that's how I am with my kids and all the other beautiful things in life."

It's pretty incredible to hear that. And I don't think we think about it. We want the Hollywood version of it. Just the simple, straight story.

My instinct is always to try to meet the person where they are rather than judge them from some position of my own.

In the case of Chris Aaron, who ends up almost in the CIA and in the drone program, his initial draw was, I want to be like my grandfather and he was a hero and he fought in World War II. And they had a sense of mission and purpose. And I want to do something for the broader society. And all of that is very admirable.

And then later, later—actually the first time I met Chris, I didn't interview him at the time. I just heard him speak. He asked a question at this panel discussion on drones. By then he was already questioning everything. He asked whether it's something in the nature of men, something deeper than politics, that leads them to be drawn to that kind of work. It's like there's some biological drive that should be identified and questioned.

So, you know, I think it's important to think about what it is that's drawing the person to that work. Right? Not impose your own *why the hell would you do that*?

But, that said, I think that if we had a more open discussion in our society about things like moral injury, if that weren't an obscure term familiar only to scholars, journalists, and military psychologists who research and write about the inner conflicts that people in security experience . . . If it were sort of thought about more broadly, then maybe it would be part of the conversation as people think about what it means to do this kind of work.

And I think also of the warning that Heather Linebaugh—the other drone operator I wrote about—got from her father just before she goes in. She thinks he's going to be proud of her because she's gone to a recruitment office and signed up. And he says to her, "Just remember, the job of the military is to kill people."

And she kind of doesn't hear it at the time, but later she goes back to it. But we don't think that way because as a society it's all kind of hidden and glossed over.

Dirty Work is an effort to complicate how we view people in security. It's not black and white. They are agents of society. But that doesn't mean I'm endorsing the idea that it's just fine, that it's all great, let's just have more and more of this, and let's pour more and more of our resources into it. To the contrary, my hope is that we question the role of security, how much of it is really needed.

I think that without a doubt in America, security is a big industry because there's a lot of insecurity. There's a dialectic, it seems. High crime, so we are heavily policed. There are lots of security apparatuses that people put in their homes and there are the guns they buy.

Everything gets amped up that way. Does it have to be that way? I certainly don't think so and I would hope not. But we'd have to change a lot and we'd have to really examine the society.

In that sense, I think security is a great lens through which to look at where we are as a society and to look at our failures and how broken things are. I will never forget my best friend growing up happened to be born in Japan because his father was in a military base there. And they would talk about the years they spent there and how nobody locked the car door. They thought it was crazy to do the things that Americans thought you'd be crazy not to do. And that is so cultural. It is so much shaped by our expectations of whom you can trust and whom you can't.

We live in a very low-trust society, for all kinds of reasons. The level of inequality and the level of racial discord and all the rest. And so, you get a lot of security with that.

I think the gap between the world—the culture, the inbred culture—of some of these professions and these vocations and the rest of society is very toxic. I'm not sure how you break that down. The military in this "all-volunteer" army ends up, since 9/11, being 1 percent of the population. And it's not a random 1 percent. It's not the sons and daughters of senators and CEOs of big companies and all the rest. It's more working-class people and people with fewer choices and opportunities who effectively are being hired to do this. And, surprise, surprise, they resent the rest of a society that judges them and that thinks that they're bad people.

It's complicated and this is why I looked at drone operators. In the case of the military, there's also a lot of putting people on platforms and honoring them. But the honoring can also be very two-faced a lot of the time because it's like, "Let's honor them at the ball game and then on with the game and forget about the fact that the wars are being fought."

I think it really has to do with the civilizing process and how the civilizing process is this process of hiding disturbing things behind the scenes. So much of security is now behind the scenes. Whether it's drones or prisons or Homeland Security. It's going on out there, but we don't really see it. And I think that that's very dangerous.

I'm not sure how you break that down. Clearly, with the whole debate and conversation around policing, that's being put on the table. How much that will change these encounters, these shootings, I'm not sure. But, certainly, there's an idea that we should make it less insular, make it less separate from the community, and, hopefully, then you get better results.

My wife is a psychotherapist, so this is her bread and butter. Not so much the graphic details, but certainly she's more attuned, I would say, than I am to the weight of being in these worlds, even as a reporter, even as a writer just going in and coming out.

On the other hand, I'm not really sure that I've fully processed it all.

The first story in *Dirty Work* is just a horrific story. The woman in that section is a mental health aide in a prison. Her hair fell out. She got PTSD. She got depressed. Ever since we met, she's been in my life as a person I talk to. I'm not sure that I've really worked through it all.

There is the impulse to write about something totally different next time.

My first book, *Absolute Convictions*, is about my father and his medical practice becoming a site of conflict within the abortion conflict.[10] I never wanted to write about it. It made me really uncomfortable. I didn't want to draw any attention to it. And I found it just creepy because these protestors would show up outside our home. They were so convinced of the rightness of their cause. They would use language like, "This is an American holocaust." I didn't want to have anything to do with it, to be honest.

And then it was in 1998, October 23, 1998, I was helping canvass somewhere. I went with a friend to this local office and someone opening the door said, "Did you hear what happened in Buffalo?" And my friend said, "No." And they said, "Oh, an abortion doctor was shot."

That's all I heard. And I knew there were about three. So there was a one in three chance that the person shot was my father. Then the person said the name of who it was. And it turned out it was a doctor my father worked with very closely. They covered for each other on weekends. I'd heard his name throughout my upbringing.

After that I could no longer shy away from it. I had to figure out how, in the name of life, people could shoot a man in his kitchen, standing there, in front of his kids.

I'd never raise a hand against my son. But I also would never think of my son being pinned to the ground by a police officer. You know, I just wouldn't think of it. It's not a normal part of consciousness for me.

If I think of Palestinians, that is a normal part of consciousness for them. They're going to, at some point, be at a checkpoint with a child, potentially. And the child is going to see the parent put in some kind of humiliating position or violence meted out to them. And what does that do to you as a parent? Do you feel like you have to toughen your children up to some extent?

I think the privilege of being in the majority in both societies is that you don't have to think about that stuff. You can just say, "All this harsh violence is wrong, and I'll never expose my kids to it." But obviously that stuff is shaped by race and by class and by your position in the society, and I don't think we think enough about the class and race dimensions that shape the lens of doing this work.

I'm not saying everyone who gets into it, gets into it because they're pushed into it by what I call the pressure of economic necessity. They don't have better options.

But it is very class-bound and race is a factor, certainly in the Border Patrol. I think that the blanket judgments are easy to make when you never think about that. It's easy to say all Border Patrol people are Nazis or traitors or whatever they are when you're on the campus of a university very far away from the world in which those people are living, from the lives of the folks who are there. That frustrates me because I feel like it misses the point. It's easy moralizing rather than really hard thinking. And it doesn't change much.

And I think it's probably similar with the police, which doesn't mean we should in any way excuse what the police do. It doesn't mean we should excuse what Border Patrol guards do. It doesn't even mean we should have those forces.

It just means, let's think a little more in a more nuanced way about the individuals, the human beings, in these jobs, and more systemically about the forces that create a demand for their services.

Eyal Press is a journalist, sociologist, and the author of three books, most recently *Dirty Work: Essential Jobs and the Hidden Toll of Inequality in America*. He is a contributor to the *New Yorker*, the *New York Times*, and numerous other publications.

PABLO ARROYO

Growing up, the only role model I really had was my mother. My father was a sperm donor. The only thing he ever gave me was his last name, period, but when I was about two, three years old in Puerto Rico my mom and dad divorced and so at about three years old we came to, as Puerto Ricans say, America. We came to the States.

There were four of us—my older sister, my brother, myself, and my youngest sister—with my mom, and this is back in the mid-'60s. You had a divorced Hispanic woman who didn't speak a lick of English with four children, coming to America with not a penny in her pocket or a pot to piss in.

We had an aunt who lived here and the intent was to come here and live with her until we got on our feet, but I guess we were like fish. After three days we began to stink, and she essentially kicked us out. Then, for about three months, going from the fall into the winter, we lived on a park bench. We were homeless and at that point and time in the '60s it would have been easy for my mother to walk away and put us into foster care and, you know, take care of herself. That would have been the simple solution, but she stuck it out.

She had a lot of strength and a lot of courage. When I talk about what I just told you, some people go, "Oh my God, that's so awful, I feel so sorry for your upbringing." I say, to the contrary. I say the experience was great because it formed me into the person I am today. It made me stronger. The courage and commitment my mother showed throughout my formative years definitely was my role model. She could do what was virtually impossible and no matter what obstacle was thrown in front of us she always overcame it and we never heard her once bitch about how tough things were. She always had a positive outlook on everything.

Getting out of high school was a major achievement in my family. But then what do you do? Do you start selling drugs? Do you enter into a life of crime? Those were the easy paths growing up in the Bronx. Or if you wanted to make a career path, you worked at a bodega, you worked at a clothing shop. And I would look at that and think: "This is ludicrous. There has to be more to this."

I came to the conclusion that the best way to move forward productively in life, first and foremost was to get out of the Bronx. If a goldfish stays in a goldfish bowl, whether or not he swims behind a castle, he's still in a goldfish bowl. If he swims behind the coral reef, he's still in the goldfish bowl. You've got to jump out of that bowl and jump into the ocean and that's what I needed to do.

One thing I always admired was the military and people who served in the military. They do something for a purpose and for a reason and it's much broader than themselves. So I decided that when I got out of high school I was going to join the military. And I didn't want to just join the military. I wanted to join the military and, air quotes, become a man.

I didn't want to go somewhere, sign up, put in my eight hours a day, and you're just some slapdick. I wanted to do something more than that and the Marine Corps offered that. The Marine Corp offered accountability and a regimented lifestyle and that's what I needed. That's why I joined the Marine Corps.

FIGURE 1.4
Pablo Arroyo, Connecticut, 2017.

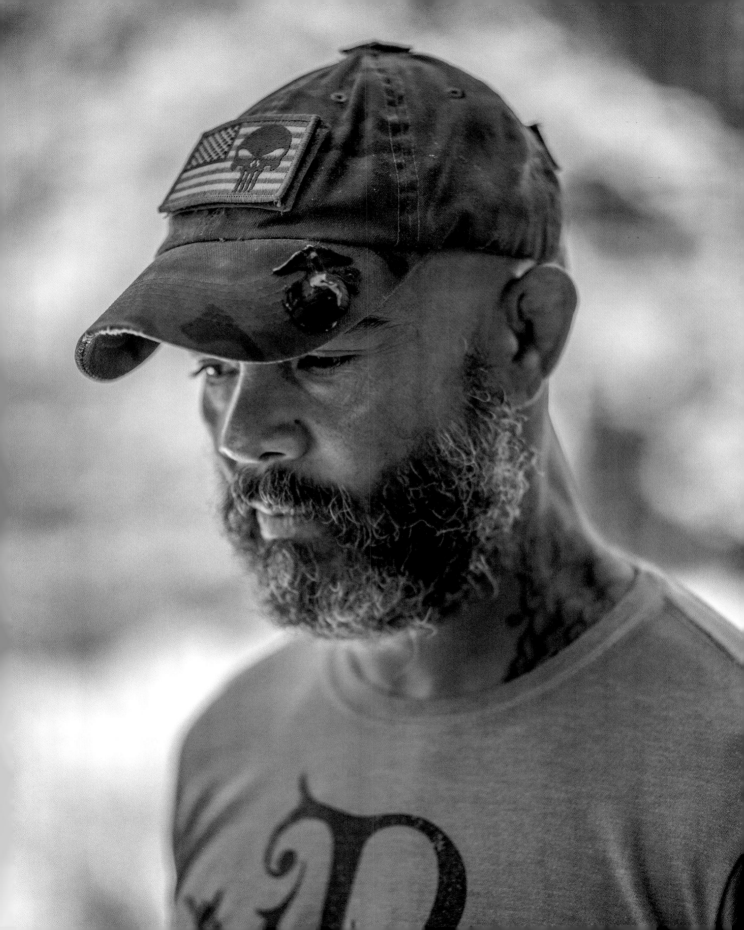

The morning after I graduated from high school, I kissed my mom goodbye and left for the Marine Corps. After four years I reenlisted. I extended for one year and then reenlisted for another four years. Love the Corps. Miss the Corps, you know. Never stop being a Marine. I joined in '79. After boot camp, I did basic military occupational specialty, or MOS, school and I was supposed to be a radio operator and after I finished that there were opportunities to deploy to Okinawa, Japan. I was like, yeah, sign me up. I'll go anywhere. I'll do anything.

So I went to Okinawa and my second day there a group of individuals came down from 3rd Recon asking to screen volunteers who wanted to be Recon Marines.[11] I said, yeah, sure, absolutely, you know. And there were about twenty of us and we went through an indoctrination program. Back then it was called RIP, the Reconnaissance Indoctrination Program, and it was six weeks of living off the jungle. By the time we were done, only three of us had made it through.

When I got done with my year over at 3rd Recon it was time to come back stateside. I was stationed at Camp Lejeune at 2nd Recon. I did several deployments from there, including a Mediterranean cruise—that's what it was called—when I happened to find myself in Haifa, Israel, at the initiation of the Intifada.

At the end of that deployment we went back to Lejeune. Did a couple more deployments and that whole thing was still going, so when it came time for the rotation to go back into the Mediterranean, we deployed straight back to Beirut.

I was in Beirut for about four and a half months until the fateful morning—well, the night of October 22nd, 1983.[12] A USO show started at about 17:00 and we—Recon platoon, twenty-four of us—were watching it.[13] At about 18:00 it was time for the nightly firefight, so rockets started coming into the compound. You could set your watch by it: 18:00, time for the firefight.

We kind of chuckled because the people who came in to entertain us for the USO show were mortified and they couldn't leave fast enough and the last song that they sang was Bonnie Tyler's "Total Eclipse of the Heart." Point of trivia. Later that evening a Recon team needed to go out and do a mission and the team did not have a sniper, so I asked the sniper on my team if he'd mind going out on this patrol with those guys. He said, yeah, sure, whatever, I'll go out and get some trigger time.

I stayed back at the compound and they were supposed to come back between 5:30 and 6 in the morning. At about 5:30 I'm up and I'm sitting by a window in my room. I have my rifle field stripped because of the firefight the night before.[14] I'm cleaning it and waiting for the guys to come back for the debrief.

I heard some shots in the distance, but it's Beirut. It's normal. It's like, you know, you're on some tropical island and you hear the rooster first thing in the morning. That's gunshots in Beirut. I heard some faint voices, some screaming and whatnot, and then I felt the building erupt and I was on the third floor next to the window. I get blown out the window and I'm looking and I'm going to the ground and I remember clearly the ground kind of coming up at me, but it wasn't from the sense of falling, like when you parachute. No, it's because the ground was coming up at me from the explosion.

So everything settled and I'm buried and I'm kind of like looking around buried under rubble and, you know, the only way out is up and at that point and time I came to the conclusion that I hadn't come to Lebanon to die and I'm not going to wait here for someone to come and rescue me. I don't want the bad guys to come dig me out. Back then French and Americans were being taken hostage. I didn't want to find myself in that situation.

I was under about eighteen to twenty feet of rubble, so it took me a while to get out. The first time I had a sense of the gravity of what occurred was I'm just standing and I'm looking around and both my eardrums were also ruptured, so I really couldn't hear anything and I'm looking around trying to make sense of what occurred and I'm trying to look for the building that I was standing at, but it's not there.

And then I'm looking at the trees around me. The night before, there were leaves on all the trees. There's not one leaf on any of the trees, but what the trees are full of is flesh and limbs, you know, and body parts. And I look at the ground and there are corpses, obviously dead, there are some people who are crawling around. I look at myself, do a self-assessment.

My right leg had about twenty, twenty-five puncture wounds from fragmentation. It looked like cottage cheese. It looked like Jell-O was oozing out of my leg. My left leg had about eleven holes. I was scorched from my head all the way down and I had a hole in my head. I didn't know it then, but I was told later that you could have looked at my head and seen my brain. That hole was about the size of a half dollar, one of those old Kennedy half dollars.

My jaw was fractured, upper and lower mandible, and I lost most of my teeth to the molars from the center line all the way back. My front tooth on top was loose and was just hanging by gum. At that point and time I was so disgusted I just reached up, ripped it out, thinking, "It's not like I'm going to need this one either, you know. I done lost all these." I just tore it out and chucked it.

So I was banged up a little, but I'm looking around and I'm like, there are guys that are far off worse than me, so the first thing I'm doing is looking for a rifle and for some boots because I didn't have anything on my feet.

But I can't find anything. There was another Marine and he was kind of like in the crater, but he had what looked like an I-beam across his lap. I go over to him and try to dig around to try and get him out. He's conscious, but there's nothing really that I can do. Try to move the I-beam. Nothing happening. I tell him, "Hey, just stay here and don't make any noise because we don't know what's going on. I'll try and get some help and I'll come right back to you."

As I start walking off I almost trip over something. I looked down. It was a torso—no head, no arms, no legs—just a torso. And I was like, "Yeah, it's gonna be a bad day at the office." I take about twenty more steps and a group of Marines rush over to me. They look horrified. I'm like, "Hey, there's a guy over here who needs help. Let's go help him." They're like, "No, we need to get you to help." I'm like, "No, we need to go help that guy. He's worse off."

A couple of them went over to try to help him and then they take me over to a triage station. The triage station was in a little building and it was in the basement, but by the time they got me there, there were so many injured that the concrete floor was tacky. It was just blood.

I was there for about an hour or two, and then they said, "Yeah, we are going to take you over to one of the hangars over on the other side of the airport and we have CH-46s coming in.[15] We'll see if we can fly you out to the USS Iwo Jima helicopter landing ship off the coast for medical attention."

They managed to do that and once I'm on the Iwo Jima they started partial treatment, but they really couldn't do anything, give me any medications or anything, because of the hole in my head. So after a couple of hours they come back and say, "Hey, we got good news for you. We're going to fly you out to Germany to the 47th General Army Hospital in Frankfurt, Germany, on a C-130."[16] I go, "Oh, that's great."

But we're on a helicopter assault ship. C-130s can't land on a helicopter assault ship, you know. So where's the C-130 that I'm supposed to get on going to land? Well, it's going to land at Beirut International Airport. So they fly me back to where they flew me out of and at this point and time there are firefights everywhere. Every time either a helicopter or an aircraft tries to land they start taking in mortar fire.

When the C-130 finally landed that I was supposed to go on, it never stopped. Four guys grab the litter[17] that I was on and start running to it and pass it to the crew chief, you know, to get me on the aircraft. They were only able to get three guys on that C-130 utilizing that method. The C-130 takes off and it was like a seven-, eight-hour flight to Germany. Again, no meds, nothing for the pain. I'm on a canvas litter and that's thick burlap, thick canvas. They put us on what looked like tiers. There were three of us. I'm in the second tier. There's a guy on the bottom, there's me, and there's a guy on top. The guy on top is doing so bad that drops of blood are coming through the canvas and falling on me. He didn't make it. He died on the flight.

We landed in Germany, but nowhere near Frankfurt and I'm hurting and I'm telling the guys, "Hey, I'm not a pussy, I'm not a bitch, but hurry up and get me to Frankfurt, just don't hit any potholes or anything."

They finally get me to the hospital and started treatment. After about three weeks in Germany, they sent me back to Camp Lejeune to the naval hospital where I spent a couple of weeks convalescing. Then I went home for a couple of days because out of a platoon of twenty-four guys, eighteen guys died over there.

A good friend of mine, Tommy Smith, lived in Connecticut and his father was a state trooper. I went to Tommy's funeral, but I was just there long enough to pay my respects and then I had to leave because, again, I had all these holes in me. My teeth are gone. My jaw is cracked. I was a hurting puppy.

I wanted to go back to 2nd Recon after my leave and so I really needed to convalesce and do physical therapy to be operational again. At that point they offered a medical discharge and I'm like, "No, I joined the Marine Corps to fight, not to take a medical discharge and do nothing."

This is the early 80s, '83, and we didn't have the ADA (Americans with Disabilities Act of 1990), so if you take a medical discharge, you are a disabled veteran. It's like you automatically limited your career potential. And, again, I want to do something productive with my life, so I want to get operational again.

They told me I could do my physical therapy where I was or I could go somewhere else to do it and that would be the end of my enlistment. They'd patch me up and send me home. I said, "No, I want to re-enlist."

So I reenlisted for another four years and then they say, "Well, if you're going to reenlist for four years, that's great. You'll come back to Recon after you get done convalescing."

But I knew I was going to be shipped off to a sick body platoon, and I didn't want that.

They said the only option was to go somewhere. Go to a Marine Corps base somewhere and convalesce there and then come back when the doctor signs off on you.

I said, "What's the worst place that I can go to?"

They said, "Well, that would be Guantanamo Bay, Cuba. It's not the end of the world, but on a clear day you can see it from there."

So I went to Gitmo for a year and did physical therapy and I was running ten miles a day in about three months. Got healed up. Doctor signed off on me, went back to Recon, did a couple more deployments and then I decided it was time to go out and see civilian life.

And one day I see a job posting for the Connecticut State Police and I thought of Tommy Smith and called up his dad. He said, "It's a good job. Put in for it. I'm sure you'll do well."

So I joined the state police and it was great because the state police also have an emergency services unit, which is comprised of the bomb squad, the SWAT team, the aviation unit, and the canine section. And I'm like, "Well, that sounds like something to shoot for." I was already a Navy-certified diver from being in Recon and a combat swimmer and I already had sufficient training in explosives, so when I got out of the police academy I had a six-month probationary period and as soon as I completed my probationary period they took me right out to the dive team.

Then the first time that there was an opening available for the bomb squad, I put in for it and I was able to get on the bomb squad. At about the ten-year mark, I took over the day-to-day operations of the bomb squad, and, of course, being in the emergency services unit and running the bomb squad, I got involved with the Federal Bureau of Investigation (FBI), the Joint Terrorism Task Force, and the Weapons of Mass Destruction (WMD) Task Force.

But when I joined the state police it was always, to me, a sacrificial job. I was twenty-seven years old when I joined and I'm like, "I can retire at forty-seven." You do twenty years and you retire. I'm going to sacrifice twenty years of my life, that was my mindset. I'll do the most that I can and be the best that I can be and dedicate twenty years of my life to this because then after this, at forty-seven, I get to enjoy life and that's what I did.

At the twenty-year mark, to the day, I retired from the state police.

Then the Department of Homeland Security (DHS) decided to start the bomb appraisal officer (BAO) program, so I put in for that and got hired to start the program in Connecticut. I was assigned to the Transportation Security Administration (TSA).[18] I joined the Department of Homeland Security and my intent was to protect the homeland and do everything for that, but there were systemic problems. I did the job for about seven years and it took me until the seven-year mark to realize that I'd become disillusioned with the program. Everyone goes in with the same concept. Everyone wants to do the best. Everyone wants to do good. Everyone is genuinely interested in Homeland Security, but you have bureaucracies and the way they go about applying the program and I don't fault them. Present day, the Department of Homeland Security is only about what, fifteen, sixteen years old? If it was a human it couldn't even have consensual sex. It's still in its formative years. It's not as old as all the other federal entities that have gone through this and have grown through growing pain. It's still teething.

When you're trying to train individuals in security postures and remediation and trying to identify the threat and you have people interrupting you, hall monitors, per se, saying, "Well, we have to consider and give consideration to our customer," my question is what product does the TSA or Homeland Security or all the agencies that make up Homeland Security sell? Literally, what is it that someone goes to the Homeland Security store, pulls out a ten-dollar bill and purchases something that qualifies them as a customer? They give you the ten dollars and you give them something tangible in return? To me that's the meaning of a customer.

My response was always, No, your focus should never be on customer service. Your focus is always on doing your job professionally. If you do your job in a professional manner all that is incorporated, but if you do your job focused primarily on customer service, that butts heads with security and you'll never be able to do your job proficiently.

The people who go into this field who do a successful and productive job don't need motivation, they don't need guidance. They just naturally do it, and those are the success stories. There are people who come into this field who have the intent, the want, the will, the motivation, but they just don't have that thing—you know, the magic sauce. They don't just possess it and it eludes them.

I would say 97 percent of the individuals who go into the security field do a mediocre job, and they excel at being second best. I go to events that have security screenings all the time. I do my own security assessment and then I determine what type of level of personal security I am going to maintain while I am there. Although they provide screening to get through, I just leverage human behavior. If I have a knife on me and I want to keep it, I'll just put it in my pocket or put it in my waistband. And when I approach the screener if it's a guy, I say, "Hi, you look cute today. I'm looking forward to you touching my junk, ha, ha, ha, ha." Now he's

FIGURE 1.5
Pablo and Stacey, Connecticut, 2017.

going to take a mental note of not touching me around the genital area where I have my knife. You develop certain skills around leveraging human behavior.

Individuals who think about coming into this field—there's nothing that I can really guide them or tell them. Hey, just stay motivated and stay vigilant. Those are the two key factors, even for someone who's going to succeed at being mediocre and succeed at being second best. But other than that, there's really nothing that you can offer to someone and guarantee that in fact they're going to be successful at the trade craft.

Still, there's a saying: "Be leery of old men in a sport where the average participant dies early." And I'm an old man, you know, but I still play sports.

I met my wife, Stacey, when she was a microbiologist, a supervisor of the environmental microbiology laboratory for the Department of Public Health for the state of Connecticut and I was still a Connecticut state trooper.

We have a great relationship. We shoot together and we also do Brazilian jiu-jitsu. She's a two-time Brazilian jiu-jitsu champion and I'm only a one-time Brazilian jiu-jitsu world champion. We started doing Brazilian jiu-jitsu together. Well, I started it. I started training and then about a year into our training, she got tired of the gym being my mistress, so she said, "I'm going to do it too."

One of the things that is kind of a running joke with my mother and with Stacey is that you can ask me any question you want. That doesn't necessarily warrant an answer. You can ask any questions. If you don't get an answer it's because, you know, it doesn't merit one. My mother knows that and she understands that. She's always full of questions. She's a mom.

When I travel, I say, "Hey Mom, going away. I will talk to you when I get back."

Sometimes she goes, "Where are you going?"

And the answer is: "Away."

"When do you leave?"

"When the flight takes off."

"When do you come back?"

"When I land. I'll talk to you then."

And we leave it at that, you know.

Pablo Arroyo is a former Recon Marine, state trooper, and bomb technician and currently the COO for a security firm.

TERRI MERZ

The story of my entry into the world of cybersecurity may sound fictional; however, I assure you it isn't.

While serving in the US Army Signals Corp in Germany, my father met and married my mother, a German citizen. They subsequently moved to the United States, where I was born. Ultimately, they divorced while I was in grade school.

After the divorce, my mother was eager to introduce me to the German side of my family. She decided we would move to Germany. This happened during my middle school years. Entering the German school system, I completed middle school, high school, and technical college. Even though my mother returned to the United States after two years, I remained with my grandmother to finish school. I subsisted on my college stipend, which was about 465 deutschmarks per month, and winnings from the occasional chess match at local taverns.

During my internship with Rosenthal Glass and Porcelain, a group of college friends and I decided to open a tavern. It was located on the outskirts of town, only a few kilometers from the demilitarized zone at the border of then communist Czechoslovakia.

On Christmas Eve of 1983, US military intelligence stopped at our tavern with a disabled vehicle. They had been patrolling the border during a heavy snowstorm. I recall being astounded by these small, fragile vehicles that were being used to brave the fierce elements of that evening. We invited the soldiers into the tavern to warm themselves by the blazing fireplace. We then conjured up an impromptu Christmas Eve dinner consisting of thawed and sauteed T-bone steaks, with various sides and warm beer.

That evening marked the beginning of a continuing friendship and my cybersecurity career. The soldiers returned to the tavern with families in tow. We became friends, and they learned I was a US citizen awaiting reentry into the German college system (as I had changed majors).

It was during that conversation I was told that if I returned to the United States and joined the military my college would be paid for by the military. However, I was not easily convinced this was true, therefore I was invited to the Grafenwoehr Army base, and shown the enlistment documents, which detailed the college benefits.

In addition to learning about my American citizenship, my newfound friends also learned I had studied photography in the German technical college, and I was a photography intern at Rosenthal (meaning I had equipment and training). They made, what seemed to me, an innocuous request, namely, if I would be so kind and snap some pictures for them of a castle. They were prohibited from entering it. They also asked if I could snap some pictures of the Czech towers which could be seen from the castle. Finally, they also asked if I'd be so kind and use infrared film.

My friends and I thought this unusual request was a simple case of Americans and Czechs being curious about each other. We happily agreed to produce the pictures. The castle was, after all, a favored destination.

On a sunny weekend, we grabbed our cameras, our tele lenses, and of course the infrared film and made our way to the castle. Without reservation I pointed the tele lenses straight at the Czech towers and happily snapped one picture after the other.

Unfortunately, this photographic field day was not appreciated by the Czechs. We found ourselves receiving new visitors at the tavern, visitors who were clearly not from "these parts." To make a long story short, the situation became quite uncomfortable. After several weeks, a couple of us took a trip to the US Embassy in Munich and shared our story. We were then brought to German intelligence to repeat the story with more details. Magically, the uncomfortable visitors disappeared. However, the American soldiers disappeared as well, with one letting me know "there had been some trouble" with their visits to our tavern.

While the events were disturbing and troubling, I was not dissuaded from exploring a return to the United States and taking advantage of that paid college tuition. I started planning my trip "home."

While my intentions were to join the Air Force, the Air Force recruiting office was perpetually closed. I found myself drinking coffee over several days with the Navy recruiter. Having lived such a sheltered life in Germany, I was swept away by this confident sailor's charm, looks, and of course the never-ending pictures of Hawaii on his walls in the background.

After enduring a month of this high-powered charm offensive, I was signing my life away to the United States Navy. Finding the right niche in the Navy was not a straightforward proposition. Translating my German college transcripts into something equivalent to the US educational system was not feasible; therefore, an officer's program was ruled out. However, I did speak several languages, so there was a strong interest in my joining as a cryptological technician linguist. That created a problem because my recruiter was unable to elaborate on what these "CTs" did. I was hesitant to commit to anything that could not be explained to me.

Much to my recruiter's dismay, the only option left was to enter the Navy undesignated and let fate determine my Navy career. Since my sole purpose was to attend college, I was not troubled by this turn of events. I entered the Navy undesignated.

My first duty station was a tugboat in Yorktown, Virginia. While most people considered tug duty undesirable, it was appealing to me. I enjoyed being on the water; the fresh air; the jovial atmosphere among the young crew members; the healthy, daily movement of the work; and of course the freedom to go to school during my personal time.

My determination to study soon became of interest to the chain of command. They structured my Navy duties around my classes. My division officer took personal interest in my class standing and I received tutoring from him in chemistry. In all, I received considerable encouragement from the command, and I excelled.

It was during this time that personal computers made their appearance in offices around the base. People moving from typewriters to personal computers was a disruptive event.

Even though I was studying biology, the chain of command assumed I would have knowledge of computers. Therefore, I was often called upon to tame the binary beasts. To my own surprise, I had an intuitive understanding of these machines and could overcome things like password lockouts, connectivity issues, and other vexing problems.

It didn't take long before I was moved off the tugboat and into a headquarters office. My new role was that of the local computer-whisperer (not sure what else to call it as there were no official titles for such jobs at the time).

In the meantime, my Navy career was moving along. I advanced in rank. With that, I received orders to transfer to Rota, Spain. With an elaborate sendoff party, my commanding officer sent me on my way. He also included a note for the receiving command. He recommended they take advantage of my computer skills.

In Spain I was forced to switch majors during my junior year of college as a biology curriculum was not available at the colleges on the base in Spain. I switched my major to computer science. While my Navy designation involved personnel management, the job I was given focused on managing the computer systems. This job was a mixture of troubleshooting and logistics (which often involved bartering for parts with other commands).

In 1987, the National Security Agency released the Rainbow Series. This set of books is often described as a "six-foot-tall stack of books" involving the evaluation of trusted computer systems. The book that pertained to my command was "The Orange Book, a Guide to Configuration Management in Trusted Systems."[19]

One day the Orange Book found its way to my desk. With no further explanations my officer in charge, Commander Hurley, simply dropped this tome on my desk with a thud and said,

FIGURE 1.6
Terri Merz, Worcester, New York, 2021.

"We need to do this; make it happen." The sheer volume of this book left me both speechless and wide-eyed. To boot, I was then officially designated the command's automated data processing systems security officer (or ADPSSO), and was told to secure the computer systems in Naples, the USS *Orion*, Spain, and Portugal. I was all of twenty-seven years old at the time.

That event marked a period of intense travel between countries, hop-scotching a ride on whatever Air Force planes were available. An at-risk system in another country meant a precarious take off in forty-mile-an-hour winds, or scraping the tips of the Pyrenees in a small C-12, or being dropped unceremoniously onto the deck of a ship by a helicopter.[20] Often I was unsure of the day, the time, or where I was. Rides on Medevac planes included stopping in every country on the way to a destination. A ride on a C-141 offered the pleasure of a tank as company in the cargo hold.[21] These trips also meant doing homework, with a book on my lap, swinging from a jump seat.

As my tour in Spain wound down, a decision was needed as to whether I would stay in the Navy. The new officer in charge recommended I attend Officer Candidate School. Initially, I agreed and began the process. However, while at my transitional duty station at Fort Meade in Maryland the civilian world beckoned, and I quickly learned my skills could command an attractive salary.

My newly minted undergraduate degree was in software engineering. Cybersecurity was not a distinct area of study at the time. The initial positions I took were therefore programming jobs. After several years, however, I found myself with the Navy again as a government civilian in Pensacola, Florida. Our tasks became increasingly intermingled with cybersecurity. Ultimately, our command's mission was reclassified, and we found ourselves wholly focused on cybersecurity. It was during this time a deliberate decision was needed: remain in software engineering or transition to a new field called information assurance. I chose information assurance/cybersecurity.[22]

From a personal perspective, choosing to enter the field of cybersecurity was the correct choice. At the time of my entry, the field had not diversified into subspecialties, and those of us in the profession found ourselves supporting the entire security engineering life cycle.

My earlier engagements had me integrating security engineering into the systems development life cycle. One such effort included taking on the role of the security interim program team leader for the US Central Command's Deployable headquarters. Another early effort involved developing a three-year IT security engineering plan for the General Service Administration. I've also executed vulnerability assessments (red team) against systems such as those found at the Defense Logistics Agency. As fate would have it, during a conference in Baltimore during the early 2000s I met an entrepreneur from Manhattan. This chance meeting led to the formation of our joint cybersecurity small business, which we ran successfully for fourteen years, averaging $9.5 million per year.

After my business partner retired, I found myself at another career crossroads. This time the choices were between a focus on managerial positions or research. I chose research and began working on my doctoral degree in computer science with a focus on information assurance.

Today I am a senior research scientist at the Pacific Northwest National Laboratory (PNNL). My doctorate and master's are in computer science, with a concentration in information assurance, and my bachelor of science is in information management.

The twenty-plus years of cybersecurity experience I now have include the areas of systems and cybersecurity engineering, research, cybersecurity testing (blue/red team testing), and management. The roles I've filled include those of a fully qualified Navy Validator (or in civilian terms a cyber security auditor for the US Navy) as well as the information systems security engineer on behalf of the National Security Agency.

In addition to security engineering and vulnerability testing, I spent several years in cyber incident response.

From 2014 onward, my specific area of research became the study of asymmetric cyber operations and analytics. I am particularly interested in advanced persistent threats (APTs) and the life cycle thereof. APTs are cyberattacks used by well-heeled adversaries and are difficult to detect and eradicate. These studies included responses to such threats, such as the development of cyber-resilient tactics, techniques, and procedures, as well as first responder detection techniques.

FIGURE 1.7
Terri's door, Worcester, New York, 2021.

For two years, I conducted research in software-enabled devices (system of systems), zero-day vulnerabilities relative to software-enabled devices, and the development of resiliency tactics, techniques, and procedures for software-enabled devices.[23]

While conducting applied research on APTs and specifically zero-day attacks, I included behavioral INFOSEC (information security) into my research areas. With humans forming the primary attack vector of advanced cyber threats, I found this area of research to be a natural fit for ongoing research.

In 2019 I started my affiliation with the College of Emergency Preparedness, Homeland Security and Cybersecurity (CEHC) at the University at Albany, New York. At the CEHC I teach classes in cybersecurity at the undergraduate, graduate, and PhD levels. In 2022 I became a joint appointee to the CEHC and now fulfill the role of a research fellow and visiting professor. It is in this capacity I hope to continue researching in breakthrough areas such as deep reinforcement learning for cyber mitigations on industrial control systems, automaticity of asymmetric cyber operations, and behavioral information security.[24]

In terms of being a female in cybersecurity, that has been a journey. Luckily, the Navy provided me with early role models. Every officer in charge I served while in Spain was a female, including our admiral in Naples. Those early role models left no doubt in my mind that women were "on the team" at every level.

While there are obviously many challenges if you are a female in a male-dominated profession, I've only encountered outright hostility on a few rare occasions. Most of the challenges come from cultural norms that permeate our social interactions and expectations. I would often joke that my male colleagues could be quite candid about an impending cyber incident and speak in dire terms without the need to worry about offending anyone. I, on other hand, seemed to be required to couch the impending doom using indirect and softer language.

However, I have seen less of those expectations in today's younger generations. Cultural, generational, and gender diversity has distilled, in many respects, cyber down to its core components of bits and bytes moving through the ether rather than a focus on our individual differences and communication styles. The cultural expectations appear to be weakening, and hopefully will result in data-driven conversations in the future.

As it relates to my family, my daughter joined the Navy while in college and entered a naval cryptological program for officers. She married a Top Gun SH Bravo Helicopter pilot. Like me, since entering the armed services, she relates best to people who are from a service community. That can include the military, law enforcement, etc.

Sharing the same context as it relates to one's perspective is important, I believe. The military creates such a unique context, particularly if you are in a field that has global implications; the need to appreciate that context is critical relative to close relationships.

I have a son as well. My son is the creative one in the family. And he has decided to "live off-grid in New Mexico," working with earth ships and the like. And he dedicated himself to art, music, and poetry.

He didn't want anything to do with this spooky world!

Terri Merz, DCS, CISSP, CISM, is a senior research scientist at the Pacific Northwest National Laboratory.

So, what inspired me to join the military? There's a short answer and a long answer. The short answer is I grew up in Alexandria, Virginia; I got into college; and my dad said, "Well, you're a middle-class white kid with no athletic ability. A ROTC scholarship is the only scholarship you're getting. You don't have to take it, but you have to apply for it." So I applied and didn't get it. I don't like being told I can't do things, so I joined anyway, and here I am.

The longer answer is it never even really occurred to me that I wouldn't go into public service of some sort. My father was a career federal law enforcement agent, who'd served in the military before he went into law enforcement. My grandfather served in the Navy in World War II. My great-grandfather served in the Army in World War I.

I was raised with this ethos. My dad was of the generation where everybody got drafted or joined the military to avoid the draft. And I grew up in the DC suburbs, where 70 percent of my friends were military brats. It was just the natural path. And then once I got on it, to some extent I liked it, and I was reasonably good at it. Not great, but not bad. And frankly, it was the path of least resistance. I was in it. I had healthcare. I had a retirement plan. I was getting promoted. I got married. I started having kids.

It was a secure job. And so I stayed at it. Then the Iraq War started and I had eleven years in. And you know, you don't take the money and the housing and the healthcare for eleven years, and then when the shooting starts, say, "Oh sorry, I'm out now. I have other things, more important things to do." There was suddenly nothing more important to do. I deployed five times in ten years and that was that.

I expected a challenge.

I was not, I am not, and I have never been a natural Army officer. I'm a political liberal among thousands of conservatives. I'm a guy from the East Coast, from the Washington, DC, suburbs among thousands of guys from the South and the Mountain West and places like that. I'm a non-athlete among guys who were all captains of the football team and the basketball team and long-distance runners. I'm a reader. I taught English at West Point. They read *Sports Illustrated* and I read Jane Austen. And you can't have a lot of discussions about Jane Austen sitting around in the office in the S-3 job.[25]

It was outside my comfort zone, and I got that because it was physically challenging. I had to stay in physical condition and be able to go on twenty-five-mile marches and hike up and down mountains in Afghanistan. I expected an adventure and I certainly got that. I think I've been to fifteen countries. Probably twenty now because I did a stint in Legislative Liaison, where I got to take people all over Africa and Vietnam and Japan.[26]

But before that, I got to go to Kyrgyzstan. I mean, if you told me when I was fifteen, I would go to Kyrgyzstan, I would have said, "Yeah, right." And of course, I've been to Afghanistan and Iraq multiple times. I served five months in the Gulf War back in '91. And then, the other forty-nine months were from 2004 to 2015. Three tours in Baghdad, two tours in Afghanistan, and then a couple of little short things, a week here, a week there. As a freshman cadet in 1986, if you had said, "Well, you're going to serve six combat tours, and the last two are going to be in Afghanistan," I would have said, "You're out of your damn mind. You know, we're not going to go into Afghanistan. The Soviets are getting their asses handed to them. Why the hell would we do that? That's the stupidest thing we could possibly think of."

So, I certainly got an adventure, more than I bargained for.

Commanding a battalion is kind of like the ultimate, as a combat arms officer, especially being able to command a battalion in combat. That's like the ultimate final exam. Are you any good at this? And I was okay. I took 512 soldiers and I brought 512 soldiers home. I accomplished every mission they gave me. I was good at it. I was not great at it. I was good enough and that is good enough. I wasn't seeking to be a four-star general. I just wanted to be good enough. And I had nine separate missions. We were the battalion that did everything that nobody else wanted to do. So, we had a whole bunch of things that had no relationship to each other, and I had to figure out how to divide up my resources and get them all done.

I had an FOB (forward operating base) with 3,500 people. It was the only year that it did not get a major ground assault.[27] We had a couple people killed by rockets. But ground assault didn't happen, because the two times they tried, we made it very clear we knew they were coming, and they decided to turn around and go home.

When I got tagged to run a detention facility, I didn't want to do that. There was a major—I almost got in a fistfight with another lieutenant colonel over it. And I was so pissed at him for dumping it on me, because he was supposed to be doing it. That's not what I signed up to do. And I was really mad about it. Abu Ghraib to me is a scar on our country. But, once I accepted the fact that I was going to have to do it, then it became an opportunity to do it right.

I don't feel a lot of survivor's guilt. I was never in one of those units where lots of people got killed. And I wasn't at COP Keating or Wanat, or one of those places. I have a lot of anger about where we were. My best friend was killed in Iraq. And I remember . . . When I'm old and senile, and I've forgotten my wife's name, I'm going to remember the conversation we had. We were walking to the gym at West Point. It was January of 2003, and there was snow on the ground. It was right after New Year's. It was that week before school started.[28]

And we were walking across The Plain in the snow, on our way to the gym, in the middle of the day to work out. He was an arch, archconservative and he had actually gone to high school with Dick Cheney's daughter, and he knew Dick Cheney and thought very highly of him. And I remember, I will remember forever the words he said. I was explaining why I thought it would be a really bad idea to invade Iraq, and why I thought that we would really regret that. And he said, "Well, I'm confident they know what they're doing. The grownups are in charge now." Because he hated the Clinton administration, you know.

Those words: *I'm confident the grownups are in charge now.* And three years later, almost to the day, he got the back of his head blown off by an EFP (explosively formed penetrator) in Najaf.[29] I mean, to the day. He died on the 5th of January, 2006, and this had to have been the 3rd, 4th, 5th of January 2003. And he shouldn't have been there. I mean, there was no reason. It was the worst strategic. . . . I'm still viscerally angry about it, and will probably always be.

It's funny. My dad and I are both history nuts, and there's always a difference when we talk about the Johnson administration. Because my dad was of that age where some of his friends went to Vietnam and he could have, except he was just a little older, so he had finished his military service. And it's funny, because I've noticed—and he actually denies this, when I said it to him—but I've noticed over the years, he cannot talk about Lyndon Johnson without a note of anger in his voice about Vietnam. He just can't. He can't look at the Civil Rights Act, the Voting Rights Act, or Medicare. He cannot look at the Johnson administration dispassionately because people he knew died in Vietnam and his whole youth was defined by that. And he just can't be dispassionate about it.

FIGURE 1.8
James Vizzard, National Cathedral, Washington, DC, 2016.

I will probably always be that way about the people who were in charge from 2001 to 2009. I just can't—I put too many bodies on airplanes. It's not survivor's guilt. It's downright anger. People were responsible for this. This was an unforced error. This was a self-inflicted wound. And the tragedy for me is most of the people I knew well, who paid the price for it, were people who were gung-ho because they were following their leaders.

There's the scene in *Henry V*, the night before the Battle of Agincourt, when a guy says, "Well, hey, if we're in the wrong, it's not my fault. I'm just following the King's orders." And the King, in disguise, says, "No, no, you're responsible for your own. It's not my fault if you get killed or if you're doing wrong. That's on you."[30] And this is it: We had all these people who led us down this road. And they're fine. None of their kids went to Iraq and got blown up. And the people who followed them trustingly paid the price.

Now, I won't stand here and tell you I thought it was an awful idea to go into Afghanistan. But I spoke as loudly as I could about what a stupid idea it was to go into Iraq. I just did the math. When people told me, "Oh, we're going to be welcomed as liberators," I said, "Listen, there's 25 million people there. Here's the math. If you tell me 90 percent are going to welcome us as liberators, that means 2.5 million are not. And if 10 percent of those actively oppose us, that's 250,000. And if 10 percent of those actually become fighters, that's a 25,000-man guerilla army with 225,000 supporters. That's going to be a hell of a fight."

And that's exactly what happened. It didn't take a genius.

When I wanted to go teach at West Point, I was advised by my battalion commander, "Don't do that. It will ruin your career." What he didn't understand was that my ambitions were quite low. And I managed to do almost all the things that I wanted to do, by being realistic about what was possible. I wanted to go teach at West Point and I wanted to command a battalion. That was it, and I got to do both those things. I wanted to teach history, but I didn't make the cut at the history department. It was slightly more competitive, and English was looking for people. And they were so desperate, they took me. And that worked out well. The English department was awesome. It was a great place to work. It was an awesome assignment.

It was also a tough assignment because the war started while I was there. And one of the things they don't talk about is: You're going to teach about 400 cadets and if that happens during a war, some of them are going to get killed. Four of the cadets I taught died before their twenty-fifth birthday, and that was hard. I mean, you know these kids when they're seventeen in some cases. And by the time they're twenty-three, you're going and visiting their graves out in the backside of the West Point Cemetery. And that was pretty tough.

But it was a great assignment. I worked with fantastic people, the cadets, but also the faculty. I always say the Army is like a pool table. You know, you tip it up and all the nuts roll into the corner pocket called West Point. Everybody there is weird, because it's not a natural career progression.

One of the things I did at West Point was teach on the Values Education Team.[31] They have a Values Education Team for every company there and it's always problematic to get people from the English and philosophy departments, because we taught ethics from a philosophical point of view, and I had a philosophy minor in college. They want you to teach this very canned version of "The Seven Army Values."[32] And we weren't very compliant about that. So one of the Seven Army Values, the very first one, is loyalty. And it was always a discussion class about, what are the problems with loyalty?

And I always say loyalty is a very problematic value. In most of the disasters you will find—Watergate, Abu Ghraib, and so on—loyalty is a huge component. Because people start to misinterpret their loyalty to lie with an individual or with their peers, whether it's the Big Blue Wall among cops, or something else. No rats. So, you've got to think long and hard about what your loyalty is to and your patriotism. I get very annoyed when people say you serve the flag. No, I don't. I serve under the flag. I serve that which it represents. I don't serve it.

And it represents peaceful protests, as much as it represents military service. It represents dissent, as much as it represents loyalty. My country right or wrong? I think just on a practical level, that's disastrous. Abu Ghraib was not right, period. My Lai was not right, period. And to defend it is to decrease your own credibility in the world. The United States derives enormous credibility and soft power. The example I use for people is: Think about in the Soviet Union, when Soviet citizens counted on the Voice of America to get their news. Why? Well, because Voice of America reported on Watergate. And if you're a Soviet listening to the Voice of America, reporting on the President resigning, and you're sitting there and you're thinking, "Well, this wouldn't happen with Brezhnev. *Pravda* would not be reporting this, right?"

I mean, it's stunning to you, if you're in a closed society. Your credibility does not come from hiding the mistakes. It comes from acknowledging and fixing. There's this debate about whether the Korematsu decision, whether the internment of the Japanese provides a legal precedent—because it's never been overturned technically—a legal precedent for a Muslim registry. You don't derive credibility and power as a nation from taking that stance. You derive credibility from acknowledging, Boy, did we screw that up. Boy, was that the most un-American thing we could possibly have done, and we're better than that now. So that to me is patriotism. It is first and foremost to the principles of the nation. Second of all, to the good, to the well-being of the whole nation. And only third, to the specific government that happens to be in power at any given moment. I think the government deserves leeway and the benefit of the doubt. You know, they are elected under the rules and laws of the country. But that doesn't mean blind obedience.

I really loved working in the Senate, one of the best jobs I ever had in the Army, and I'd love to go back up there, but I have this weird thing. I was an artillery officer technically, but I have an advanced degree in English. I did legislative affairs. I actually spent my last year in public affairs. I did joint planning in Afghanistan, my last tour, and was the chief of plans for US Forces Afghanistan. During my last tour in Iraq, I did intelligence work. So I have this very hodgepodge resume, opens a lot of options. I would love to get into national security policy, but it's a tough world to crack into, especially at my age. I'm forty-eight years old. It's tough at my age to get into it.

One of the sad things that you learn is: if you want to influence national defense policy, the worst thing you can do is go into it at the bottom and work your way up. There are very few people at the top who started out as second lieutenants or as ground-level CIA agents or analysts. Most of the people running things went to law school, got a law degree, went to work for a campaign, got into Congress or the White House as appointees at twenty-eight years old, and are assistant secretaries by the time they're thirty-five. That's just the unfortunate truth. So getting into national security policy level is very tough for me now and I have zero interest in the path that will provide you with a $150,000-a-year job and allow you to live a very nice life in the DC suburbs. You'd have to go in, look people in the eye, and tell them that the National Defense will fail if they don't buy the Gizmo 3000. And oh, by the way, we need a cost-plus contract, with very loose requirements. And if it fails, it's not my fault, you know.

I can't do that. We spend way too much money on hardware, and not enough on people. As a student of military history, the one thing you cannot generate quickly is competent, qualified people. We can make a lot of stuff really fast, if we really have to. We're good at that. But creating competent leaders and technicians takes years, and there's no shortcuts.

So, I'm a little disturbed at the route I think we will end up going, and have gone. Some days I think, Screw it, I'm just going to become a high school history teacher in Arlington. If I could only pay my mortgage. . . . Unfortunately, you can't teach in Arlington and afford to live in Arlington.

Still, it hasn't been a terrible way to raise a family. Now, we got incredibly lucky. When I was a major with the Command and General Staff College in Kansas in 2003, my wife got a job with a big consulting firm here in the DC suburbs. And they hired her on a temporary basis, because they couldn't find anybody else qualified for the job. And then when we went to move, they said, "Hey, we still can't find anybody else qualified. Would you telecommute?"

And so she's been working for the same company with one nine-month break since 2003, and she's had a professional career. She's a senior manager now with a major billion-dollar-a-year consulting firm. She has not gone through the displacement that a lot of other spouses do, always had a job. That made life different, because she was not one of those people who wanted to just stay home and be the military spouse.

So, it was a lot of security for us, because she didn't have to give up her job. We had healthcare. When we were trying to have kids, and it turned into a high-risk twin pregnancy, I wasn't sitting there stressing about, "Oh my God, how are we going to pay? It costs $25,000 to have kids." It cost us $75. Those things were great. On the other hand, I didn't join expecting to be deployed for fifty-four months. To spend fifty-four months in a combat zone, that's actually extraordinary.

We were at dinner last night and my son is actually taking psychology in high school. They were studying the Stanford Prison Experiment, and he was talking about it. I said, "Well, yeah, that's why when I ran a detention facility, these were my rules." And my other son looked at me and said, "What do you mean when you ran a detention facility?" I said, "Well, when I ran the detention facility in Afghanistan for a year. And the unit before really screwed it up, and they made these mistakes that had to be reported to the Secretary of Defense. And so, I came in and took it over, and these were my rules to make sure this—and that's why. To make sure these things didn't happen again."

"You never told me that," my son said.

They had no idea what I was doing. It was a great discussion to have. But I couldn't have that discussion with them when they were ten, when I was doing it. And now they're sixteen, so now they're asking questions. And now it's all in the past, so I can kind of discuss a lot of it.

My dad was in federal law enforcement. But to the extent he could, he actually talked a lot. He and I were very close. And I probably knew more about what he was doing than any other agent's kid I ever met. Others were like, "I don't know what my dad does." I paid a lot of attention, and we discussed it quite a bit. I was one of those kids who always hung around with the adults and wanted to talk to them. My kids are less like that, but they're getting more like that now that they're in their mid-teen years.

But at the time, they were like, "Oh, my dad, you know, he's in Afghanistan." That was all they knew. They didn't know the difference between Fort Hood, where I was on a Division Staff, and Fort Knox, where I was a battalion commander.[33] They didn't have any idea what any of that meant. And to this day, and I don't think they really care.

They're both sixteen now. They're already talking about moving out of the house, going to college, and it's going to be weird. I'm teaching them to drive and we're starting to look at colleges, and they just took their PSATs. And I'm thinking, "You know, it's over. This is over. My kids are going to be gone in the blink of an eye. I mean, two years—it's like we moved

FIGURE 1.9
Digital recorder, Washington, DC, 2016.

here, and they weren't even in middle school. And now, we're talking about colleges and it's just happening so fast."

And I'm going to look back and I will have missed four and a half years of that. That's a big chunk. They were three and a half when I deployed the first time, and they were almost fifteen when I came home the last time. So from three and a half to fifteen . . . There are huge chunks of their lives I missed. They talk about people they knew in Texas when we lived there, but I never met those people. By the time I came home, they were in school. My wife had to find the daycare, get them to daycare, and do all the parent things.

But if you want to know what the costs are for families and for family life, you've got to get it from all sides. Maybe you should talk to my sons, or my wife. Because I don't know what I don't know, and I don't know what they don't tell me.

And there are people out there who have been through this from all sides. I mean, my friend who was killed in Iraq, his wife and his kids have a perspective on this, on "Here's the real cost of this at the high end." He left behind four kids and the youngest one was two,

FIGURE 1.10
James Vizzard, National Cathedral, Washington, DC, 2016.

and the oldest had her tenth birthday today. She hasn't had a good birthday since her father died. And yet that family has also managed to survive and thrive, because they had a solid foundation.

Every once in a while now, things will still come up at home and I'll say, "Well, I did it yesterday." And my wife will just look at me and say, "Five deployments." Then I say, "Yes dear, I'll go walk the dogs. I'll do the dishes." She doesn't do it often, but every once in a while, when she doesn't want to do something, the answer I get is "Five deployments." And I will never pay off that debt, to the day I die.

James Vizzard retired from the US Army in 2016 after more than twenty-six years on active duty and is currently pursuing a PhD in political science.

2

PORTFOLIO: SIMULATIONS

ON SEPTEMBER 19, 2019, Ed and I made the trip to Oriskany, New York, to photograph the $50 million, 1,100-acre New York State Preparedness Training Center on the site of the former Griffiss Air Force Base.[1] These sprawling simulacra include a bank, a high school, a drug store, a motel, a hospital, a county courthouse, and several retail establishments. Active-shooter drills, improvised explosive detection and disarming, and various natural and human-crafted emergencies and disasters are pantomimed. All fake but all too real. There's a trailer park where meth labs are sniffed out, an elevator shaft for rescue training, a massive rubble pile simulating the after-effects of an urban bombing, and a city block that can be flooded with "swift water" at a moment's notice. Although the attention to detail is striking, it is the conspicuous absence of certain details and the odd presence of others that lend these images their eerie resonance.

FIGURE 2.1 (previous pages)
Bean County Courthouse, CityScape simulator, New
York State Preparedness Training Center, Oriskany,
New York, 2019.

FIGURE 2.2
City Drugs, CityScape simulator, New York State
Preparedness Training Center, Oriskany, New
York, 2019.

FIGURE 2.3
Rosterfield Motel, CityScape simulator, New York
State Preparedness Training Center, Oriskany, New
York, 2019.

FIGURE 2.4
Swift water simulator, New York State Preparedness
Training Center, Oriskany, New York, 2019.

FIGURE 2.5
Urban Search and Rescue simulator, New York
State Preparedness Training Center, Oriskany, New
York, 2019.

FIGURE 2.6
First and Main, CityScape simulator, New York State Preparedness Training Center, Oriskany, New York, 2019.

3

BORDER PATROL

I was twelve years old when my father passed away. My mother ended up working in pretty much a sweatshop in El Paso where they would get subcontracted to make high-end clothing. She worked there forty hours a week, probably for minimum wage, and was raising five of us on that. She would ask her boss for a raise, but there was a line of illegal aliens waiting to fill any spot and he would say, "There's no need for me to give you a raise when there's eight or ten other people waiting just to take your job."

She would tell me that the Border Patrol would show up from time to time and raid the place. People would scurry behind bolts of material or out the doors. The Border Patrol would take a bunch of employees with them. There'd be open spots for just a few hours, and then they'd be filled.

What could I do to help my mother and people like my mother in that situation? She was here legally and she died as an American citizen. She was very proud to be an American citizen, but she was a lawful, permanent resident years back. I figured I needed to do something to help people like her who are doing the right thing, the right way.

I was a paper boy, delivering the newspaper, back when kids did that. One of my customers was a Border Patrol agent. One time when I went to collect the monthly dues, he was rushing out. He was in uniform, in a hurry to get the job done. And that set a high standard, I guess, of what a Border Patrol agent was. There were plenty of Border Patrol agents around El Paso. You'd go downtown and they would always be out there driving around, chasing people. But this guy, you know, it was more of a personal interaction—he was one of my customers— and that just planted the seed.

Going through high school, I had an older sister in her twenties who started dating a Marine. I talked to him about the Marine Corps a little bit, and started getting the idea of, Well, I don't want to go to college, I want to be a Border Patrol agent, and maybe some law enforcement experience will help me get there.

So, I joined the Marine Corps right out of high school. Tried to join when I was seventeen, and my mother wouldn't sign for me. She didn't want any part of that. I joined after I turned eighteen and that got me a good foundation. I did four years in the Marine Corps as a military policeman. It wasn't the traditional role of a military policeman at the gate, the ones who wave you in or check your credentials. It was with the field unit, which, during combat, you maintain the POW camps, and you escort POWs, do some route reconnaissance. I was with the field unit my first three years at Camp Pendleton in California. We did a lot of field training. We would go to Twentynine Palms, California, to do desert training. It was a combat-type role. When I went overseas my last year, it was with the aircraft wing unit, which was not as much a field unit. We were there to secure the flight lines in time of combat. Did very little law enforcement, traditional military police law enforcement type work. We did a little bit of that, but it was mostly flight line security.[1]

Hadn't gotten out of the Marine Corps yet when I submitted my Border Patrol interest card. It was kind of like the postal service back then. You would submit a card of interest, and I guess they kept them until they had a big batch of openings, and then they'd send out the appointments for a written test. After I got out of the Marine Corps, I took my written test, and went through the hiring process. June of '92 was when I joined Border Patrol and went through the academy.

I'll tell you right now, for an individual who went in not knowing Spanish, it was a completely different Border Patrol Academy than for an individual like me that knew Spanish. It was two to three times the workload for them, I would guess. They had everything we had to learn on law and statutes, and the Border Patrol history and this and that, *and* a new language. I had three housemates and two of the three didn't know one word of Spanish when we showed up. They'd come to me to help them conjugate verbs, and they had all the patterns and the conjugations and stuff pasted to their walls.

We had to learn a lot more law than I thought we would, but I enjoyed the time there. It wasn't a cakewalk. It was a lot more academic than the Marine Corps. And there were a lot of trainees there at the time. And you'd see people just start to disappear when they were no longer mathematically able to make it through. They'd pull them out and send them home. It was tough on those of us who were married at the time. It's three and a half months away from your home. Whether you got a wife, a wife and kids.

Most of us were young. There were a couple of older trainees—they were thirty-five, thirty-four. They were the old-timers. You looked to them to share their wisdom with you. But the majority of us were twenty-four, twenty-five. And there were some really young ones at twenty-two. There were several who had gone through before and hadn't made it, and they would give you insight: "Hey, this is coming up, we need to prepare for this or prepare for that." Whether it was physical conditioning or the big progress exam in Spanish or law.

You go through the academy knowing where you're heading. I was going to Deming, New Mexico. I had to look at a map. I'd driven through there, but never even stopped to get fuel there, I don't think. It was a little town of 10,000 people and I was coming from El Paso where we, at the time, probably had 600,000, 700,000.

My first day at work was November 13th, a Friday the 13th in 1992. I showed up in the morning for a day shift. The acting supervisor said, "Hey, you're riding with this guy." And the guy told him, "I don't want no damn trainee." They pulled me from that guy, and put me in with another guy. And I thought, Oh, man, this is terrible. Nobody likes trainees.

Back then, nobody liked riding around with a trainee, because then you just had somebody else to look out for. So, my first day I went to El Paso with a guy to pick up tires for the trucks. That was my first day as a Border Patrol agent. It was a letdown. We brought eight or twelve or sixteen tires back to the station.

But, generally, in Deming we did a lot of desert tracking of aliens, which is classic Border Patrol work. And I loved it. I had an outstanding time there. We had a lot of desert—about sixty miles—to cover with very few agents. When I got there in 1992, there were thirty-eight agents.

We would work trails down in the desert. Dayshift would usually start, you get some tracks across one of the tracking roads and then work the trails, and you'd see who's got the biggest group, and work that one first. Try and catch the big groups, because they were a little bit slower and easier to spot, easier to track. Every now and then we'd get an aircraft out of El Paso to support us, but it was pretty infrequent. As time went on, traffic picked up. Staffing grew—I think at the high point it was probably about 400 agents at the station. The traffic required it. Most stations grew to be huge stations compared to what they started out with.

Times have changed, and promotion timeframes have changed, due to the volume of staffing. But back then most of your journeymen would be a journeyman for eight or ten years.[2]

Depends on what station you were at a little bit, but let's say eight or ten years. And then they'd become a supervisor, if they wanted to. Some agents were journeymen their entire careers because they enjoyed doing what they did. There was no mandate to promote like in the military, where if you don't get promoted you'll get booted out after a certain number of years. The Border Patrol, you could do your entire career as a journeyman if you enjoyed it. I did. I really enjoyed it.

Toward the end of my journeyman time, I was a dog handler, and that was a lot of fun. I had a great time. I ended up doing about fourteen years as a journeyman because once you're a dog handler, if you get promoted you have to turn the dog in. That kind of extended my time as a journeyman, which I was fine with.[3]

Toward the end of that I had gotten divorced and gotten remarried and had my first child with my wife. I said, "Well, now that I've got a family I'd better start thinking of my future." Because even though you were a journeyman, and as a dog handler you got paid a little bit extra for taking care of the dog at home, that didn't calculate into your retirement pension. It didn't calculate into the formula. So, I said, "I better get a couple of promotions under my belt before I retire, being as now I'm starting to have children and my family's going to grow."

That was after sixteen years in Deming, and I never thought I'd leave until we started having kids, and my wife and I discussed moving to a bigger city to raise our kids in, just so there were more positive things for them to do. There wasn't a lot to do in Deming. When I first moved there, there was a small movie theater. But it got to the point where they had to have at least six customers or they wouldn't show the movie, because they were losing money. And they ended up shutting down. There was also a bowling alley that shut down.

In 2006, I became a supervisor. Then I got promoted again in 2008 to a second line supervisor. I bounced around at that level—it was a GS-13 back then—at a couple of stations during that time.[4] A couple of years away from my family, which was tough on my kids, tough on our marriage. But we got through that.

When we left Deming, my family moved here to Las Cruces, and I was working in Fabens, Texas. I would commute and I'd come home on the weekends. Once I left Fabens, I came to El Paso, then to Tucson. Same thing in Tucson. I'd just come home on the weekends. Finally, I got back to Las Cruces, and then back to El Paso. And then I was coming home every day.

I ended up in a station commander position, a patrol agent in charge position, in Truth or Consequences, New Mexico, and then I was coming home every day as well.

Generally, a dog handler had one dog. I had two dogs because my first dog was retired. He just was no longer engaged, so I received a second dog to work. Once your dog is too old to work or no longer engaged, then you get another dog and you train with that dog for a period. The training academy was very difficult. You had to get a 90 percent or better to pass. They expect excellence on your academic portion and your performance portion. You get through that, and you have to train every two weeks with your dog to maintain proficiency, with an instructor. The training is always there.

There's no maybe with a dog. You've got to be 100 percent sure of what your dog is telling you so you can relay that.

It was a great time because one day you could go do red ribbon week where you would go to the schools and show students how your dog works. It's amazing to watch a dog work. It's probably more fun when you're a dog handler sitting back and watching another dog work, because you can appreciate it so much more than when you're working your dog, having to concentrate on what you're doing. It's amazing to watch the minuscule amount that a dog will alert to.

When you do a presentation you can tell people: "When you walk into a hotel room there's nobody smoking in there, but you can tell somebody smoked in there, right? You can tell. That's what a dog smells when they have just tiny, tiny amounts of marijuana, or any concealed item that they've been trained to detect. When you smell beef stew cooking, they can smell the individual vegetables and the meat in the stew. Their olfactory glands are just nothing that we can imagine." So, it's amazing to watch them work, and if they could drive, they wouldn't need a handler. That's the bottom line. Or if they could type, they wouldn't need a handler. Because they do the work and you do the reporting.

You go out there and get in the middle of it with your dog, and do some amazing searches with your dog. You find people in the desert that the agents can't find. They say, "Hey, man, we've tracked these people into this cornfield, and we can't pull them out of the brush." And your dog rolls in there and finds them for you. And your dog's a hero. You find stranded people in the desert who are not doing really well. There was a case of one of our dog handlers in Deming. He found a child who had been abducted and was still in a car seat. It was a little child. And he went and found her in the desert. She was sunburnt, she'd been out there a full day. It was a real bad case, but he found her. Things like that make it excellent to be a dog handler.

A dog will alert, and that's something that happens to a dog naturally. Just like when you see two dogs at the dog park, and you see something change, and all of a sudden they're fighting. That's an alert. That change is something natural that they do. Their tail will go up like a scorpion tail, or their hackles will stand up, or they'll get increased respiration. There are certain things you look for that tell you something's going on here. Then you have that followed up with a trained change of stance. You have them sit or you have them lay down.

They'll alert, they'll say okay, there's something here, there's a concealed person here. And now they'll narrow it down to, "This is where I'm smelling the odor." And the dog will sit or lay there. Some agencies have an aggressive alert or an aggressive indication, which the dog will start to scratch, but if you've got a bomb dog naturally you don't want that.[5] If you've got a bomb detection dog you want a passive indication, which will be the dog will sit and stare, or point, or whatever you train them to do. To tell you, "This is where it's at, partner."

The dog does the work. What you have to learn is to read your dog, to be able to tell what your dog is telling you. And the dogs are right on. Generally, it's the handler who'll make a mistake. And that's where you have to be right on. You can't tell a state police officer, "Hey, I think there's marijuana in the gas tank." That's not what he wants to hear. He wants to hear either yes or no.

They don't want to hear, "Well, I see some anomaly here." That doesn't tell them anything. Yeah, sure, it could be there's a natural void in the car. What they want to know is if there's a person concealed in the trunk or if there's some kind of narcotic in that natural or manmade void. And that's what the dogs do. That's what they do. It's an amazing tool.

I have dogs at home. I do. I always seem to get a German shepherd. It's funny, my kids, they've seen me cry at my mother's funeral and when I buried our dog. My boy didn't even recognize me. "Dad's crying? What?" But, yeah, you form a super tight bond with your partner.

With my first marriage, our divorce wasn't work-related. But being away from my family, it puts a strain on it. I worked for another chief and when I was done with my time in Tucson, he told me, "Adrian, I've spent a lot of time away from my family. When you get home tread lightly because Mama's been running the show for over a year. Be prepared for that."

And it's true. I would come home on the weekends and it wouldn't be right for me to try to change something that's working at home five days a week, for me to do it in two days, and then leave again on Sunday night. So, it is very stressful on a marriage. Your kids develop differently from other kids. My kids know to look around for exits at a restaurant when they sit down. It's things they've shared with me. My wife does it. Did she used to? Probably not. But my kids do it. My middle daughter is proud of some defensive tactics that she knows. They pick that up just from Bring a Kid to Work day.

You raise kids a little differently. You want to shelter them. Because you see what happens. You get the bulletins on all these kids you're looking for. You see that stuff, more so than what you see on the news. You see the kids who are coming across the desert with their families to make a better life, and here we have the life they're looking for. We need to appreciate that. But yeah, your kids, they are raised a little differently. When I first got to Deming, my classmate who went to Deming with me, I had to take his kids trick or treating the first three or four years, because he stayed late at work. You miss birthdays, you miss the soccer games, you miss a lot of that stuff. Because you can't schedule that stuff into your work schedule as much as somebody who works a traditional Monday through Friday.

You do, you miss a lot of things. But your kids appreciate it more, I think, when they see you there at their events.

I've got a sixteen-year-old daughter, a fourteen-year-old daughter, and a twelve-year-old son.

They would ask me for Border Patrol bedtime stories. I could give them good stories with good endings and whatnot. Then there's all the stories that you don't want to share with your family. You see people die in the desert; they really don't need to hear that when they're little babies.

My wife was eight months' pregnant when a guy tried to run me over. That was a real bad situation. I almost got hit. And it's weird because my wife called me and asked me, "Hey, is everything okay? A bunch of ambulances just left."

And I said, "Well, I'm okay but not everything's okay." And that was an incident where a vehicle had rolled over, and it was loaded full of people who were fleeing from another agent. And I deployed the tire deflation device, and he swerved and tried to run me over. And then he swerved back, and the vehicle rolled. There were thirteen people in the truck, and six of them died. The guy ended up going to jail for like twelve years.

Is that enough for the families? I would think no. I knew I was where I should've been, I knew I deployed the device correctly. But still, it's something you've got to live with. And then you start thinking, "What if I wouldn't have been at work that day? This may have not happened." Those feelings come across. But, you know, I was the good guy. The guy behind the wheel who didn't get a scratch on him, who got out of the truck wanting to fight, blaming it on us, that's the bad guy. I knew I was in the right that day, but the next few days were tough.

My kids know about that stuff now that they're a little older. They know the dangers that these guys are in, and they know that any time we go through a checkpoint I tell whoever is working to be safe, whether they recognize me or not. My kids get a kick out of it. They say, "You're still telling them to be careful."

My boy didn't speak till he was three. He had a hard time speaking. He has apraxia. I explain it to most people that it is like when somebody has a stroke they have to learn how to redo everything out of repetition. And that's kind of how he had to learn to speak. He wouldn't repeat a word. He learned sign language before he could speak, and then he communicated that way. We had to try to catch up to him most of the time with sign language so that we could understand what he was trying to tell us. But he's dealing with that.

My oldest daughter saw how much that helped him. He was getting up to sixteen hours a week of therapy. She saw what that did for him. Now she wants to go into special ed or speech therapy type work. I'm really proud of her for that.

My middle one wants to be a massage therapist like her mom. A medical massage therapist, not the kind where you go to the resort and get a massage, but the kind where it has some medical impact.

My wife is a big believer in Chinese therapy, the lines in your body and that stuff. I make fun of her being a hippie, but she believes in that, and for anybody that's sick she'll try to offer them a lymphatic pump to clean out all your lymph nodes—it gets fresh blood pumping all around. My middle daughter wants to follow in her footsteps in that.

My boy, he wants to be an animator or game designer. He draws really well. I said, "Well, boy, we don't have a basement so you're not going to be living here in the basement forever." But our local university, New Mexico State University, now offers an animation course. If he sticks around for that, he can live in the garage or something. But not in the basement.

So, they've got their ideas kind of lined out. You know how that's subject to change when you're that age. When you're an adult it's subject to change. I'm hoping they all do what they want to do. And it stems from something a chief told me when I was talking about my retirement with him. He did consulting, and now he's in education at the university. And I asked him, "Hey, chief, I'm thinking about retiring. Do you recommend that consultation stuff?" And he goes, "Adrian, if you have to think about it, don't do it." He goes, "Do something that you're having a fun time at. Because you're making the money. You made your money. If you're retiring, it's because you can. Do something that you're going to have a good time at."

I started young, and I was able to retire young. And people say, Man, you're too young. I went to a financial adviser, he told me not to retire. He said, "Hey, you came to talk to me about money, not about what your heart is telling you." He goes, "You're leaving too much money on the table." I operate a tractor now. I bought myself a little backhoe, and that's what I do, because it's soothing. It's relaxing. Sometimes I come home and think, "Man, I got paid for this today. This is awesome." But my financial guy told me, "No, you're leaving what is an over $100,000 a year job, with all kinds of goodies, and the 401(k), and this and that, to go drive a tractor for $40 an hour?" I said, "Yes, I am. You know why? Because I want to spend more time with my kids."

That financial guy was real blunt. I was like, "Man, you're right. That's a lot of money." But I want to spend time with my family before my kids are too old to want to hang around with me. The Border Patrol gave me that opportunity. Whether I'm broke or whether I'm rich, I'm spending time with my kids. And my wife.

During my career, if anybody was abusing people, it was the smugglers. That's where people got hurt the most. That's where they got overworked. That's where they got robbed. Raped. Whatever the case. That's generally when it occurred.

Yeah, you see it. You have a job to do, you have laws to enforce, you have an oath you swore to, and you have the expectation of the American public to do the right thing. Is it

FIGURE 3.2
Adrian Aizpuru, University of Texas at El Paso, El Paso, Texas, 2022.

always easy? No, it's not always easy. Is it what you signed up for? Whether you like it or not, that's what you signed up for. There's an expectation. There's a risk that comes with the job.

There are tough times that come with the job, and there are also very good times that come with the job. Not everybody you encounter is an illegal alien. You encounter American citizens who are in distress and you find them and take them home to their families. That happened too. I've been through that.

You get calls: "Hey, my husband or my grandpa or dad, or whomever, left, and he's diabetic. He hasn't been back."

We found a couple of people who were lost. They just got disoriented. Down here all the time people are getting lost on mountains, and it's the Border Patrol search and rescue that's finding them. Because they're ready to go, they stay practiced, they do their job well, so they go out there and find people. The other day a group of like twenty-eight hikers got lost on the mountain. There are cities on both sides of the mountain. If you keep walking to the light, you'll get there. I don't understand how you get lost on that mountain. I think they may have gotten scared or something; it got dark on them and they got scared.

One of my favorite days was when I found a World War II veteran who had fallen and broken his hip and couldn't get up. He'd covered himself with dirt to stay warm overnight. His wife had called, and said he walked out, collecting aluminum cans. My best friend and I tracked him for a couple of hours down into town and back, and sure enough, he was hitting the trash cans, picking up aluminum cans, and he headed back home just to make his whatever money, and he fell down into the bottom of a bar ditch. It was sandy so he didn't get hurt too badly, but he did break his hip, and couldn't get out.

We found him, and when you can call people and say, "Hey, we found your husband, your father, your dad, your grandpa, he's down here, the ambulance is taking him in" . . . well, that's a good day.

Don't think that I think that everybody's coming over to look for a good life. Don't think that. That's not the case. Let me make that clear. But some people want a better life. We can go to Las Vegas and still get a room for twenty-nine bucks. How does that happen? I could tell you why that happens. Why does it happen that sometimes we can get a head of lettuce for sixty-nine cents and sometimes it's three dollars? That has a lot to do with it. There's still a lot of produce that is harvested by hand. In my entire career, there were very few American citizens out there. And that's a ground truth. But this was twenty years ago.

Is it the same now? Go check a Tyson chicken plant. That's a very undesirable job. And I can guarantee you you'll see very few American citizens in there working. So, are there people coming to fill those jobs? Yes, there are. Is everybody coming for those? No, that's not what everybody's coming for. Some people are coming just to do bad stuff.

I think different communities tolerate the Border Patrol differently. Like when I first started, you'd get ranchers who would call the station: "Hey, we're leaving town for a week or two. Come by and get the newspaper, and just drive around and check on the house." And that just doesn't happen anymore, really. It's just with the growth of the Border Patrol and the growth of the volume of traffic, and politics and stuff, that has changed. Just like it's changed everything else in our country. It's changed the relationship of the general public with law enforcement and the Border Patrol.

Still, today, sometimes somebody will pay for your lunch. But then sometimes you'll be sitting down to have lunch, and people question why you're sitting down and having lunch on their dime. Just because you're a government employee doesn't mean you deserve a lunchtime. You probably deserve lunchtime, but it shouldn't be here in the restaurant. You should be sitting out in your truck.

There are just so many different dynamics. And it seems to change from community to community. It's kind of weird, and hard to explain. It just depends on where you go and how receptive they are to the Border Patrol. If you're within the 100 air miles of the border, you're trying to do this job, and you go talk to the people in Green Valley, south of Tucson, and your checkpoint's just a pain in the butt because they drive through it every day. The job that we have to do isn't conducive to everybody's schedule, or what they think we should be doing. Not everybody, but a lot of people say, Hey, Border Patrol, you should be on the border.

Everybody's got their idea of what everybody else should be doing, and so you have to do it until you've walked a mile in their shoes.

The badge is not a piece of tin, it's not a brass star, it's the American trust that you're going to do the right thing. That was always huge to me. And it's hard sometimes. It's hard to do the right thing. When nobody's watching, is the important part.

But that's what you sign up for. It wasn't hard for me but it's hard for some people. I was never confronted with an upfront bribe. It's not usually, "Hey, I'll give you a million dollars for this." It's, "Hey, come over to the house and we'll drink a beer," and then you end up talking about—not that you have to do something, it's that they want you not to do something. Which I guess makes it seem easier. Hey, "I'm not asking you to do this, I just want you not to take appropriate action on this." And people fall for that.

I'm big on the oath that we took, the trust that the American people put in you that you're going to do the right thing. And I'm big on Border Patrol history. People don't know about when we helped desegregate Mississippi State and when we helped stop the first hijacking that happened in the United States.

James Meredith was the first Black student at Mississippi State. And there were about 300 Border Patrol agents that got deployed out there. Just like you see in *Forrest Gump*. That's James Meredith going in the building. And he was taken to his first day of school in a beat-up Border Patrol car that had gotten beaten up in the riots the night before.

People don't know that. To me that's huge.

The first hijacking happened in El Paso, and President Kennedy told the FBI to do whatever it takes. "Do not let that plane leave El Paso."

The Border Patrol shot out the landing gear, and one of the engines. The hijacker, he had to let that negotiator on. And when the negotiator came on, a Border Patrol agent who was in the airplane punched the hijacker out.

People just don't know about that kind of stuff, but it means a lot to me. That's part of who I was. Who I am.

Adrian Aizpuru is a retired patrol agent in charge with the US Border Patrol.

I wish I had this beautiful story that says as a kid I wanted to do this, and things of that nature, but I really don't. Quite honestly, I was very fortunate. I had a job. I was looking for a career. I look back, and I kind of went into it blind.

I had a two-year-old son, and my wife and I really did not have two nickels to rub together. So, it was out of necessity. I was going to the University of Arizona at the time. I was majoring in criminal justice, so I knew I wanted something in that law enforcement field, but I had never heard of the Border Patrol. Then these ads came out. Back in 1987, the Border Patrol had this big recruitment. They were going to double in size. They were going to go from 4,000 agents to 8,000 agents. Nationwide. They had these commercials, and they had these ATVs, horses, jet skis—all the cool stuff they show you. And so I decided, I can do that.

I like the idea of service. The idea of doing something bigger than I am.

I submitted an application to the civil service. They scheduled me for a civil service exam. I went out and looked for a textbook that I found about forty miles away from our town of Tucson. And it was outdated—didn't help me, but gave me a sense of confidence, I guess. False confidence. I went and took the exam with about 500 other people.

Afterward, we sat there and if they called your name, you didn't pass. I was sitting in this conference room in a hotel by the airport in Tucson, Arizona, hoping that I didn't hear my name. And I didn't hear my name. Then, lo and behold, they set me up for an interview about three weeks later.

But I still didn't know what the job was. I didn't know what the job entailed.

My aunt's neighbor's son was a Border Patrol agent. I remember calling him. He was probably about three years in. I explained who I was and said I got this hiring board appointment. Any advice you can give me?

His only advice was, "Hey, during the interview, don't shoot anyone in any of the scenarios." Could you imagine? That's on my mind. What kind of scenarios are they going to give me? But he started telling me more about the job. I started getting an idea of what to expect. And he was really the only person I had ever spoken to about it. I didn't even meet him.

The interview was with a normal hiring board of two individuals, and I didn't know what to expect. Then, before you know it, it's 2011 and I'm ready to retire.

The whole concept probably came from my father. My father wasn't a police officer; my dad was a meat cutter. My parents are from Mexico, they came as immigrants and naturalized. My dad worked at a wholesale place. They would make the cuts and they would sell it to restaurants and chains, and things of that nature.

I remember as a little kid I would go with my dad. I'm the oldest of two and he would take me. It almost sounds morbid now. He would take me to go slaughter and cut goats and calves and stuff. That's what a rancher or a farmer wanted done, and I would go. And my dad would always tell me, "I'm bringing you here because I want you to know what an uneducated man does for a living."

He and my grandfather also said, "You're going to have a position where people salute you."

I said, "Come on. This is Vic. No one's going to do that."

But my dad planted that seed. He said, "You're going to do something bigger and better."

The academy in Glynco is called the Federal Law Enforcement Training Center (FLETC). Glynco doesn't even have an airport; you have to land in Jacksonville and they bus you for two hours. I remember on that bus ride going, "Man, what did I get myself into?"

Everything was kind of a shock. You get to Glynco—and I had never smelled the odors of a paper mill before and I go, "What in the world is that?" Then they issue uniforms, your gear, going through that whole process. Learning the various types of immigration, naturalization, criminal law, everything that you would teach at a police academy. And still, you're training, and they're teaching you law enforcement functions. You're getting a better idea of what the job is, but you really don't know.

After twenty-one weeks, I got out of the academy and they flew me back to Tucson. I hooked up a U-Haul trailer with everything we had in storage that we owned. It was my three-year-old son and my wife. We leave Tucson for San Diego. We arrive in San Ysidro, California, which is right on the border, at two or three in the morning. And as we're going down the main drag, I see these individuals running across the street. Then I see a Border Patrol agent chasing them. My wife goes, "Is that what you're going to be doing?" And I go, "I have no idea." That's after twenty-one weeks at the academy. I have no idea.

That was my first a-ha moment.

Then you start dealing with people. Most people that we dealt with—and today too—they're economic migrants. The poorest of the poor, coming up. And you're just like, "Jeez, you know, I'd be doing the same thing." And that was a kind of a different a-ha moment. You look and say, "Wow, they're poor. They're the poorest of the poor." And generally they're really good people.

What I found in my career, usually 10 or 15 percent of the people have other intents than working. But the vast majority are economic migrants. In that mix you can have some really bad people. How do you treat someone with the compassion that you ought to treat them, but at the same time don't make yourself vulnerable?

Those are hard lessons. When someone's chucking a rock at you, or someone decides that they can take you on. I had some of those a-ha moments, like, "Man, if I'm not careful I'm going to get hurt."

I also remember—I must've been about three years in on patrol—I was working an overtime shift near the port of entry. And there was this family group from somewhere in Middle America. I think they said Kansas. I'm in my green uniform, at that time the vehicles were a sea foam green with white. And I remember the man came up and said, "Excuse me, are we in Mexico?" And I looked at them. "Better not be," I said, "because I'd be in a lot of trouble if I was in Mexico."

They looked at the insignia, the emblem on the vehicle, and my patch on my left arm, and they go, "Who are you?" I said, "Border Patrol." And it dawned on me: Middle America doesn't even know who we are. They not only don't know who we are, but they look at the issues on the border as being a California, Arizona, New Mexico, and Texas problem.

I've had several a-ha moments like that.

That family wanted to take pictures. I felt like a museum piece, you know. That's when it struck me. They had no idea.

In 1988, I started out, like most of my peers, as GS-5.[6] I still have the appointment letter I received from the government. The annual salary for a GS-5 was $17,529. And my wife goes, "Jeez, is that all of it?" But it was the benefits and the retirement stuff that we were looking at.

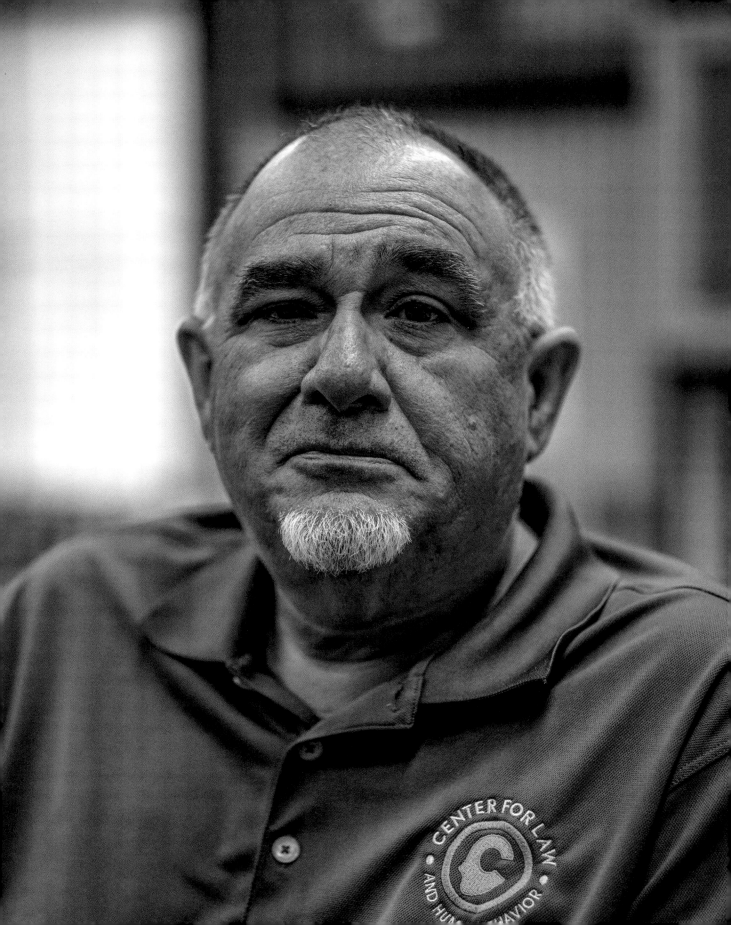

I remember when I showed up at post-academy, they asked, "Who's married? Raise your hand. Who's got children? Raise your hand. Fill out these forms."

And I qualified for food stamps.

I was like, "I can't tell my wife this."

After the completion of the ten-month exam, I'd be a GS-7 automatically. And then a year later I'd be a GS-9. After that it became competitive. My goal was: How do I prepare myself to be a GS-11? GS-11 is a senior agent, very few of those. You had to have a lot of time.

I had aspirations, but they weren't really based in reality. I didn't have a whole lot of time in. But I was fortunate that the agency started to grow, and they had positions open. I said, "Well, I'm going to put in for a supervisor position," because the announcement was GS-11/12, which made me eligible to apply.

I applied with the idea that if I get my paperwork in, it means I made the points. And then the next time I'll hopefully get an interview. And then, maybe the third time I'll combine good paperwork, a good interview, and I'll get that job. Well, I go to the interview, and it surprised the heck out of me. I did well. And they offered me a supervisor's job.

Brown Field Station in San Diego, where I was, was very desirable. Imperial Beach Station where I went to was not a desirable place. No one wanted to go there because they were overrun. It was not uncommon to make anywhere from 600 to 800 arrests in an eight-hour shift. Then you had the processing and things of that nature. Anything bad that could happen, would happen. It seemed like everyone wanted to fight. We had vehicle accidents. And then when you have the poorest of the poor, they're also exploited by the criminal element. You're dealing with all these things. But the beauty—if there is beauty in a place like that—is that you get a ton of experience in a very compact time.

I got a ton of experience at that place. In other positions, when I started seeing things, I'd go, "This is nothing. I've seen it all."

So, I spent some time at Imperial Beach. Arizona was starting to open up in terms of positions, and my wife really wanted to go back. And I didn't. I'll be honest. I didn't. I thought, "I finally made supervisor." The second level was the field operations supervisor. I got a chance in about five to ten years, but she says, "No, I want to go home." So, we went home. And it seemed like the activity level followed me. Because like a year later, it's just getting busier and busier again.

When it really got busy, our station hit it in stride. We dealt with it really, really well. And I became a field operations supervisor. About a year after that, I became the head of that station.

I was very young in terms of the length of service to get in there. But there were not too many people in the Tucson setting who had my kind of experience. And as we got busier in Southern Arizona, it was just more experience. But it was at a different level because I wasn't doing the fieldwork every day. It was more the vision, the planning for growth.

Then we had tons of CODELs—congressional delegations—coming out, and I knew Southern Arizona really well. I grew up in Southern Arizona. So, when our sector chief—who's responsible for a large geographical area—would have these CODELs come down, I'd go to

Tucson, get in a helicopter, and I'd give them the air tour. I could point out things from the air and the whole bit.

That provided me with the ability to understand the bigger picture better. What resonates with these CODELs? How can I get that in a twenty-second snippet that they'll remember as opposed to a long briefing? I started to understand what they were looking at, some of the approaches, what worked, and what didn't work. And they're all different personalities. Some are really gruff, some just had no clue. And you had to educate them.

I got to brief senators, the Speaker of the House, out in the field like that. Those are the highest folks, and you get a better understanding. The more I did it, the better I got at it.

And then our sector chief became the national chief of the Border Patrol. And he said, "I'd like you to be part of my staff at headquarters." So, I went up there as the director of planning and analysis. We did strategic planning, a hiring push, congressional preparation for our national chief, and then I did a lot of back-seating congressional preparation for Secretary Chertoff, who was secretary of DHS at that time. And that even provided a bigger understanding, a bigger scope, of that picture.

Of course, along the way you go from GS levels all the way up to GS-15. I became part of the senior executive service in DC. I would've never imagined it. When I was filling out that application, and I just wanted to have the civil service exam. I just wanted a 70. And I would've never imagined that, from that letter, that $17,000 that I was making in the beginning of the career, it was just . . .

I didn't have a plan. It was just the idea that I could take additional responsibility. I sought that.

My dad's got early onset Alzheimer's, and to this day I do things hoping that he's proud.

When you get to certain levels—agent in charge of a station or a sector—they have change of command ceremonies. There's a lot of pomp and circumstance with that. There's a guidon that's switched over. Every single one of them, my mom and dad have been there. And my dad looks like a peacock, you know. He's just so proud, and the feathers are out. It's priceless.

I remember one time when I was the sector chief in Tucson, he and my nephew came over to have lunch. I had an adjutant and he had them in my office. It had glass walls and you could look into a conference room. I went to go see my dad and my nephew real quick, and then I had to go back to a meeting in the conference room. And when I walk back in with the staff, they stand up. They stand up.

I just glanced over back through the glass walls and looked at my dad. He had this grin, from ear to ear. It was like my dream, you know. Well, his dream.

Of course, I'm also fortunate that my son and my daughter got to see all those things. And my spouse, obviously. She's been super supportive, because there's no way I would've gotten to this point without her support and without, sometimes, honestly, a good swift kick in the ass to get me going.

My son's a radiologist now and my daughter is a special ed teacher at an elementary school. They trail-blazed their own paths.

I think we made a very good team the last thirty-five years.

Definitely the hardest part of my career was conducting death notifications. That would just turn my stomach. If I never have to ever do that again for the rest of my life, I'm okay with that.

I remember when I was an agent in charge of the Douglas Station. I was driving home, and at the side of the road there were two young ladies. I pulled over and to me it was obvious that they had just crossed. But they were crying. The rest of the family was up in the hills and one of the woman's brothers had passed away. It was just me and the two women speaking, and you can't help but try to have some kind of compassion. They're in a country where they can't speak the language, they really don't know where they're going to go. We found out later that the brother was given diuretics, which makes you get dehydrated. It's the last thing you want to give someone in the desert.

She had no idea what was going to go on, what was going to happen to her, how she was going to get her brother's body back to—I think it was Guatemala.

That's what I went home with. I drive home on that, and it takes a toll on you. You think about someone who's coming here as an economic migrant because they have aspirations. And it ended this way. How is she going to tell her parents?

Death notifications, you know . . .

This is a card. David M. Webb. He was a Border Patrol agent in Ajo. Now, I retired in 2011. I have this one, and I have four others on my wall, pinned up. And they call these the silent partners. The Border Patrol Academy started giving these out, I want to say, in 2008/2009, as a part of not forgetting the sacrifice and the heritage of other agents who have come up.

The idea was to put that in your uniform pocket. You say, "Hey, never forgotten." The trainees at the academy were given these cards, and it's got the name, the picture, the birth date, entered on duty, the date they passed away, and on the back side a short story about how they passed away in the line of duty.

David Webb was the first one that I did the death notification. He was in a car accident. I was a deputy in Tucson when I got called, and they said, There was an agent killed on duty. I get the particulars, call my boss, let him know. I remember it was a Friday, because we were having dinner. And my wife saw my face.

I saw her go upstairs, and she was getting uniforms. She said, "When will you be back?" I said, "I'm not sure. I got to drive to Ajo, and it's like two, two and a half hours away."

I drive over there to go with the agent in charge, to go speak to his spouse, Celia. Of course, she already knew because you have agents who are friends of David's, or whose spouses were friends of hers. They'd called and said, "Hey, David's been hurt really bad." She didn't know any particulars.

I remember knocking on her door, coming up in uniform. And her two little boys, Cedric and Andrew, come up and say, "Hey, my dad's going to come home. He's got a uniform just like yours."

That is the toughest thing because you hear the stories. You sit there and chat with them a little bit, you know. What I've found is it's therapeutic—especially with the parents. They have pictures of different stages, little kids . . . You go to their parents' house, and I start to ask, "What was this picture?" And, man, they would really get into talking about the stories.

That is definitely the hardest part. I will not ever, ever miss that.

We'd go there prepared in terms of having some people they could speak to. Down the road there's a lot of planning. Things that they don't ask, right? Because their lives stop as they know it.

You've got to carry them for a while, just to make sure that they get back on their feet and don't make any bad decisions in terms of the government's going to pay out, because you have options, and things of that nature. You try to help them and guide them through that process. But it rips you. It rips you apart.

I kept five cards, all the time. David's mom, I called her November 24th. That's the day he was born. He passed away in 2006. And even to this day I give her a call, just to let her know that at least one person hasn't forgotten.

About six months ago, I had this idea in my mind. I wasn't brave enough to tell my wife till about three months ago. Then I asked her, "What if we went to Costa Rica for retirement?"

To my surprise, she said, "Let's do it."

I said, "Man, who are you? I don't know you."

I thought it was a trick. Funny thing is, neither one of us have been there.

But I was doing a lot of research. In our backyard, we have a pool, and I have all sorts of tropical plants. I never knew I was building Costa Rica in my backyard. The plants, that whole idea, right?

We started looking at housing, what it costs. It's very inexpensive. And they have retirement visas. We actually had a trip planned, but the trips were being cancelled or postponed because of the COVID travel restrictions.

We thought of doing three or four trips next year. One of them is where we meet with immigration attorneys and real estate people, medical staff, doctors, things that we have questions about, you know. That is my next step, to do that.

I'd like to sit there and write my dad's book. His story.

And I wrote a journal my entire career. I don't know if you're familiar with these green leather books that the government has that say "Record." I have eleven of those from my career. If you were to go through them, you'd see all the way from when I was a GS-5 step nothing to my last days as sector chief in Tucson sector, and everything in between. My mom is always encouraging me. "You should write a book," she says. And I say, "Mom, there's only one person who's going to read it. That's you."

Maybe that's what I'll do.

Dr. Victor M. Manjarrez Jr. retired as the chief patrol agent of the Tucson sector after twenty-two years of service. He is the director of the Center for Law and Human Behavior at the University of Texas at El Paso.

FRANCISCO CANTÚ

What led me to join the Border Patrol is probably pretty out of the ordinary. It's a more uncommon path.

I grew up in Arizona. I followed a standard trajectory from high school to undergraduate studies. I decided to study international relations. Then I left home to go to school in DC, the epicenter of international relations and US diplomacy. For me, growing up in a small town in Arizona, it was such a big shift. I think part of my response to the disorientation of being in a place like that was to turn back toward what I felt I knew a little bit more, or a place and a subject and a topic where I had a little bit of skin in the game. And so, within an international relations degree, I started to focus on US-Mexico relations and border issues.

Studying the border at a place that was so far from the border, through books and studies and research papers and ethnographies, I really had this strange look at the topic and the place. It was like understanding a place that you maybe intuitively know through the eyes of a lot of outside rhetoric, looking at the place as a problem or looking at the place as this question to be answered.

I think my reaction to that when I was coming out of college was that I wanted to go back to Arizona. I knew my interest in the border had only grown. I had studied abroad in Mexico. I had worked at a migration policy institute. I was in this strange situation. When I started to look at how I could go be close to all these issues in a way that was radically different from all the books I'd been reading, I thought, "Who's out on the border day in and day out, twenty-four hours a day?"

I thought about different advocacy jobs or volunteer work. I imagined that those would be weekend trips or that you'd only be out there under certain conditions. And then I was walking around at the university job fair in a huge stadium and going to all these different booths. I remember walking by the Department of Homeland Security booth, the Customs and Border Protection booth, and almost laughingly picking up one of these brochures. That idea weirdly planted itself in my head. I thought, "Well, actually, there are very few people who spend more time out in it."

There was a lot of naivete and privilege that went into my thinking at that moment. When I look back on that time, I had this idea as a young person in my early twenties that I could be part of this system. I could step into this system and not partake in the uglier aspects that I knew about and was familiar with. I imagined that I could see and learn, but not be implicated. I imagined that I could be a force for good within this agency that I already didn't agree with, but I sort of accepted as inevitable. I accepted it as this inevitable part of shaping the reality of the border.

Today, as a writer and a literary critic and thinker, I'm thinking about narrative all the time. And when you look at the narrative of the stories that we grow up with in this country, I think there's this uniquely American idea that the individual can overcome anything and is the most powerful social unit. We grow up on these stories where one person steps into a system and, against all odds, they're able to overcome or change it.

As a young person, I had this idea that I could step into this job and that I would learn all of these things and come out with all these answers that nobody else who was a policymaker—or who had written the work I'd been reading in college—had come up with because they'd never done work like that. I imagined I would be able to go on to be this policymaker or this immigration lawyer with a totally different toolbox or bag of tricks.

If I'd gone to a small liberal arts school it might have been different. But the school I went to in DC was very oriented around government services jobs. Very oriented around service. The people who came out of my program were angling for State Department jobs, government jobs, or research and think tank jobs. That was the abbreviated menu of career options that I think a lot of people like me coming out of a program like that were thinking about.

Now I've lived in Tucson for a very long time and I'm involved with so many groups that are doing work on the border, day in and day out, in a completely different capacity. In a moral and ethical capacity. That world just wasn't as available to me back then. I think that if I had gone to school here, if I had stayed in Arizona, it might have been very different.

I had this foundational, early childhood experience of living in a national park with my mom about an hour and a half or two hours outside of El Paso in West Texas. It was Guadalupe

Mountains National Park, one of the least visited national parks in the country. Remote, Chihuahuan desert landscape. We would go to El Paso for shopping. That was the city where we did our urban things. It was an early childhood of being very connected to desert landscapes and caring a lot about the natural world and coming to understand myself in relationship to the outdoors in a big way.

That was early childhood, up until the age of five or six, I think, when we moved away. We moved to central Arizona, an hour and a half north of Phoenix in a small—well, it's not that small anymore—town called Prescott. My mom got a job with the Forest Service there. It's a high desert, piñon, juniper, Douglas fir kind of landscape in the middle elevation mountains.

But when I think about the demographics of the place where I grew up . . . now, this is the heart of Arizona's Trump country. Paul Gosar is our representative. It's a very white town, where the cowboy myth is larger than life. It's home of the world's oldest rodeo.

That was the backdrop to how I grew up. A lot of that sort of mythology. It was an interesting place to grow up in relation to the border because the border was not close like it is here in Tucson. It was not an everyday consideration. It was not a place that people thought about and were involved in on any day-to-day basis. However, it was also not completely foreign or abstract or so distant that it wasn't at all comprehensible.

My first job was as a busboy in an Italian restaurant. I started in middle school and I kept that job all through high school. Everyone in the back was from the same community in central Mexico, in Guanajuato.

I was growing up in this kind of small, white, cowboy town, and then I started to travel, first in Mexico and then in Europe. Seeing the world beyond this town became this really exciting thing for me as a young person and definitely was kind of the subtext to me choosing to study international relations.

One of the first places I went to when I traveled in Mexico, maybe my freshman year in college, was to the village where all these guys I worked with in the Mexican restaurant were from. I ended up going to the dishwasher's brother's wedding. I just happened to be there when he was getting married.

I stepped off the bus like 2,000 miles from where I grew up and I knew somebody, and nobody questioned who I was—it was like, "Oh, this person works with this other person who left." That was my first experience of seeing the interconnectedness of migrant communities, this living, breathing connection that I think is probably unique to the tail end of the twentieth century. There were immediate wire transfers and communication was easier and it still wasn't so impossible to cross the border in the '80s and the '90s. There was still a more fluid exchange, I think, between a lot of these communities. That was all the stuff maybe swirling behind what became a more academic fascination as I went further into my college years.

I always knew this academic question pointing me into the Border Patrol was uncommon and I think when I talked to friends or family (other than my mom) about the decision, I always did a lot of explaining: "Oh, I'm doing it for these reasons and I'm going to find this out. I'm not doing it because I want to protect the country and keep out immigrants or something like that. I don't believe in that."

Different people bought it or pushed back in different ways. The other people I was going to school with in DC, they were doing these same kinds of internships at think tanks and government entities. I remember one friend who had an internship at the State Department who was like, "There's this Border Patrol liaison who seems really nice in our office. I'll ask, if you want to talk to that person." That was one of the few people I talked to before applying who was actually from the agency.

We got coffee somewhere in DC and had this pretty normal-seeming conversation. This person had grown up in Arizona, wasn't a recruiter or anything, not your typical Border Patrol agent. They were part Asian-American, part Mexican-American. I remember they just talked about, "You'll be outside all the time. You'll be hiking trails all the time."

And there I was, fascinated by the desert, and having these questions about how do these policies and this enforcement shape our ideas and notion about the landscape? And how has it changed the desert and how is the desert being weaponized in all of these ways? And before those questions were maybe fully formed, it was also just like, "Wow, that sounds pretty great to be out in the desert all the time and exploring the outdoors."

When I showed up at the Border Patrol Academy, there were lots of guys who'd been in the military or in law enforcement. I signed up in the beginning of 2008, but by the time I showed up at the Academy it was November. This was the tail end of the George W. Bush hiring push and the economy was crashing down. A lot of people who were there were just looking for a good steady job with benefits. There was everybody from eighteen-year-olds who had only worked at fast food restaurants to early forties, late thirty-year-olds who had run a business for a decade or two before it collapsed because of the economic crisis in 2008.

I remember the first couple of days when we were showing up in Tucson before they sent us to the Academy. They brought us to the station. I remember being with a lot of guys from the Midwest and the East Coast who'd never seen a cactus, never seen a cattle guard. To them this was like the ends of the earth. It was like a purgatory landscape that they were getting sent to patrol at the gates of—you know, like *Game of Thrones*. The wall, or something like that.

I had studied in Mexico. I'd been to different parts of the country where there are traditionally migrant-sending communities. I imagined that I would be able to help and have conversations and put people at ease and be a more humanitarian-minded agent.

That idea—yes, it was naive, but it also wasn't. It didn't come out of nowhere. The Border Patrol itself cultivates this idea. There's a journalist, Debbie Weingarten, who talks about "the militarization of humanitarian aid," this humanitarian enforcement myth where Border Patrol agents and the Border Patrol in general—especially in the Southwest—talk about the search and rescue component of their work, like, "We're the first ones out there who are rescuing people and saving people from the desert and giving them water."

The Border Patrol talks about that a lot and I think that was also something that some of the recruitment literature, or the conversation with that Border Patrol liaison, had given me. Recruiters might see that you're not a guns-and-badge kind of a guy and so they pivot to that.

Even once I joined the Border Patrol, I signed up to be trained as an EMT. So, there were these tangible ways in which I was able to prolong my time there and feed this idea that I was doing "good work," or something good, by providing first aid and doing search and rescue work.

But, of course, all of that comes at the expense of casting into the back of your mind, or not even entertaining the idea, that the reason people need rescuing has completely shifted because of the enforcement policies and the enforcement tactics of the agency. Thirty years ago, people didn't cross through the middle of the desert. They didn't make five to ten to fifteen-day treks through the most remote parts of the Southwest border because it wasn't necessary. The whole idea of prevention through deterrence—that wasn't present in my mind.

Now, I think this idea of being able to feel proud of rescue work as a Border Patrol agent is like being a firefighter and feeling proud about putting out a blaze, but it turns out that blaze was actually started by the fire chief. That's kind of what it comes down to. These people are there to avoid your presence. They were out there to avoid my presence. So even when I show up and I'm bandaging somebody's blisters or giving them an IV, bringing them back from a dehydrated state, it's like, in a very real way, I—or any agent out there—is the reason that that person ended up in that state in the first place.Still, I would cling to the moments when I was able to come home and feel like I had helped someone. I could cling to those moments as a way to not feel morally implicated or to feel like I was doing something good within the job.

That would happen in my waking life. But all of that would get torn down and torn asunder by dreams and subconscious, unconscious preoccupations. I think that my body, my mind, my spirit knew that was a bunch of bullshit. Or knew that it was this small consolation.

Grappling with that was something that led me to put together *The Line Becomes a River: Dispatches from the Border*, or it led me to do writing in the first place.[7] I think there's an accumulation in the first part of this book of small encounters, small moments with a different person each time. And a lot of those moments are moments that stuck in my mind because I was having an exchange or a conversation with somebody or "helping" somebody or having someone express gratitude to me. That was always very strange. Because there was this part of you that was like, "Wow, that person is thanking me. They feel like I have done something humanitarian to them or helpful to them."

But then you know in the back of your mind that it's off, that that's not the whole story. That that's not where it ends. You're still sending them back to do it all again.

There were glimmers of wanting to, or trying to, find consolation or some kind of pride in the job. And maybe there were moments. Maybe my hindsight is obscuring moments where I did come home and feel proud. There were definitely moments where you felt exhilarated. A chase and catching a bunch of drugs. It's easy to imagine that, "Okay, well, the drug dealers are the bad guys and I'm keeping them out."

You could try to feel good about that for a minute before you realize that the drug war is a bunch of garbage. Even a lot of other agents I worked with realized how silly it was and how small it was.

The Border Patrol instills a military hierarchy from the moment you show up at the Academy. It's run like a boot camp. They pride themselves on being like a paramilitary police force. They really bill themselves as being somewhere between law enforcement and military.

Your critical question-asking impulses get intentionally broken down during the training process. When I look back at some of these moments when I was observing my colleagues crushing people's food or slashing water bottles or dumping people's backpacks out in the desert, that kind of thing . . . I think I imagined at the moment that by not participating, that that was a moral act or something, just not participating.

But it's not. You're completely complicit. You're wearing a uniform, you're standing aside while this is happening. A lot of this stuff was happening on my first week in the field. I would see supervisors taking part in this or supervisors literally teaching it and giving the okay. And that hierarchy made it so you didn't feel like you could speak out or ask questions. I still wonder what would have happened. Would it have been totally futile to speak out?

There are all sorts of moments I didn't ever write down in my journals. A lot of them are moments that aren't even in the book. There was this one moment that made it into an op-ed I wrote a few years ago. There was this girl, Jakelin Caal, a twelve-year-old girl from Guatemala, who died several years ago.[8] It came out that she was arrested at one of these forwarding operating bases in a remote part of New Mexico and was brought in from the field and detained in this little operating base before agents came to pick up the group that she was apprehended with and take them into the larger station. Probably what happened is that she wasn't given food and water or any sort of medical attention at the small substation. And so, she died being transported to this bigger station.

I remember reading about that and having this memory return to me of being, again, in the first or second week in the field, apprehending a group of men in the desert, maybe five people. Bringing them back to the station. I'm a trainee. They could tell that I'm the one who speaks Spanish and they ask me for some water. I say, "Oh, yeah, sure."

There was a case of water bottles in the storage room right outside the processing area. I went to bring it into the processing area and my supervisor—my field training agent—sees me walking into the processing area with this case of water bottles and is like, "What are you doing?"

I said, "Oh, these guys asked for water."

She said, "They're fine. Leave it."

I said, "I already have the water bottles in my hand. It's fine. I'll just go drop it off, don't worry about it."

And she said, "No, that's an order. Leave it. We need you in the computer room. Come over here right now."

Today I wonder what the fuck could she have possibly done to me if I had said, "No, I'm going to give these guys water. Write me up for it. I dare you to write me up for giving these guys water."

There are all sorts of ways that they try to get rid of people or push people out. Are you really going to try to push someone out who is saying "No" to those things? There were only a few instances where I ever spoke up, told somebody to shut the fuck up because they were saying something racist. It was always a calculation of, "Do I have the rank or social standing to call this person out or try to humiliate them?" or something like that.

It's the culture of the agency. It's such a toxic culture. It's such a toxically masculine culture. You don't show compassion, or talk about feelings. You don't show weakness. You don't hesitate or express vulnerability or any of those things.

There were other people. That's the interesting thing about the Border Patrol. I felt at the time that there were a handful of other like-minded people that I got along with. A lot of the connecting happens through humor or something like that. You develop a sort of dark sense of humor.

There were people who recognized some of the rhetoric and you're able to poke fun at the idea of, "Oh, yeah, we're fucking heroes because we're keeping these bundles of schwag marijuana that some middle school kids are going to smoke in their bedroom during a sleepover." You know, like, marijuana? I mean, that was the only thing I ever had a hand in stopping.

Today it's hard to imagine. Now in Arizona, where I live, marijuana is legal. It's legal as a recreational drug. You turn eighteen and you can buy the stuff. Or maybe it's twenty-one.

But, at the time, it was absolutely not like that, and there was this idea that I think a lot of people had where it's like, "Okay, we understand that these migrants are not criminals." I think there were plenty of people who drew lines that separated the migrants or the people who were coming looking for work from the people who were smuggling drugs. And the drug smugglers are the bad guys and that's what we're able to feel good about. That's where we're able to believe in this myth that we're keeping America safe or that we're standing guard or whatever the hell rhetoric they feed you to make you feel heroic about your job.

But the reality is that the Border Patrol—and this is true for most law enforcement—if you look at the numbers, this is not a dangerous job. These are not violent encounters. The overwhelming majority of your encounters are humanitarian encounters. And if you're willing to look at it or to have conversations or to think critically, you begin to understand even the people who are smuggling these bales of marijuana through the desert, they're not hardened criminals. A lot of them are people who struck out on two or three prior attempts to cross the border the normal way with a group and a coyote leading them across. They don't have any more money to pay for another crossing.

So, you have guys who can't pay to get across. The smugglers, human traffickers, human trafficking networks are now the same as the drug trafficking networks. That's a shift that our own drug policies and border enforcement policies have facilitated. Those people will say, "Well, if you carry this bundle of marijuana on your back, we'll let you cross for free or we'll give you a discount once you get there."

You're not dealing with violent, hardened criminals. You're not dealing with the smuggling networks. You're not dealing with El Chapo Guzman out here crossing the desert. These are kids a lot of times, eighteen-year-old kids or something, who are trying to make a buck leading groups through the desert and bailing the first opportunity they get.

You're looking at people who are in an extremely precarious situation. The people who are being smuggled, the people who are crossing the border—they're a lot of times being taken advantage of or victimized—their bodies are being commodified every step of the way. From the moment they leave their doorstep in Central America until even past the time that they arrive, if they successfully arrive. Then they have to pay off the debt they incurred just in order to get to San Francisco or Chicago or wherever they're trying to go.

There were definitely people I think who saw through that. But I think a lot of people, even people who arrive at or who maybe know the whole time the silly or scary aspects of this work, they might have a family. And they might have a mortgage. And they might not have the option to leave. Or they might not *feel* like they have the option to leave. Everybody always had the option to leave. But they might not feel like they have the option to leave.

That's not accidental, either. The Border Patrol, especially in these remote stations like the one where I worked, they know that it's a hardship for people to be out there. And so, they sweeten the pot. You're able to climb the ladder quickly. You're able to get raises quickly. You're able to promote quickly, especially if you're out in these "undesirable" stations.

I think there are plenty of people who see the problems, but don't feel like they have an easy way out. I had a college education. I went into it from the beginning with the idea that it would only be something I would do for four or five years as an extension of my education. I went in with all sorts of privilege. And it was all sorts of privilege that enabled me to so easily leave when I did finally decide to leave.

I imagined I would go into policymaking or that I would become an immigration attorney or something like that. I imagined that I would be coming out of the experience with answers to these intractable questions. I imagined that I was going to get answers to these questions and that I would be uniquely positioned to use those answers in some kind of work or job that I would have afterward.

But by the time I left the Border Patrol, I think those questions seemed more unanswerable than they had even when I joined. I left with more questions than I came in with. Just the idea that there is an answer to any of this . . . it was obvious that was a fallacy born from afar.

And these problems are also imposed from afar. This border enforcement regime, and the whole way that we think about the border as being problematic, and the whole way we think about this landscape as being hostile—all of that is borne from afar or imposed from afar.

Coming out of the Border Patrol—there are several different alternative ways that could have gone. It could have gone in a direction where you just want to get as far away as possible from the place or the subject. I applied for a Fulbright to go to the Netherlands. The Fulbright was to study immigration and asylum seekers in the EU. So it was still connected.

At the end of the day, maybe because of how I grew up, and because of this question of the landscape that was ingrained in me from such a young age because of growing up in the park service, I've always felt accountable to this place. Even after I left, leaving the border behind never felt like an option. I was trying to process and make sense of my participation in this violent institution. My complicity. It would be more convenient and easy to leave it behind, but that would also be a continuation of this idea of bottling it all up.

This is all a long way of getting around to my being involved in humanitarian work on the border. Right now, that mostly takes the form of working on projects in detention centers with detained asylum seekers. I don't know if it's atonement. There must be an element of that. There must be an element of that subconsciously, implicitly. You know, feeling like it is a way of putting a few weights on the other side of that scale, slowly trying to put in more time and more attention on that side of the scale than I ever did on the other side.

But, really, I think of it now more as a practice. The same way that people think of a religious practice or an intellectual practice or if you practice yoga or meditation or anything like that. It's just something that you have to show up for daily or weekly or whatever.

This whole system functions by us feeling that the border is far away and that the border is an exceptional, othered landscape that we're not accountable to. But I live here. It's a topic, it's a landscape, that runs through my family. It runs through so many people's families in this part of the country.

Being involved in some sort of teaching, education, service, volunteer work—I don't think I'll ever not do that. I hope I will never not do that as a practice. I don't know if I believe in this idea of atonement or that idea of balancing the scales. I think that's probably a false construct. But the idea of it being a practice is much more appealing to me. And of it being about accountability. Being accountable to this place. Being accountable to your life before where you are now. I think we should be accountable to who we were and so that feels important too.

I would really caution anyone to never underestimate these institutions of power that have accumulated their power over the course of centuries. The idea that we can step into them with our own ambitions and our own set of questions and come out scot-free, or the idea that we can change these systems from within—I think that a lot of that is rooted in underestimating those systems and overestimating our power and influence as individuals. I think that the American mythology of the individual is a really toxic one. And I think it's a myth. I think it's a complete myth.

What I would tell anybody who's interested in affecting change is that if you look at history, these institutions rarely, if ever, truly change from the inside. They change in reaction to, most often, intense, sustained people-powered pressure from outside, over the course of many, many, many years or decades.

I think that's what we are seeing in the last decade with the Black Lives Matter movement and with a lot of the conversations that we're having about policing in this country, more publicly, more broadly. Not that those conversations are new, because they're not. But a lot of us are learning about them in ways that we have not before.

FIGURE 3.5
Francisco Cantú, Pima County Cemetery, Tucson, Arizona, 2022.

The idea that I think a lot of people have after participating in the uprisings in 2020 is like, "Oh, why hasn't this changed? I showed up at my city council meeting. I showed up in the street. I went to these marches." It's easy to get disillusioned because what has meaningfully changed a year later? Not a lot. Culturally, conversation-wise, a lot has maybe changed. Awareness-wise, maybe a lot has changed. But politically? Policy-wise? Not a lot has changed.

But this is generational work. It's going to take a long slow shift—a consciousness shift—and sustained involvement and attention. With the border, the biggest thing—and what makes me feel good as a writer—is giving more language to the ways that we think about and talk about the border, enabling people who aren't from here to have emotional engagement and investment in this place and to be able to think of it the same way that they would think of their home. Or to think about what happens here the same way that they would think about what happens in the next neighborhood over from them.

That seems like the important work moving forward: not letting the people whose lives are affected by this place be othered. Not letting the place be presented as this dangerous, other-worldly, exceptional landscape, because it's not. People have been living here in the desert for a very long time and it's not an inherently violent place. It's not an inherently hostile place. That comes from what we bring in from the outside.

Francisco Cantú is an author who teaches at the University of Arizona. He is the author of *The Line Becomes a River: Dispatches from the Border*.

CARLA PROVOST

I was raised in Burlingame, Kansas, a small town in Middle America. It sits literally in the very center of the country. In the last fifty years, it's always had between 800 and 1,200 people. My father and brother still live there.

I did not have a family with a history of law enforcement; however, my father had always been interested in it and I am certain that had an influence on me. Also, my best friend's father was the city marshal. When I say "city marshal," I mean there were one to two cops at any given time in Burlingame. I had always thought about either being a teacher/coach or doing something in law enforcement.

I think the patriotism of the small town that I grew up in had a huge impact on me as well. July 4th was always a big event. I still go back home every year to celebrate July 4th with my father and my brother. I also considered going into the military at one point. The Air Force Academy was recruiting me before college as well. I was always brought up to be proud to be an American and to feel blessed to live in this country. I think law enforcement was always in the back of my mind.

When I went into college at Kansas State University, I was originally a business major because I didn't know what I wanted to do. But at Kansas State, business just wasn't doing it for me. I found out that Kansas State University had a criminal justice program, and after my freshman year, I transferred into it and I never looked back. A very good friend of the family was a homicide detective in Topeka, Kansas, for years and I ended up doing my internship my last year at Kansas State at Topeka Police Department and I got to work with him. I still go back and visit him to this day. He has been a great mentor and friend.

After graduating, I hired on with Riley County Police Department in Manhattan, Kansas. The Little Apple. I'd tell people I was a police officer in Manhattan. They're like, "Oh, really?" I'm, like, "Kansas."

I loved being a police officer, but I wanted a federal job. I loved the Riley County Police Department. I loved working there, but I had the concept that federal jobs were bigger and better. FBI or DEA or one of those. I knew nothing about the Border Patrol. I grew up as far away from the borders as I possibly could have, but I was going through a hiring process with the US Marshal Service in the 1993/'94 timeframe and I was almost through the process when they had a hiring freeze.

It was a US Marshal who told me, "Hey, you should put in for Border Patrol because they're hiring and you can get your foot in the door." And that was my intent. I thought, "Well, I'll apply. I'll see if I can get in." I took the exam, I scored fairly well on it, but I did not speak Spanish. I actually received three denial letters from the Immigration and Naturalization Service. I'm thinking to myself, "Okay, I get it. You're not accepting me for the job." At that point, I never gave the Border Patrol another thought. And then in December of '94, right before Christmas, I get this call. I thought it was a practical joke. They were calling and they wanted me to enter on duty within just under two weeks.

I had to make a very quick decision. It was difficult for me. I had just turned twenty-five years old, had lived my entire life in Kansas, and had never really been anywhere because of growing up in that small-town community. And I loved being a police officer. But I wanted that federal job.

I thought I would use it for a stepping stone to move on to something bigger and better in the future. They offered me a job in Douglas, Arizona. I had never heard of Douglas, so I got out my Rand McNally atlas—now I'm really showing my age. Douglas looked like it was close to Tucson and I'd heard of Tucson, so I thought, "I can do this."

And then I got to Douglas, Arizona. It is really not that close to Tucson, about two hours away. It was a sleepy little border town, but I think because I grew up in a small town in the Midwest I really didn't struggle being assigned there. Still, when I entered on duty and they put us on the bus—it was a detention bus that they drove us down to Douglas on—there was a little part of me that thought, "Technically, I'm only on annual leave from my police department. I could go back." But I got to Douglas and I stuck with my commitment, and I ended up going off to the Academy, which was about six months long. I graduated from the Academy and arrived back in Douglas, Arizona, in May of 1995.

Once I was on the ground, working with the men and women I was blessed to work with in that sleepy little border town, I quickly fell in love with the Border Patrol and I swore I'd never leave. That's what it really came down to: the mission, the work, the men and women, what I saw them doing on the ground, the sacrifices they made. At that point in time, the Border Patrol was only about 6,000 agents and when you think about 2,000 miles with Mexico's border and another 4,000 northern border miles, that's a pretty small agency. The work was thrilling. It was the kind of job where you really controlled your own destiny, and, if you were a worker, there was so much to do.

My police job was very reactive, meaning you're responding to calls. Dispatch is sending you the calls. With the Border Patrol, when I started, you'd come in and we'd have six or seven guys or gals on the shift. They'd throw you a set of keys and give you an assignment that was several miles long and you just went out and you found the work yourself. Don't get me

FIGURE 3.6
Carla Provost, Boerne, Texas, 2022.

wrong, there were sensors and such, but you weren't being dispatched from call to call. You were proactive versus being reactive.

I transitioned from dealing with some illegal guns or narcotics where you pull one weapon off of somebody to thousands of pounds that come across the border, large weapons seizures—those kinds of things. I just fell in love with it. I fell in love with the mission of protecting the country.

I hired on in January of '95. I retired twenty-five years later at the end of January 2020. So, I did twenty-five years. I am a planner and that was my plan all along. Well, I actually had two plans. I always said if I was stuck in DC—because I didn't like the politics—I would go with twenty-five years at age fifty. If I was in the field, I would potentially stay until age fifty-five and do thirty years. I have a teenager and part of it revolved around high school, wanting to keep her in one location throughout high school because I've moved her around so much throughout her life. I knew she'd be hitting high school age right around the time that I retired, so I wanted to plan for that in advance.

And I did. I planned for it financially, personally. A lot of people may make a last-minute decision; this is something I had planned for over the years.

When I joined the Border Patrol, people didn't move much. All of the senior agents who were at my station had been there for most of their entire careers and you didn't promote until you had ten to twelve years in. That was just the Border Patrol.

But from '94 on, the Border Patrol just started hiring.[9] Boom, boom, boom, boom, hiring, hiring. I gained instant seniority, meaning I got off of probation at a year and was put on specialty units like bike patrol, firearms, and I was a law instructor. All these things didn't used to happen because there wasn't much growth in the Border Patrol. But because of what was going on along the southwest border, it just started growing rapidly and I was lucky enough to be at the forefront of all of it.

Myself and two of my classmates were the first in Border Patrol history to promote to first line supervisor with three years in service. It was unheard of. Obviously, the three of us had previous experience and had proven ourselves, but it caused a big uproar in the Border Patrol. Part of it was people didn't want to come to Douglas, Arizona. A lot of people didn't apply for supervisor jobs before then.

The promotion system had also changed. There was an old system where everything was based on experience. Then they went to a balance of experience and taking tests, leadership tests. So, I applied not intending to get promoted to supervisor with three years in service, but because this was a new test process and I wanted to take the test and see how I would do on it and to prepare for the future, as did my classmates. Well, because of the rapid growth, the number of supervisors they needed to hire, and not tons of other people putting in, the three of us were promoted. We were known as the three-year wonders and, boy, did that spread across the Border Patrol.

It really did cause an uproar. I remember specifically having one senior agent come up to me and he was mad at me for getting the job and we had always been good friends. And I remember distinctly having a conversation with him and saying, "You're upset with me for getting this job. Did you put in?"

"Well, no, but whatever."

I said, "Okay, wait a minute. So, if you're me, yes, I applied. I applied because I wanted to be prepared for the future. They offered me the job. What would you do?"

It really worked because he kind of backed off and took it from my perspective. But then I was very cognizant that I needed to prove myself in that position. And there was a lot I didn't know. There really was. Douglas was out of control at that point and that's why nobody wanted to be a supervisor. We were literally getting run over with traffic in the area.

When I look back there's a lot of things I could have done better. It's hard to transition to being a supervisor. You're trying to balance friendship with, okay, if someone's not doing their job, I still have to hold them accountable and I have to be that supervisor. I was also terrible at delegating. We were getting so overwhelmed and everybody was working sixteen- to eighteen-hour days and if someone couldn't do a report or this or that, I'd just be, like, "Step aside and let me do it." And I finally had to step back and go, "Wait a minute. If I don't ever teach them to do it, they're not going to learn and I'm never going to truly be able to do my job." So, it was really a big learning experience for me in that first line supervisor job.

And then three years later I promoted again into a second line supervisory position.

The Patrol really started changing at that point because of the rapid growth, because so many people were coming in. The stations were growing, manpower was expanding into the tens of thousands, and we needed more supervisory personnel and the opportunities were there.

When I came in, I was expecting, "Well, in twelve years I'll maybe make a supervisor and maybe if it all possible I might have my own station at some point." By no means did I ever expect what happened.

When I put in for the senior executive level back in 2010, I certainly wasn't expected to get it. I was never a GS-15 in the government. I jumped from a GS-14 to a senior executive position. I believe there was one other; myself and one other, we were the first ones in the Border Patrol history to jump from GS-14 straight to senior executive. But part of that was the position I was doing ultimately ended up being a position that is now a GS-15. I hit good timing. I liked a challenge. I never shied away from it. I always stepped up and raised my hand to take on the additional work and those types of things. And the opportunities just came. It certainly wasn't something I strove for. I didn't go, "I'm going to be the first female chief of the Border Patrol."

But I might be a little competitive. My siblings and I were all athletes and it was always about grades and sports. I was raised by my parents telling me, "You can do or be anything you want, but whatever it is you better do the best that you can." And that has stuck with me. My poor daughter, I drive her insane with that, because I pass it on to her. "You can do whatever it is you want to do. I'm not going to push your future on you, but always do your best." What can I say, it's a family trait. Whatever we do, we work hard at it and try to be the best at it that we can be.

It was not an easy time to be the chief of the Border Patrol when I held the position. It really was not. Lots of politics around the Border Patrol, a lot of scrutiny around law enforcement. We were called every name in the book. Media was pushing a lot of blame on my men and women, but I felt like I at least got the opportunity to be their voice and to come out and, whether people picked it up or not, tell the truth about what it was that they were doing and how they would go out of their way to care for families and children. Which was not by any means what they were hired to do, but because it was left in the hands of my men and women, we did the best that we could do and we had to care for them.

I testified more than a lot of chiefs did in prior times because we were called up to the Hill so often. I tried to squash some of the false rhetoric that was out there because, whether people believed it or not—and there are plenty who don't—I watched agents bringing in food, clothing, toys, to family members. I watched them try to care for people who were in overcrowded facilities because our facilities weren't meant to house families and children. I watched them do the best they could with limited resources. And I watched them struggle because they felt like nobody else was supporting them.

I was able to go say, "Don't give more money to CBP (US Customs and Border Protection) to house families and children. Give it to HHS (US Department of Health and Human Services) and to ICE (US Immigration and Customs Enforcement) because that's their job and that's not the role of my men and women."

And, you know, the Border Patrol, it's a family. It truly is. It's an organization that always stands up. We've had tons of tragedies over the years and agents lost in the line of duty. It's a very dangerous job, but everybody comes together and supports one another. And I think in the law enforcement world sometimes that gets misconstrued as, "Oh, they come in and cover up for when their guys and gals are doing bad things," and that's just not true.

One of the jobs I held, the one time I stepped outside the Border Patrol, I was the deputy assistant commissioner for the Office of Professional Responsibility for a year, 2015 to '16. And, you know, bad agents, bad cops, nobody wants them out of the organization more than the good men and women working in the organization. Every profession has good people and bad people. There are good teachers and there are bad teachers; there are good medical professionals and there are bad medical professionals. In the law enforcement realm, unfortunately, yes, there are a few bad apples, but law enforcement, like nobody else, gets painted as, "Oh, one bad apple, they're all bad." And it really pulls on the hearts and souls of the men and women who wear the uniform. It's hard. It's hard to deal with and there's been so much of that over the last few years. It certainly has been a struggle for the men and women because 99 percent plus are good, hard-working, kind, generous people who are parents themselves, who understand the plight of the migrants but are stuck dealing with the situation.

I testified in Congress—this is public information—that, yes, we had 2,700 children that we were housing in facilities not meant to house them, but that's because by law the only people we could turn them over to were Health and Human Services. And Health and Human Services said, "We can't take them." So what does that leave the Border Patrol agents left to do? We had no option. I needed Congress to act. I pleaded with Congress, "Please fund Health and Human Services." My agents were being blamed as these horrible people who had kids sleeping on mats on a floor. And, yes, we did have children sleeping on mats, because we had no other option, but it also shouldn't have fallen on the shoulders of my men and women.

So much of the public didn't realize. How many people know that by law the only people that Border Patrol could turn unaccompanied children over to was Health and Human Services? Most people don't know that. They don't understand the concept, and it was, "Well, you've got them in these crowded facilities." Not because we wanted them there, but because there were no other options.

The Border Patrol really is a family and they step up and they do good things for the kids. Nobody would publicize Santa Claus coming on Christmas when we had kids in our custody and care. Santa would come to a lot of the stations and bring gifts that were purchased by the agents. That stuff didn't make the media because that wasn't the story the media was interested in telling. But those were the things I saw throughout my career. Agents stopping at a McDonald's and spending their own money to buy food because a family they had picked up out in the middle of the desert said, "We're really hungry and thirsty." Back in the '90s, I did that, as did all of my colleagues. Agents still do it today.

I certainly missed a lot of things over the years. It was tough. I missed my daughter's entire second year of life because I was sent off to the War College, which was a great experience, but my family was in Yuma, Arizona, and I was in Washington, DC. And then I missed a lot of family time while on detail assignments. So, a lot of things missed. And I think that's why, when I said I was a planner, I spent a lot of time preparing to retire early, because I wanted to be around during my daughter's teen years. The years that, you know, she doesn't want me around as much, but I knew how critical it was that I be there.

My partner was a Border Patrol agent as well and, as our daughter was growing up, we were very, very blessed because both of us moved up through the ranks. We both worked a lot. When our daughter was little, another agent's wife basically took care of her while we were working and we worked different shifts at different times. But not long after she was born, we moved to Yuma, Arizona, and we both moved into day-shift positions at that point. We had the same nanny there for her from birth basically until age nine. Well, there were a couple years we went to El Paso that we didn't have them.

And they had their own kids, so she was raised around others. It was very much a big Border Patrol family. And then my daughter just turned ten when we went to DC. And she was always mature for her age and very responsible. The bus picked her up one block away and she would walk herself to the bus and walk herself home afterward. If she had not been so mature, I don't think we would have done that. She was happy because she got a phone much younger than I'd intended. I was like, "I have to know where you are," which made her happy.

On the immigration side of the work and the basic border security, she always asks good questions. She's debated on the issue in school. She's, of course, a lot brighter than I am, an honor student. With the tough things, I think she knew that wasn't something that you asked about. It just wasn't something that was ever brought up. She knew the overarching mission—what we did on a day-to-day basis—and she got to see a lot of it, unfortunately, in the news. We would have long conversations about, "Okay, here's what the news said and here's what actually happened," because those two don't tend to match up exactly. But she always asks and we still talk about it. I'm still, with my retirement, involved in certain aspects of it, and she still, to this day, if she sees something in the news she will ask an educated question about it. "Okay, so I saw this. What's going on here? Is this actually the case, or is it not?"

I think the key was she liked moving around. I was terrified because I was born and raised in the same town, never left, had friends from kindergarten through high school. I was worried about that, but she actually liked moving around, until I retired and we moved out of DC. She really liked school there. They moved in 2019 because she started school, so they moved before me. She started her freshman year out here where I've retired in Texas. And she liked the city life a little bit more. I'm small-town, so I like the small towns and we moved her into a smaller community. But she's a very resilient kid. Smart as a whip, and a bit of a smart-aleck. I'm not sure where she gets that from.

My other half had top secret, SCI (sensitive compartmented information), you know, all the clearances and stuff.[10] Now, obviously, there's certain things you don't talk about—but general conversations we were always able to have. And I do think when you have spouses who work in the same field it does ease some of it because they understand what you're doing. You understand each other and you understand the stress of the job and you understand why, "Hey, I've got to go on TDY (temporary duty travel) for six months and I'm leaving tomorrow," because we both experienced it throughout our careers.[11]

And I think that does make it easier on the family. Easier and harder, because if both of you are rising up, then it's balancing the challenges of you going here and I'm going here, but at the same time there's that understanding that you don't always get when you have a spouse who does not work in the field.

I had no plan [to marry someone in the Border Patrol]. It just happened. But I think it made things better. I think part of it happened because I was working. I mean, for the most part throughout the '90s and early 2000s, it was sixteen-hour days. We were overwhelmed. All you did was work, so who were my friends? Border Patrol agents. And they truly became a family. And when you live in a small community, a border community, there's a lot of corruption in border communities. Law enforcement hang out with other law enforcement because it's a safe environment. Even on the off-duty time, if I was going to a barbecue, it would be at my supervisor's home.

And it was the same when I was a police officer. It just becomes kind of that community. Because you feel safe there. Now, don't get me wrong. I've got some other great friends, but as a whole, most of my close friends are agents or retired agents. . . . I went and played golf with two other retired chiefs the other day because they've become good friends. And I've watched their kids grow up over the years, and our kids all hang out together.

The Border Patrol was right around 5 percent female when I came in. It's been around 5 percent the whole twenty-five years I was in. Most law enforcement has progressed quite a bit over those years. Most police departments were only about 10 percent women when I joined the Border Patrol. Those numbers are a lot higher now, I think at least in the 20 percent realm. So, it wasn't a huge change for me when I joined. The police department was mostly guys. I think we had seven women in my police department. I was the only one who worked midnights, so it was me and all of the guys then when I worked at Riley County PD.

My Border Patrol class was unique because we had five females in a class of forty-something, so we made up over 10 percent. All of us made it through the academy, too. One ended up not passing her ten-month exam. The other four of us spent our whole careers in the Border Patrol.

I was used to working with mostly men. It really wasn't something I thought about. I also had an older brother who liked to pick on me when we were kids. My sister was in between us in age and was apparently a lot smarter than I was. She didn't let him beat up on her. I was six years younger than him so he beat up on me because he didn't have a little brother. Ironically enough, he's like four inches shorter than me now. I have fun with that when I go home. Being the only female working with a bunch of men was never an issue for me and I think part of it was maybe my size, because I was a six-foot-tall female.

I also think this goes back to when I ran cross country. I was a very competitive runner and I would run in meets where they would combine the girls and boys together. This was back when everybody ran two miles. Now the boys run further. And I remember running on this one golf course. My dad got into an intense argument with a guy because he was cheering for me to pass this other boy. And that father got upset, saying, "You shouldn't tell her to do that." Of course, I ended up beating the boy at the end of the race.

I was brought up to think it doesn't matter what your gender is; you do your best and you can do anything you set your mind to. So, I never worried about the fact that I was a female in a predominantly male profession. It wasn't something that weighed on my mind. It wasn't something that I thought about. I never thought about myself as a female Border Patrol agent. I was just a Border Patrol agent.

Now, that being said, I think women in the Patrol do have to prove themselves a little bit more. And advice that I haven given to female agents over the years is: "Like it or not, you stand out, because there are only 5 percent of us. You stand out. Now, you control your destiny of how you're going to stand out." And I always explain it to them in Border Patrol terms: "You're either a slug, which makes you lazy and not a hard worker, or you're 10-8." You know what "10-8" means in the law enforcement world: I'm operational. But it also means you're a hard worker. If somebody says, "Man, he or she is 10-8," that means they're a good agent.

Throughout my career, I've told female agents this: "You control your destiny. If you are a hard worker, you're going to stand out more than all of the guys who are hard workers because there's so few of us. At the same time, if you are not a hard worker, you stand out more than the guys who are not hard workers." So, female agents who maybe don't cut the mustard, they get ridiculed more, I think, than male agents who don't. But I also think that when females go above and beyond and work hard and do a good job—and this was my experience—that the guys get behind them. And I've heard it numerous times, "Man, she is 10-8." And if they say that about a female agent, that girl is golden for her career.

And all that it takes is proof. Yes, you have to prove yourself, but I think you have to prove yourself whether you're a man or woman in law enforcement because people's lives depend on it. Partners depend upon each other, and if you show that you're not afraid and that you're there and you're going to back them up and support them, you get their support in return. And I always felt like I was supported throughout the years.

I had one supervisor try to give me some job, I called it "the girl job." When I was a supervisor, they offered me an administrative supervisory role and I just politely turned it down because I didn't want it. If females go the admin route, they do get stereotyped a bit in the Patrol, and I think that's also kind of in law enforcement in general. I wanted to make sure that I proved myself as an operator in this field, so, I guess, subconsciously I made certain choices because of that, but it was also because that's what I liked to do. I didn't like the administrative stuff. I like the operational stuff. I wanted to be out doing the job.

An ongoing joke is that the gentleman who ultimately ended up being my deputy when I was the chief, he's the one who called me and wanted me to come to Washington, DC, when he was up there. He offered me a job. There's the chief, the deputy, then there's B-3, as they call it, the third position, which is the position he held, the operator position, and then there was B-4, which was the administrative position. And he kept trying to pull me up there and I said, "Don't call me and offer me the girl job." I said, "When you promote into something else, I'll take your job." And that became an ongoing joke because, of course, a couple of guys ended up in that administrative position afterward.

So, there were those instances, but I guess I was always comfortable in the role and I think it started with my parents in the aspect of, "Hey, you can do anything." Yeah, you might not go be a professional football player because there's just certain limitations that girls have, but if you set your mind to it and it's something you want to do, you can do it. It was that way in sports and because I have a family that was supportive, it didn't matter whether I was competing against girls or boys, you know; you do the best you can do. I came into this job in the same mindset. And I just think it's served me well throughout the years.

And it wasn't something that weighed on my mind, "Oh, only 5 percent of us are females." That being said, I would love to see more women in the Border Patrol. I think diversity as a whole is good for any organization, and whether it's diversity in gender or race or whatever, I think we need more of that because different people bring different perspectives, and we can always use more of that.

But it's a hard organization to recruit for because of the locations. It's hard to get anybody into the Border Patrol because if you didn't grow up in border communities, it's a big move to the southwest border where you don't have necessarily the best education, the best medical care—all these things. And I think for women, in general, especially if you're a mother, the hours, those family factors come into play. I think it makes it harder to recruit females into the Patrol versus other law enforcement jobs. But I will tell you this about the women who are in the Patrol, they are one of the proudest groups of women I have ever seen because they go through the exact same training, physical, everything, that the men go through.

And the fact that they get through it—and it is one of the toughest academies out there—and that they pass . . . it's like a badge of honor. It really is a badge of honor. We need to do more and it's been a difficult thing recruiting for women. We've had targeted recruiting over the years, but for some reason we just can't get those numbers up. Most of the women we recruit do come from the border communities, but it is something that the Border Patrol struggled with over the years. I think a lot of it truly does have to do with locations and working with the family life, which maybe, I don't know, maybe we look at it a little bit different than men do when it comes to making sure that kids have a good school system and the proper healthcare and those types of things.

But for my career, I really just was blessed. And I felt like I had good support. The guys knew me. It was funny because when social media first started up and I was promoted to the chief in El Centro, I remember somebody saying to me, "Hey, you're being talked about on some site." And this comes back to if you prove yourself as being 10-8, you stand out. And there were some guys who were complaining that she got the job because she's a girl—whatever. Well, I can't tell you how many people, guys whom I've worked with over the years, came on, and, man, they shut those guys down in a heartbeat, and were, "Hey, we have worked with her, that's BS, you don't know her."

That was just something that it was nice to see, because, yeah, there were a few who were insinuating I got promoted for being a female, but I mean they came out of all corners, people I worked with in Douglas, and in Yuma and El Paso, you know, came out and just really shut down the conversation the guys who didn't know me were starting.

Actually, I have no issues retiring. I know a lot of people struggle with it, but because I was a planner and I had been planning for it, I didn't have an issue with it. I am doing some work on the technology side because I see how much of a role technology plays in national security and border security. I am working with a couple of companies when it comes to the tech that supports the men and women on the front lines.

I believe in technology and what it brings to the table. And when I look at the federal government and I look at the adversary (the cartels, human smugglers/traffickers, others who seek to harm the United States), the adversary doesn't have the constraints of finances, rule of law—you know, all of those things—when it comes to their ability to leverage technology to support their effort. I want to be able to support more how we counter their efforts by getting the technology into the hands of our security and law enforcement professionals that is needed to help them do their job more safely, efficiently, and effectively.

I am doing some other work that's in support of the frontline operations with the men and women, something that I've been passionate about from the time that I was the chief. Families and women and children don't belong in Border Patrol facilities. And I am doing some support to help get them out of those facilities. I've been doing some work with ICE and HHS with another contract that helps get unaccompanied kids into a better space until they can be reunified with family. If you read the media on me, I'm this horrible person because of the position that I held and what was going on in immigration and people's false beliefs about the Border Patrol. What people believe and what's the truth are two completely different things.

I look at it in two ways. The families, the children, they don't belong in these facilities. We don't leave our humanity behind. I want to put them into a better situation than what they've been in, and, at the same time, it helps the frontline Border Patrol Agents because they need to focus on the true threat on the border and not be dealing with this humanitarian crisis. And they need to be back doing what they should be doing for their jobs, worrying about actually securing the borders, not caring for families and children.

So, those are the areas that I've been working in. It's funny, because in retirement, sometimes it's like there's no work and then I'm going, "Oh, my God, this is too much work." I certainly do focus on trying to get more time with the family, but I have been a little busier than I had planned to be in retirement here in the last few months. The Border Patrol is in my heart and soul and if I can help the men and women who are risking their lives to protect us all, then that's what I'm going to do.

Carla Provost is national chief (retired) of the US Border Patrol.

4

PORTFOLIO: BORDER STUDIES

IN 2022, FOLLOWING our interviews of several people engaged in work related to policing the US-Mexico border, I made these environmental portraits of the architectural contrivance itself: the Wall. As the string of steel bollards wends across the landscape, it variously divides previously holistic communities, as it does Ambos ("both") Nogales; while in other stretches it provides a physical manifestation of separation that, plopped in the middle of the Sonoran Desert, can only be described as arbitrary. In the case of its termination in the shallows of the Pacific Ocean, it serves as a poetic sculptural embodiment of heedless hubris and dysfunctional policy.

FIGURE 4.1
Ambos Nogales (Arizona/Sonora), 2022.

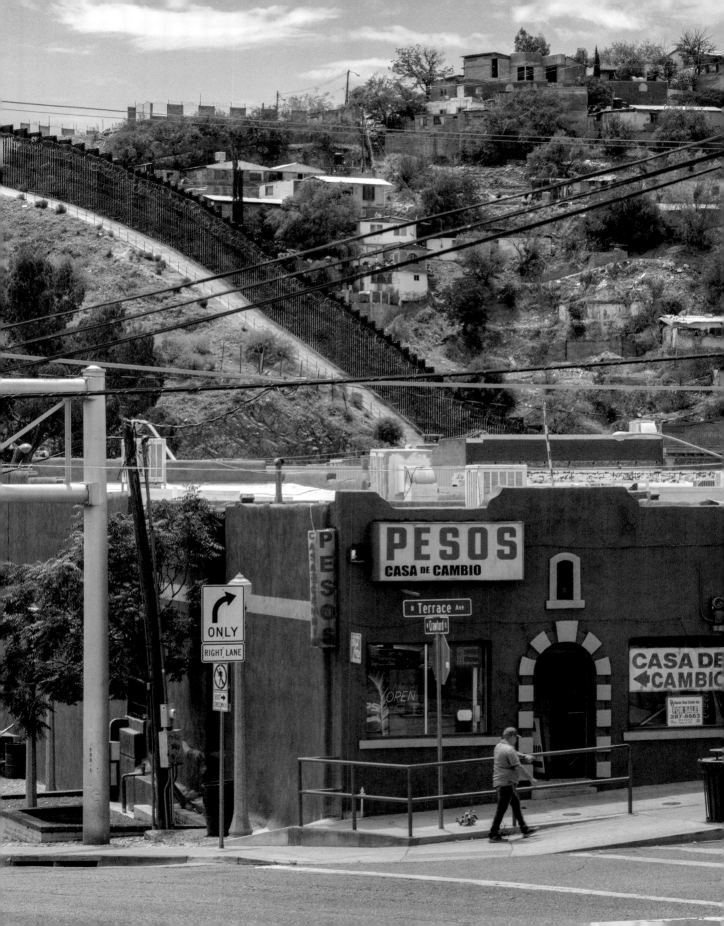

FIGURE 4.2
Pima County Cemetery, Tucson, Airzona, 2022.

FIGURE 4.3
Unidentified migrant grave, Pima County Cemetery,
Tucson, Arizona, 2022.

FIGURE 4.4
San Diego–Tijuana border wall, 2022.

FIGURE 4.5
Border wall, Border Field State Park, San Diego,
California, 2022.

FIGURE 4.6
Border wall, Border Field State Park, San Diego,
California, 2022.

FIGURE 4.7
San Diego–Tijuana border wall termination, 2022.

5

CIA, FBI, SECRET SERVICE

It'll be fifty years in January that I've been involved in intelligence—conducting analysis, leading analysis, managing analysis and operations, and evaluating intelligence products. Most of that time—thirty-three years—was in the CIA. For the last twelve years, I've been teaching intelligence.

I've always been a service guy. I don't know why, but it was baked into me. Maybe it's the Jesuit education. I went to St. Louis High, which was a Jesuit prep school. Then I went to Georgetown University, and my plan was to get a PhD in economics and teach economics. I eventually did get a PhD in economics, but I don't teach economics.

I graduated from college in 1968, the year that 500,000 young men were drafted into the military, and I wanted to go in as an officer rather than an enlisted man. So I applied for and got into the Navy Officer Candidate School. I found out in the spring of '68 that I was going to be going in in January '69. That gave me time to, by hook and by crook, get a master's degree in economics before I went in. I still hold the record at Georgetown University—six months—for getting a master's. Part of that was I had taken extra courses as an undergraduate because I'm cheap, and you could take as many courses as you wanted. I mention that only because I'm probably one of the few people who went into the military, and the military looked at my background, and they matched it. I had my master's in economic development in Latin America, and the next thing I knew I was assigned to Panama.

The general there was responsible for all of Latin America. My job was to provide a daily briefing to the general every morning at 7:00 a.m. and I enjoyed it. It was a challenge. Information would flow in from all over South America together with stuff coming down from Washington, and you would write what amounted to a half-hour briefing. Kind of episodic. Here's what's going on in Uruguay today, and here's what's going on in Peru. That was in the period of all the insurgencies and terrorists in South America. It was pretty exciting. I did that for two years, and then I had done my duty. I got an early out because the war in Vietnam was phasing down. I went off to graduate school. After about a month of graduate school in economics I said, "This is silly. I don't belong here."

But if I was going to work in intelligence, I wanted to work on the big issue, and I wanted to work at the right place. So I applied to work on Russia—Soviet Union at that time—at the agency. In September of 1972, I entered on duty, and I spent the next thirty-three years there, and 90 percent of the mornings when I woke up it was, "Oh boy. I can't wait to get to work."

I was an analyst and then a leader of analytic teams and then a manager of analytic organizations. Then I did a tour at the State Department where I briefed the deputy secretary of state every day and was actually a deputy assistant secretary of state.

I had regional responsibility for Central Asia, and I had responsibility for countering corruption, organized crime, and that was fun. I did it for three years, led some delegations, found myself on TV, but couldn't understand what I was doing as a State Department officer. And then when I came back to the agency after that I had four, five, six jobs at fairly senior levels of the organization. My last job I was director for transnational issues. I had 700 officers and a $100 million budget, which inside the Beltway is a pretty significant body of analytic power.

On the way there I was deputy director for crime and narcotics. Smaller number of people, about the same amount of money, doing a lot of stuff. We did a lot overseas that I probably wouldn't talk too much about, but that was the most operational job I had. And then 9/11 happened. I had a big bunch of people who were looking at illicit finance, and gray arms, and things like that, and I just took all of them, and they went over to work on counterterrorism.[1] I stayed in the agency for a year after that, and then I got one of the greatest assignments of all time.

The agency used to have an officer in residence program where you would go to an academic institution and essentially teach and be a resource. Not to recruit, but you would be available to talk to people who were interested in careers in intelligence. So I spent three years at Georgetown teaching courses, and doing some writing. And then I got out of the agency in 2006. I spent a little time teaching down at the FBI academy in Quantico, and then came up here to Albany.

They were setting up the New York State Intelligence apparatus, and the guy running DHS intelligence at the time asked me to come up here and help with that. I did that for about three years, pretty much full time, while also teaching at UAlbany part time.

Around 2013–14, I shifted to full time at the university. I've been teaching here ever since. I teach courses in Homeland Security intelligence, and there was no good textbook. A publisher said, "Write one," and I did.[2]

There were two jobs that really stick out for me. One was in the early '90s when I hit the level of division chief. At that point maybe eighty people or so were working for me. It was an area that I'd been working in for over ten years. And it was a time period when no matter what the subject was, I knew it. I was steeped in it.

For me, that's about the perfect span of control if you're a real practitioner and you want your hands in it. You're still leading. You get much beyond that and you start managing. And, frankly, leading is much more fun than managing. In that job, at that level, I got promoted to the equivalent of a general officer. I really enjoyed that and I reached the pinnacle of it with testifying to Congress, and I was on the C-SPAN predecessor. So my wife and kids could look at it. I had good control, and I could see what was coming next in my area. I felt really good about that.

The other job I had that I really enjoyed was being deputy director for crime and narcotics, and part of that was I had come up the analytic route rather than the operational route. At the agency there's really two cultures, the analysts and the operators. During the Cold War the operators were doing much more human source reporting and recruiting assets. There was covert action like Afghanistan, of course, but it was not all-consuming. Whereas at the agency today counterterrorism has been pretty much all-consuming. Now that's starting to change, but that's a problem. Anyway, in the crime and narcotics area, I had the analytic stuff on one side, but then there were the operations. I was not directly involved in planning the operations, because I had not come up in that world, but I was there, and evaluating, and giving the thumbs-up or thumbs-down on whether to go ahead. And operations are fun.

To me, intelligence at its core is providing information to a customer so that they can decide what to do when it still makes a difference. Timely flow of analyzed information. Operations, especially covert action, which is everything beyond diplomacy but less than sending in the Marines, that's a policy tool. That's not information. That's action, by its very name.

The raid on Bin Laden, capturing Bin Laden, that was a covert action, even though it was not very covert obviously. But when the United States does things overseas and doesn't want the United States recognized as doing it, it falls to the agency to do that.

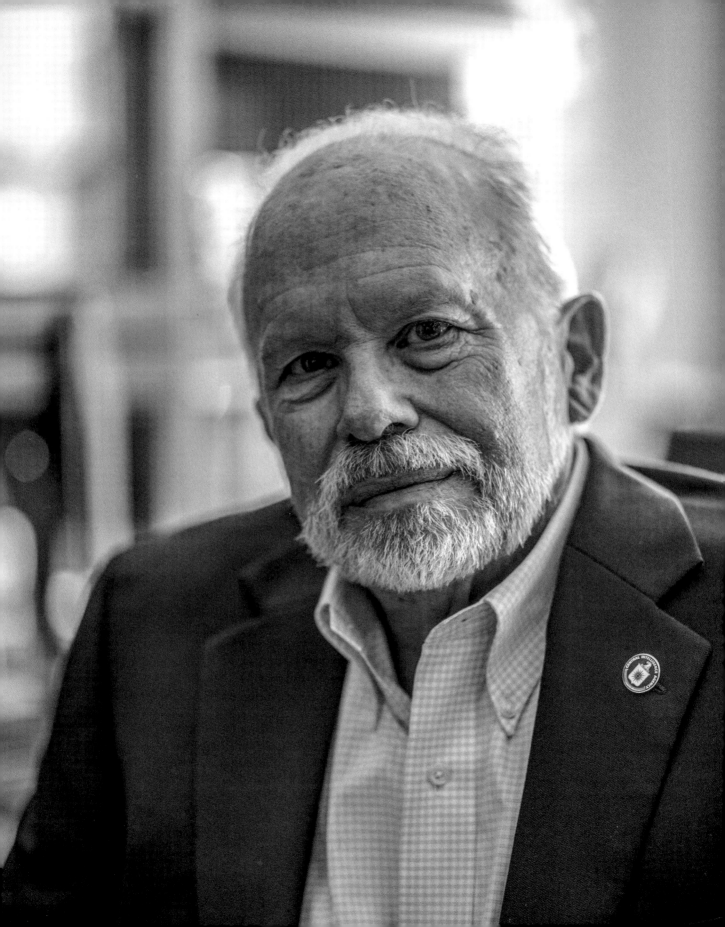

FIGURE 5.1
Jim Steiner, Albany, New York, 2018.

So when I was involved in covert action on counter-narcotics, frankly, it was a lot of fun. You get to see results right away. You've got really motivated people taking risks. The interaction with the policy community is really dynamic, because oftentimes when the State Department and Department of Defense can't figure out what to do, either because it's beyond what the state can do and we're not quite ready to send in the troops, they punt and say, "Okay, you intel guys do covert action and take care of it." So, as far as a fun job, and a lot of travel globally, the crime and narcotics job was really good.

CIA analysts make their money in Washington. I can count a few days when I briefed in sequence the secretary of state, secretary of defense, and that's a head trip. But that comes at the pinnacle of your career and you're not doing that when you're just conducting analysis. Analysts spend a lot of time sitting at a desk with the classified network. You do get to travel a bit. We try to get our analysts to spend some time doing a tour overseas, but it's still analytic work.

You are essentially gathering, analyzing information, and providing it to someone so they can decide what to do. Whether it's a general officer in the military, whether it's a senior law enforcement person, whether it's the president and the National Security Council. Covert action, on the other hand, you're actually doing it. In fact, you task intelligence analysts to provide you information to enable you to conduct your operations.

Give you an example of crime in crime and narcotics. We had what were called target analysts. So they might be assigned to look at a certain drug organization somewhere where it's probably warm, okay, and they would analyze the heck out of that. And they'd put together what's called the target study, which identifies how big the organization is. How's it structured? What are their main product lines? What are the flows? How does it go? How do they work the money side? And where are the vulnerabilities? Then that study might go to the covert action people to go do something with it. Or it might go to the Drug Enforcement Administration, or it might go to certain law enforcement entities in other countries. And this is all foreign. Nothing domestic. When it crosses the border it's not ours. Belongs to the DEA.

Those target analysts get closer to operations. Analysts who really like operations might take those jobs. Whereas analysts who like to inform policy formulation would take the policy job. If you're conducting analysis for policymakers, you're probably going to do a tour, a rotation, a three-year stint with one of the customers. We sent people all the time to work at the National Security Council. I worked at State Department. We had people at the Department of Defense, because it's important to understand the customer—what they do, what they need—all the way along.

But analysts mainly make their money in Washington. Operators make their money overseas. I don't mean money, but that's where they make their bones.

These days, I've got a variety of old friends. Surprisingly, I don't have a lot of close friends from the agency, and I find it interesting, because there were times at the agency when I put lots of stuff on the line for people and they did for me. But I've been out now for about fifteen years. I went to Georgetown at the end of 2002 and retired in 2006. So it's been twelve years retired, and actually fifteen years or so completely out.

And I think this is, once again, the analytic versus the operational. I think most of the analytic people think, "Okay, that was a fun career. What am I going to go do now?"

The operators, it's more like the military. Also, they had, I think, a tighter relationship with each other. Putting everything on the line for an analyst is very different from putting your life on the line the way the operators do. So those are much tighter relationships.

I try to give my students an accurate picture, and I try to help them think about what type of career they want. The MPA (master of public administration) is a great program, because it's essentially an MBA (master of business administration) for those who want to work in the public sector. You've got a lot of service-oriented people who want to go into some form of government service, federal, state, local. For those who know they want to go into intelligence, I have them take a course. I never talk careers to anyone who hasn't taken one of my courses, because the first three classes are essentially here's what intelligence is, here's how our intelligence community has grown, and here's how it's structured today. And you have to have that foundation to talk to a student who wants a career in intelligence.

Then the real discussion begins. Okay, do you want to do analysis, or do you want to do operations? If you want to do analysis, are you sure you want to do intelligence analysis, or do you want to do policy analysis? And if you want to do policy analysis, do you want to be a political appointee, or do you want to be a career policy analyst?

Because of what I did for thirty-five years in Washington, I'm able to give the students a pretty good firsthand understanding of the national security apparatus and Washington, where they might find a job, where they might enjoy it, where they might not, and a way to think about it. And I do a lot of that, because I feel that's a big part of my job. In many ways, I'm motivated, because I see this as the next generation. That's a big reason why I teach.

Most of what I was involved in I could describe to my family, to a certain degree. Also, it's a different environment when you live in Washington because the neighbor kids got the same damn thing. It may not be so true anymore. There's a lot more contractors and lawyers in Washington, but when I was first there with the family, up and down my street there were no other intel people, but there were people in justice, and there were people in law enforcement. In Washington, you're just one more person going down the street. And where my kids went to school they could talk about, "Oh, my dad works at CIA."

I was always able to say it. In the old days, you couldn't do that. In the old days, in the '60s and early '70s, the only people who wore lanyards were CIA and NSA. So if you did that, you know, what is it? Do you play the saxophone or something? There were little things like that. NSA, the National Security Agency, was frequently called "No Such Agency."

You had the jokes.

I'm seventy-two. If you were a little bit older, it was a more restrictive environment. And if you were involved in operations, then that always gets very, very sensitive. I was not involved in operations until—well, with one exception—until the mid-'90s. By which time one of my kids was through college, and the other one was a senior in high school. So all the way up until then it was "My parents worked at CIA," because my former wife worked there for ten years.

So, for us, I think it was easier. It was certainly easier for me in that if I had to be at work until ten o'clock at night for a month, my wife understood. She wasn't thrilled about it, but she understood. She still had friends there. She'd go to lunch with them. She didn't have a clearance, but she really didn't need a clearance for the type of stuff we would talk about. She was more interested in people and the internal politics. So that made it very easy.

The hardest part was when I traveled, because then she'd be home with the kids, and I would probably go maybe four or five times a year, for ten days to two weeks at a shot. And then she had the kids. It was especially tough if I was going to a nice place at a nice time of year. For example, every year in March NATO would have what was called MC161, the military committee project 161, which was at that time sixteen NATO countries would send representatives to work on all aspects of the Soviet threat, and we'd be there for two full weeks. Well, that meant for years and years I had to go to Brussels for two weeks in March. My former wife's been around and she was smart enough to know that, yes, you may work there during the day, but you guys all go out all night and eat rich food, drink too much, and essentially have a good time.

And we did.

But it was part of the work. There's nothing like going into a restaurant in Brussels with a couple thousand dollars in cash in your pocket, hosting a dinner for people. But there was good reason to do it, because while you're there you're also—well, I won't go into that. My wife understood what was going on. So what I found myself doing was if I knew I had to go to Moscow, and I needed to be there within six months, I would schedule it for February. Nobody goes to Moscow in February.

If I had to go somewhere where it was hot, I would go there in the summer, and that worked out.

Still, spouses usually know most everything that's going on. Let's face it, they do. Most government organizations understand that, but there are still things you don't talk about. There are a handful of things that I'll never be able to talk about. So I just don't. You just put them over there and turn the key.

When I was executive secretary for the agency—one of my more senior jobs—there were meetings downtown and it would all come through my office, and I had a two-drawer safe under my desk where I had documents that only the director and I could see. That was it. It just goes with the job.

My current wife never had anything to do with intelligence. So this was all new to her, but eight years later she has a good idea of what I did. She's amazed so much of it was routine, but that's life. It is routine, but there are still things I obviously can't tell her. I don't go around saying, "I can't tell you this." I just don't mention it.

You learn very quickly what you can talk about and what you can't talk about. And then when you teach it, it's even clearer. I teach three different courses on intelligence. I tell my students, "I'm going to tell some war stories. There's nothing classified. But I don't want to see the war stories end up in the paper." So that's why I'm not sitting here telling you guys war stories, because I wouldn't want it to end up in print. I'd get my hand slapped or possibly worse. But absolutely nothing classified, and I find that after fifty years, it's just natural.

There is one thing I really regret: when my younger son graduated from college, shortly before I retired, he wanted to go into the Peace Corps. And they wouldn't take him because of me. Now I had always known that if you work for the agency you can never work for the Peace Corps, and if you work for the Peace Corps you can never work for the agency. And it's a good rule. But I had never heard about this generation-skipping crap before, and we appealed it, significantly, and they said, "You're just too public. All you got to do is Google the name. So we just can't take him." And I always felt bad about that, because I think he would have been really good in the Peace Corps, and he really wanted to do it, but some things you can't control.

When I was actually doing the work and raising a family, I didn't have time for anything else. It was as simple as that. But when my older son went off to college and my younger son was starting to get to middle school and high school, I actually had some time, and I grabbed that for fishing. I really like fishing. In the summer, I'll probably fish five or six times a week. I keep a boat up on the Mohawk. That's the first real boat I had, a Ranger with a 115 horsepower engine. Before that I had a plastic boat with an electric motor on it, but the idea was just to be able to get away from everything to be in the middle of nature. I didn't really care if I caught fish or not.

Even that, though, occasionally got ruined because I always had to have a phone with me. Got a fish on the line, and the phone rings, and it's the office. I'm like, "Damnit. Okay, I've got to take it."

Then there's meditation. You know, I was raised Catholic. Stopped going to church like a lot of Catholics do in high school. Did some church stuff when the kids were growing up. More of a modeling-type thing rather than the need to do it. When I moved up here, it was really a life shift for me. I actually started thinking about mortality and things like that. So meditation and thinking about what comes next became big issues for me.

One thing I've been able to do, which is kind of weird, is I teach a course on analysis, intelligence analysis. Part of it is intuitive thinking, but part of it is non-intuitive. It's deliberative, where you use different structured techniques to essentially avoid the cognitive errors. And it occurred to me I could take one of the techniques—analysis of competing hypotheses—and use that to look at what comes next, after life. My wife says, "So you're using analytic techniques to understand spirituality."

Fishing and meditation, those are my two hobbies.

Jim Steiner is a former senior CIA officer. He recently retired after more than fifty years of conducting, leading, managing, evaluating, and teaching intelligence.

DIANA BOLSINGER

I blame my dad. When I was very young, he was the chief of personnel at Keflavik Air Base in Iceland. We actually spent a little short of five years when I was growing up not just living in Iceland, but, since we were there, we were always taking R&Rs (rest and recuperation) in Europe. At one point, down the road, my mom laughed and complained because I was serving in Pakistan, my sister was with her Spanish husband in Madrid, and she said, "It's my fault. I warped them young."

I always liked foreign languages, foreign cultures, and seeing places. Initially, I'd started school in physics and engineering. Freshman year at Reed College, I was a physics major blowing off the physics homework due the next morning to do extra extra extra credit reading for my history class in fourteenth-century peasant revolts. I knew in my mapped-out schedule that this was going to be my last social science class in quite a while because of all the physics classes. And I was really depressed.

Suddenly, I realized: Am I an idiot? Why am I doing classes that make me unhappy instead of classes that make me happy? It was a transcendent moment.

That was the next to last day to drop and add classes, so I switched over to anthropology and creative writing, and a bunch of stuff, and ended up as an interdisciplinary international studies major. Never looked back, and never regretted it. The funniest thing of all was my mom was initially appalled. She had been so proud, as a feminist, of her daughter in a tough, masculine field, and she threatened, "You're going to end up a secretary!"

Something I tell my students is, Don't plan too hard, because you never know what can happen.

Well, Homeland Security didn't exist. Criminal justice, that kind of thing—I was a liberal arts major, it never occurred to me. I decided I was either going to be an anthropologist or a Foreign Service officer and diplomat. Because, again, Iceland was a small enough community that even though we were over on the DOD side, my parents socialized with the ambassador and the two or three Americans in our embassy in Keflavik all the time.

Senior year, I took the Foreign Service exam. And this is one of the flukes. Before they started factoring in experience, before it got a whole lot tougher, as a senior taking economic classes, taking the history of Asia, history of Europe, et cetera, these questions on the Foreign Service exam were from exactly what I was taking and what I was reading. So, I passed the exam, went on to orals, and that was where being twenty years old suddenly turned around and worked against me. I did make the accepted list, but, oh, I was down there. I was way down there.

At the time, I interviewed with this brand new startup called Microsoft, but the job that they offered sounded terribly boring, so forget that. This was before they went public. God, if only . . .

I applied to Tufts and Kennedy School, and a couple of others. My parents were not going to pay for a master's; it was undergrad only. The schools put me on their waitlists and offered no money. There was this waiting game. I saw a CIA ad and I figured, What the heck? What does it hurt? They won't take me, but, if they do, I'll work for a year or so and make some money for graduate school. So, I went ahead and applied.

But there were two things I didn't know.

One, my senior thesis project was decided on the last day before I was in real trouble; I had to declare a topic junior year. And I had seen an article that Pakistani president, Zia-ul-Haq, was banning interest payments from the banking system as part of his Islamization program. I had been looking for an interdisciplinary topic that set culture against modernity and modernization. So, banning interest? That is so bizarre and so weird that it worked.

I did my senior thesis, a hundred pages of gobbledygook that's really embarrassing, but it did involve a whole year of studying Islamic movements in South Asia in 1984 and 1985. And the CIA saw this, and the chapters that I submitted, and this was just as they were planning to introduce the Stinger missile into Afghanistan. This was just as they were really starting to realize, "We don't have a handle on these Mujahidin groups and what they want," et cetera, et cetera. They hired me at twenty years old before I knew what was happening.

The second thing was that they offered to pay for my master's while I worked, so, I was there.

They put me into the career training program, and it was cool. It was fun. I did a trainee stint helping to start up this brand-new thing called the Counterterrorism Center. And then

FIGURE 5.2
Diana Bolsinger, Lhakhang Bhutanese Temple on the campus
of the University of Texas at El Paso, El Paso, Texas, 2022.

in 1986 I was working on Afghanistan. I'm twenty-one, twenty-two years old and I'm briefing people in the NSC (National Security Council). Briefing cabinet members. Having what I've written included in the president's daily brief. Getting familiarization trips around the world.

Why in the world would I leave it?

In 1986 I also started working on my master's degree at night at George Washington. Of course, I was going to stay at least until I finished my degree. Then I got the opportunity to do a rotation to the State Department to actually work as a political analyst, religious affairs, in the political section of our embassy in Islamabad. I did think for a little while about switching over to Foreign Service permanently—that had originally been my goal—but during the Gulf War evacuations especially I saw, frankly, how much better the agency treated its people than the State Department. What can I say? At that point, I had a career.

My age was a deep, dark secret. I remember my first day out of training, members of my branch just laughing over my year of birth: "Oh, I was in college," "I was in the Air Force," et cetera. But the female factor was terribly hard. Before me, the number of women whom they hired as professionals were few. They existed. At one point during my training, I worked for one woman, a case officer. I adored the woman, but she was tough as nails. She had somehow made it into the Directorate of Operations (DO) and was in the thick of it.[3] But overwhelmingly the women who were hired my year—my peers—were hired as support.

I remember several moments of feeling guilty. There was one woman who was hired a month before me. She was short, she was slim, soft-spoken, maybe ninety-five pounds. She had killer degrees in economics, and papers to her name. And she was hired as a secretary. Now, come on. But that was how it was.

I'm delighted to say she went on to become a senior SIS, as well she deserved. It's not as if she stayed in the basement forever.[4]

I can also tell you about another internship over in the ops side. As a trainee, I worked for a woman who had been around forever. She knew, metaphorically, where the bodies were buried. She knew everything, she knew every procedure, she knew everything you can imagine. I pictured her as a GS-15 or something, for her level of experience, time, and knowledge. And at one point it came out that she was a GS-10, and she told me, "Oh, you're not going to like me anymore."

I said, "My like has nothing to do with it. But GS-10 for what you've done?"

I will also say that, yes, single female, non-stop hits, and it was worse on the DO side without question. There were innumerable DO gentlemen, the majority of them were gentlemen, but I can think of one character in particular. . . . Idiot, naive twenty-one-year-old that I was, he took me out to lunch. You know, we'd go to the cafeteria for lunch. And he told war stories. He told the best stories. He was interested in what I wanted to do with my career. He gave me career advice.

And, naive little girl, I was thinking grandfather figure. Grandpa figure. Until the day he said, "My wife is out of town. Let's do dinner."

Where did that come from? And he was shocked that I was shocked. But we were reading such totally different scripts.

That was the end of a beautiful friendship. It was a betrayal.

And I laugh to think that was now thirty-five years ago.

I don't even remember his name, so I'm obviously not too scarred.

There probably will never in my lifetime be a moment when it's exactly equal, gender-blind male and female, et cetera. I just don't see it. What I do see is, when I got to the DI (directorate of intelligence), all credit to my office management. They genuinely tried. They were solid, clichéd, white males. To be fair, I like white males. I'm married to one. But the thing is, they gave women opportunities. There were times when it was pretty clear they were specifically choosing younger women, and a couple of our analysts of color, to have a shot to do something a little bit more prominent, a little bit to show ourselves. It wasn't 100 percent consistent, but there was an awareness.

I can also tell you a story twenty-five years in that's hilarious in hindsight, though it was infuriating at the time.

I wrote a long article. A male, very new, very young military analyst wrote what's called a box, which is, basically, a couple paragraphs of text that don't quite fit in with the main flow, but it's useful information. The article involved hard stuff. Military stuff. The military and politics. Our group chief called us in for editing, and I brought the young analyst—Mike— along because he had made a contribution. And that group chief spent the entire time talking to Mike: Mike, you've got to do this. Mike, you've got to do that.

I was less upset with my group chief than Mike was. I thought, "Oh, here we go again." Mike kept saying, "It's Diana's, it's Diana's, it's Diana's."

Afterward, Mike apologized to me so profusely. And I said, "No, you did everything you could." And he said, "Is this what it's like?"

I said, "Sometimes." And here's the good news. Here's the thing of it. Mike went on to be a senior manager. He may or may not still be working there. But I trust that working for Mike was a whole different universe. Because, you know, he and his generation are not perfect. But I have a lot of faith that it's better.

I can tell dating stories. If I had a penny for every guy who thought it was funny, asking, "Well, what do you actually do at this company? Oh, wait a minute. If you tell me, you have to kill me, right?"

But, basically, long story short, the stereotypes really made it hard dating outside the agency. The "Oh, you must be incredibly tough" and "You know fifty ways to kill me with your pinky, don't you?" Blah, blah, blah.

Even more than that, though, and what's really important, is I was working counterterrorism. I had no control over my time. Really. Constantly. If something happened on the other side of the world at 4:45 in the evening, our time, I'm spending the night. If I have a date, forget it. That's it. Or, if I pull an all-nighter two, three days in a row, I don't want to go out and do something energetic for the weekend. I want to catch up on my sleep. I feel for the guys, because several of them really thought I was trying to avoid them, and I had to say, "No, I have no life. Sorry, it's not you." But between those couple of things, dating within the agency just was so much easier.

I know so many wives and some husbands from outside and I have so much respect for them, because there's so much trust there. They're trusting their spouse, rightfully so, knowing their spouses, but they're really doing it on faith.

I met my husband when we were trainees together back in early '86. We didn't start dating until years later. So, we were good friends to start with, which also smooths dating, if you're already dating somebody you know and like and trust. We understood each other's language, some of the jargon. Basically, it's as easy as that. If I can't tell you, I can't tell you. And we both know to respect it. There's a commonality. It's so much easier and more familiar.

You could say I made the terrible career error of falling in love and getting married. I understand it's much easier now for tandem couples to find positions for two, but what

FIGURE 5.3
Diana and Dan Bolsinger, Lhakhang Bhutanese Temple on the campus of the University of Texas at El Paso, El Paso, Texas, 2022.

happened was my husband would get a shot at a position, and there was nothing there for me. I would get a shot at a position, and there was nothing there for him. This went on for a couple of years and it was really, really frustrating. Because, ironically, when he proposed to me, I was in line to take language training to go to an incredibly beautiful spot in Europe. I actually took a bit of a career hit when I backed out of this position. But newlyweds . . . At the time it was like, "Well, he can find another country. There's a lot of jobs in Europe." And I'm like, "No, I didn't marry him for an immediate separated tour."

Years later, in the spring of 2001, I was working as a manager at the Counterterrorism Center (CTC). I saw that Marymount University had a program where you could get both a master's of education and do your student teaching, and get your teaching credential, all in one year. Even better, the site where you did the student teaching was a short walk from our townhouse.

The reality is, counterterrorism can burn you out. During the millennial threat, I led a group and we really were 24/7 for more than a month. Just insane burnout.[5] And it never went back to normal after that. We were screaming and shouting. And I do hold somewhat of a grudge for the incoming Bush administration, because you could feel the difference of the level of interest. There was a point, for example, during the millennial threat where Cofer Black was literally in the White House and talking to the president.[6] He got us resources we needed, just like that, that the bureaucracy had been fighting. And then there was nothing like that anymore. And some of the questions that we did get—I can't go into details other than to say they were very naive. They weren't from the president. I'm talking staffers, advisers, et cetera. This was somebody who was a smart person who had never thought about the issue before and was asking the ABCs. Then not even really listening to the answers.

So, the timing is terribly ironic and it's bizarre. I was one of the very first people in the late 1980s writing about the risks of these foreign Arab fighters, and tracking them. But in May 2001 I resigned from the Counterterrorism Center to teach middle school.

I then spent a decade teaching. One of the irony of ironies was I had students who lost their dads on 9/11.

I volunteered to go back to CTC on 9/11 itself, but they were aware I was out of pocket more than $10,000 for my classes, and they were aware that I had students who had lost their dads. I only found out after the fact that was why they didn't call me back. I spent the rest of that school year teaching little girls who had lost their dads how to write their names in Arabic, and other things like that, to try to support them.

I worked as an elementary middle school teacher until 2008 when my husband was assigned to Korea, where I worked in the embassy, and then in 2011 I went back on board with NCTC (US National Counterterrorism Center) at ODNI (US Office of the Director of National Intelligence), and spent some time there working my way back up. Retired as an acting group chief there in 2014 to move to New Mexico, get my doctorate, and teach some more.

Basically, it is a fabulous career. I was blessed with the opportunities. I was privileged to be part of history. Honestly, there were people alive because of my work. I'll never meet them, I'll never know their names, but that's an indescribable feeling. There are some fabulous positives. And national security matters, it's important, and we need good people. Public service is an honor and a duty. I mean, going back to Kennedy and his, "Ask not what your country can do for you. . . ."

My students here in El Paso, the majority are Latino, quite a few first-generation Americans, quite a few first-generation university students, and they want to serve. They want to give back. I'm so impressed. In terms of things for them to think about, I work to make sure they know it's not just hard work. It can be incredibly long hours. It can mean living in places that aren't fun, living in places where you are your own resource, especially if you're in a small place in a developing country. You may only have a handful of Americans there, and you may or may not like them. They're still the people you're going to be with every day of your life for two, three years. Knowing that you are going to sign a pledge that what you write will go through the publication review board; there will be limits on what you can say to your family about what you do. Knowing, frankly, the agency and the intelligence community does have a diversity problem. It's gotten better than it was. And one of the best ways to resolve that is, I believe, training up the next generation of people from whatever background to go there and be so damned good that nobody can hold them back. And, to be fair, I have a few friends who are still fighting that fight inside the organization, and I'm in awe of their courage.

After decades of service on three continents with the CIA, Department of State, and ODNI, Dr. Diana Bolsinger is now the director of the Intelligence and National Security Studies graduate programs at the University of Texas at El Paso.

FATEMA AHMAD

One essential thing to know is my parents are Egyptian. I was born in New Jersey, but we moved to western Maryland when I was pretty young. When I say western Maryland, I mean like the Appalachian Mountains, nowhere near DC/Baltimore, which is what people usually think of. It's a skinny part of Maryland that's ten minutes between Pennsylvania and West Virginia. That's where I grew up. Cumberland, Maryland.

I was watching the show *Succession*, which is about very wealthy people, and one of them is potentially going to go to prison, and he's debating which prison, and he talks about Cumberland. This is the only time people ever hear about Cumberland. If you listen to the podcast "Serial," the person, Adnan Syed, he was incarcerated in Cumberland. I grew up with a prison truly down the road from my house, just a mile away, that I saw all the time. A lot of people around me, their options were to go work there or to join the military to try to get out of Cumberland, maybe even potentially go to college that way. There are multiple prisons in a place with a population of under 20,000 people.

Obviously, immigrant parents didn't necessarily know what it would be like living there.

Even before 9/11, we experienced plenty of racism and Islamophobia. That's just what I knew to be normal living there in a very white, very economically disadvantaged place.

9/11 happened when I was in the ninth grade, really my first week of high school, just rough timing for anybody, but especially when you're *the* visible Muslim girl for miles, for like towns and towns. It was just me. That had a profound impact on my life. I was a shy, quiet kid, and suddenly I was expected to speak about this either because teachers, well-meaning but misguided, would ask me to talk about Islam in front of everybody, or because kids were harassing me verbally and physically.

So, I started to find my voice in high school. But I just saw that as a part of my life. I didn't know what to do about it. I didn't talk to my parents about it because I didn't want them to feel worried or feel bad about what was going on. They also wouldn't understand. They just hadn't lived through that. And there was really no one around me who could talk to me about anything like that.

The goal was to get out of Cumberland.

I studied biomedical engineering. I went to Duke University, moved to North Carolina. And I was like, "This is who I am. I'm an engineer. I'm really great at math and science, total nerd."

Living at Duke and in North Carolina was the first time I was around more Muslims my age, and diversity in general. I started to understand what it meant to be connected to community, connected to Muslims. I was engaged in the Muslim Student Association, but engineering was still my thing.

I eventually moved to Wisconsin to work at a big company and I was making great money and doing great work. It was fine, but it just didn't align with my values. As a manager, I was like, "I don't want to rank my team members. They all deserve a raise," not in a naive way, but in an anti-capitalist way. I didn't have the language to say that I was anti-capitalist at that point, but I was coming into my politics.

I was living in Madison. Everybody there thinks they're progressive. Slowly, I was like, "Oh wow, you all are actually racist. You just don't know it." Like, the things people would say to me as a Muslim woman. I thought I was losing my mind a little bit.

I had grown up with neo-Nazis in my hometown. It was just so clear and overt. That sounds wild to other people when I'm like, "Yes, I know people who got swastika tattoos and came to high school." I had grown up with them and was friends with them in the past. We knew that the KKK was active in our hometown. I know that's absurd to other people, but at least it was clear. At least it was obvious what was happening versus experiencing liberal Islamophobia and liberal racism.

I got to a point where I just couldn't do it anymore. I couldn't fake it. I could've kept making lots of money and living in this nice city and brushing off the things that people were saying. But deep down, I was like, "I actually need to do something about this."

I'd thought I was an engineer, as if that's an identity. If you're an engineer, people are like, "You don't know how to talk to people. You don't know how to do anything else." But I was always unique in being able to do public speaking and to engage community. So, I thought, "Even though I haven't studied this stuff, this is what I care about. I want to actually do something about these issues." I quit my job and decided to try to find a way to make a bigger impact.

I got into community organizing. This was right before Trump got elected. When he did get elected, it was even clearer that I needed to keep doing this, especially as somebody who knew that he was going to get elected. I was like, "Yes, everyone in my hometown is going to vote for Trump. I know what this looks like. I know where this is coming from." I felt like, "I have to keep doing this." Again, even though I didn't have an organizing background. I had never experienced that, never learned about it. I grew up in Appalachia. It was very much like freedom versus communism. That's politics. Your understanding is these are the two things. You have freedom here, and everything else is terrible.

On my own, I started learning, and finding people.

From the start, the main thing, for me as a Muslim, was the national security state. For me, our issues have never been just get Muslims civically engaged, get people voting, or make sure that the good immigrants can come in. I was like, "No, it's absolutely the surveillance state. It's the policing. It's the actual, literal borderless war that is happening globally."

It wasn't like I had a particular awful thing happen to me individually. But I've always been so community-based, so I've always had a good sense of what's happening to people around me. When 9/11 happened, I was mortified by how we went to war in Afghanistan and Iraq, and I could do nothing about it. I was a kid. I was a little bit too young to vote when George Bush ran again. That was the worst feeling, to be like, "These adults are really voting for this person again, and we're going to continue this."

I had people that I grew up with say, in front of a whole classroom, "Well, we should carpet bomb your country," without knowing what country I was from.

I saw how the war wasn't just about people wanting to murder my people, though there were so many instances of people saying that directly to me, or saying that around me, or people putting signs in their yards about murdering Muslims. And these were the same people who were going to go and impact people.

The craziest part of this story is that the military troop that committed torture and all the atrocities at Abu Ghraib, they're from my hometown. That's where they were based. It was either my senior year of high school or freshman year of college that that news had come out, and all these people were talking about Lynndie England. And I was like, "This person is from here."[7]

The years after that, when I was in places with mosques or I met a lot of other Muslims through college and other places, it was really very common for people to talk about informants and spies, like to the point where it was becoming a joke. Like, "Oh, this new person at the mosque who's so eager to talk to you is probably a spy." It was so clear within the community that that was going on a decade before the media would really pay attention to it.

These spies were sometimes undercover agents (FBI or local police) or sometimes paid informants—meaning a community member convinced and paid to be an informant. There have now been documentaries on this like *(T)error* (2016), about a community informant, and *Watched* (2018), about an undercover NYPD officer.[8] One story that has gone all the way to the Supreme Court is about this bodybuilder informant, who Hasan Minhaj covered in his latest comedy special too.[9] It became so common that Muslims started joking about new people showing up at the mosque who were super eager and then eventually want to talk to you about politics. There's an example of this in the first season of the show *Ramy* and a lot of Muslim media now.[10] But it's deeply psychologically traumatizing to feel that you can't trust anyone in your communal spaces, not even familiar faces who may be paid to turn against you, or people who have developed a close relationship with you. And that it happens in our most sacred spaces. Media is finally covering it but I think it's still not widely understood how damaging this is to all Muslims, and there's been no accountability. Many law enforcement officials responsible for those early war on terror policies have led very successful careers and these agencies have been empowered more over time.

To know that the FBI may come to your house at any point—to grow up with that—has a huge psychological impact on the community. I knew that at such a young age. That's how common it was, especially for people my age, millennials and so on, who saw it happen to all of our parents.

My father worked for the government—the USDA—pretty much my whole life. Far from law enforcement, although I'm sure food enforcement is like a thing. But I remember, I think sometime in college, he said that the FBI had come to our house. This might have been slightly after college. But I remember he said, "Yeah, they stopped by." My parents weren't home, and they left a card or something. My father called them and was like, "You know where I work, so why are you showing up at my house? You can come to my office." And some FBI agent came by with an NSA agent or somebody else who I'm sure was part of the Joint Terrorism Task Force.

My father didn't understand why this was bad. He obviously felt weird about it, but I was thinking, "Oh man, even my dad. They know truly everything about him. What do they need from him?" And it was very much them going and saying, "You're a leader in the community. We know that you're really trusted. We'd love to hear your thoughts in general." But then, suddenly, they're asking him about a specific person. And he told me he was like, "Yeah, this person was kind of weird." And I was like, "Oh, no. No, Dad. You don't know how those few words are going to impact that person's life."

The surveillance state has such deep psychological impacts on Muslims that people are not willing to talk about. Usually when journalists reach out to us, they're like, "Can you connect me with somebody who was impacted by national security?" And I'm like, "Yes, you are literally talking to one of those people." I don't have some crazy sob story. Those exist. Guantanamo still exists. You could go and find so many people who have had awful, awful impacts on their lives.

Every Muslim you talk to in the United States is impacted by it. All of us are constantly thinking, "Can I text this? Is it okay to share this on the internet? Can I say this on the phone? Is this person whom I just met legit?"

There have been informants who have either built friendships or romantic relationships with people. And to think that your partner or someone you thought you were intimately involved with is actually an FBI agent or actually being paid by the FBI, that is so devastating and such a unique thing that's happening to Muslims. I think about that all the time. And I definitely told many people in my life. I was like, "Oh yeah, when I met you, I thought you might be a spy." I tell them this after I'm pretty sure that they're not. But that's how I have to engage with the people around me.

Being really public as a Muslim woman talking about these things, talking about the police especially, people get very, very mad at you. I'm always kind of thinking about, "Yeah, what if somebody follows me home? What if somebody figures out where I live? What if somebody comes to our office? What do we do about that?" Safety is a real concern for us.

I'm a very hopeful person, but I'm also very realistic. Muslim or not, most people don't know what it's like to live in a place like Cumberland. So, I think my understanding of how deep the problem is is a little bit different than other folks'. Because again, I was like, "Yeah, of course, Trump is going to get elected. My best friend from childhood is voting for Trump and thinks that she loves me." Maybe people saw me as pessimistic, but I just thought, "I know how bad it is, and there's so much to do, and I just have to do something about it."

I came into it really annoyed with the rhetoric around Muslims at the time. The Muslim ban and Trump rhetoric was all about "love trumping hate" and about, "Oh, these people just don't know any Muslims. If they get to meet a Muslim, they'll be okay." There were "Hug a Muslim" tables, or whatever. And I was like, "This is nonsense." I was very well known and loved in my hometown. And most of those people still voted for Trump. They also still were pro-war and all of that. Not absolutely everybody, but truly I was like, "No, my family was known and loved, and that doesn't stop anything."

I want to help the Muslim community understand that this was structural and systemic. It's not about convincing one individual person that you're human. And that whole process itself is very dehumanizing. I was like, "I really want to do organizing within the community to help people understand there's a long history of this. This is not all happening because of 9/11. 9/11 happened because of this long history of US foreign politics and domestic politics." That has always been one big goal for me: building power within the Muslim community and making sure people understand what has actually brought us here so that they can also understand what we can do about it.

Just getting people to vote is not the thing. Throwing money at the Democrats is not the thing. And definitely, with the Trump election, there was a lot of hullaballoo around people wanting to stand with Muslims, but then not really. Even outside the Muslim community, I really want to make sure that liberal and progressive folks understand the same thing, that you can't just say, "We love Muslims" and then accept the national security state. These things go hand-in-hand. During the Trump administration, it was interesting because in some ways his overt racism and Islamophobia made people pay attention. It made people question programs and things that he was doing. It made people stand up to the Muslim ban. If that Muslim ban had happened under Obama, I don't think people would've been protesting at the airports. And it could've easily happened under Obama. It could really happen under any of these presidents.

It's always been frustrating to see how people still think these issues are just right-wing issues and don't understand that Islamophobia is so normalized across the board. If you look at polling of people's opinions on Muslims or people's opinions on security policies, it's horrifying. Every time those polls come out, many people will highlight the gap between Republicans and Democrats. But I'm like, "That gap, sure, but both numbers are too high. The fact that all of you hate Muslims is the terrifying thing. Don't pat yourselves on the backs because you see this slight difference in each side."

In the wake of January 6th, one of the most frustrating things is people think that expanding national security is going to address white supremacy. We're seeing DHS and DOJ get more money. We're seeing all of these programs that have targeted Muslims and people of color get expanded, as if they're ever going to go after white people and also as if that's the answer, going after individual white people. That has been truly crazy-making. Because again, as somebody who grew up with people who became neo-Nazis, I'm like, "Yeah, this is actually a real issue. And some FBI program that tells you look out for someone who is getting really political and starts dressing this way and has lost their job, that's not going to find the kid down the street from me that became a neo-Nazi."

If that kid maybe wasn't surrounded by people and media and politicians spewing all of these same things, or if that kid's only option wasn't to become a prison guard (where he's absolutely going to become more racist) or to join the military and go abroad and again enact violence on people of color . . .

After Charlottesville, after January 6, after each of these incidents, we see people going, "Oh, yeah, that thing that just targets Muslims, we should make it target everybody instead.

Let's do equal-opportunity surveillance." And I'm like, "This is not helpful for anybody. This is only going to make it worse."

Boston is truly one of the most racist places in the country, and it also historically has been an incredible place for resistance. I draw a lot of strength from that. On May 15th of 2020, I did not think anybody in a few weeks would suddenly care about abolishing the police. That moment around George Floyd and that uprising was just wild. We had been told for so long, "You're so radical. Those ideas are too much. People can't handle the thought of abolishing the police." And we were like, "Yeah, yeah, yeah. We know, but we're going to get there. We're totally going to get there." And then, suddenly, it took off.

It was maybe the craziest month of my life to see so many people engage in this work. It was fascinating, too, because again I think people's understanding of these issues is like, "Oh, Muslims, they must be dealing with that Muslim ban thing and Islamophobia." People's conception of how these issues impact different communities is pretty basic. I'm sure for a lot of people it was surprising that, "Oh, Muslim Justice League (MJL) is the abolitionist organization that's talking about defunding the police and at the forefront of this conversation as Muslims."

For us, it's like, "Yeah, Muslims are the most diverse community." We are policed and surveilled. We're impacted by truly everything. And for us, again, national security goes hand-in-hand with global policing. We've always worked on those things across the board.

BLM (Black Lives Matter), that had been a thing for a while. It was just that finally everybody got it. Everyone was like, "Oh yeah, you're right. This isn't a one-off thing. This is happening too much." You don't want it to get to that point, but it is incredible when you see people decide to do that. In the same way, when people protested the Muslim ban, it was incredible. I was in North Carolina at the time. Our airport there was not big enough to have a significant thing going on. But I was watching all these videos in SFO, here in Logan Airport, and seeing my brother go to the airport. He was texting me that he was going to the airport there. Those moments of resistance are one of the things that can keep me going.

I was taking the train to work, and I called my dad. My dad and my stepmom live in Richmond, Virginia, now. And I called them because there was this whole national "Hurt a Muslim" day. I think this was a British thing, but people knew that it would impact Muslims here in the United States, too. I called my dad to be like, "Hey, this thing is happening. You and my stepmom should probably stay in the house today. Maybe just don't go places, because you're in Virginia."

Richmond is diverse, but there's plenty of people who might do something like this. And his response was, "Oh yeah, that's fine. We'll be fine." But he said, "Are you doing anything about this man who was shot in California?" And I said, "What are you talking about?" He said, "You know, there was a Black man who was shot by the police in Sacramento." I was like, "Oh, are you talking about Stephon Clark?"

I think the police shot him in the back when he was running away. But my dad was asking me if I was doing anything about it. And I was like, "Huh?" I said, "What do you mean? What

do you know about this?" So, he told me. He said, "Yeah, we were at this conference, and they had a protest about it during the conference, and people spoke about it." I said, "What were people saying?" And he said, "You know, there was a lot of chanting, like 'No justice, no peace.' People were talking about the fact that he was Muslim. But I know, obviously, when they shot him, they didn't know he was Muslim. They just shot him because he's Black." And I said, "Yeah, that's true."

I was sitting on the train thinking, "What is happening right now that my dad is actually asking me about this and explaining it to me?" And I was so grateful that it wasn't just that he heard it on the news, but he was at a Muslim conference, and they talked about it. He was hearing about it in all these different ways. And he was asking me, "Are you doing anything about it?" I said, "Well, I'm in Boston." I said, "Our organization is two people in Massachusetts, so I can't do much about this thing in California." I hung up and I was crying on the train, which is a very Boston thing to be, crying on the train.

I had called my dad about this thing that I thought he needed to know about. And I was so shocked that he then engaged in this deeper conversation about Black Lives Matter, about police shooting, that he had heard about it from other people. Because, prior to that, it was always me saying, "Don't you know that this is happening? Haven't you heard about these things?"

I don't want to do this work forever. I'm doing this because it has to happen. I would love to go back to doing healthcare. If we end wars and create real community safety and all of that, I won't be out here doing this anymore. So, that's always the goal. The goal is to make it so that we're not needed, to make it so that we don't have all of these issues.

I think more tangibly, I think in the very near future, at least for MJL, a big conversation is getting people to understand we can't use white supremacist agencies to fight white supremacy. The FBI and DHS are not going to solve QAnon and Proud Boys and all these things that people are worried about. That's a big thing where I feel like people really don't get it and are, unfortunately, expanding the national security state under the Biden administration. As people think about us as more polarized or whatever or both sides being extreme, we're out here like, "No. You can be against white supremacy, and that's not extreme." I always quote this 1930s surveillance from the FBI. They called these Muslims "fanatics of racial equality."[11] And I'm like, "Yes. Yes, I am. Go ahead, call me that."

I really want to see us talk about ending wars and decreasing the scale of these institutions in ways that both benefit the people we've hurt abroad and here. Some progressive people will be like, "We shouldn't be spending money on the Department of Defense, on this military budget. We could spend that on healthcare here, Medicare for all here." I'm like, "That's cool, but, actually, you should pay for Medicare for All for everyone in Iraq and Afghanistan first. Do you not understand what we've done?"

The level of harm that has happened and violence that has happened is profound.

Right now, we can barely even recognize how the domestic policies are bad. We can barely even recognize Islamophobia in our own progressive spaces. How do we get from here to where we need to be, which is really having a strong anti-war movement that connects domestic policy to foreign policy? When Pete Buttigieg says, "We shouldn't use the guns I used abroad here on our own citizens," I'm like, "Fuck you, man. You shouldn't have used them anywhere."

That can't be the progressive movement. On a personal level, I really want to get past working on the FBI stuff, the domestic policy stuff, and really look at what our foreign policy means. How do we help people understand that we are globally the bully? How do we help people understand that violence abroad impacts millions of people and generations of people, and that that is one of the root causes for all of the things that we see happening with national security here?

I had my phone stolen once in Wisconsin, and it was this really weird situation where the police wanted to set up a sting operation to get my phone back and to arrest the person who took it who was asking me for $200 for it. A bunch of friends were like, "Yeah, you should do that. That person should go to jail." And I was like, "What is wrong with all of you? You all sit here, and you're making great salaries, and you think I should send this person to prison who needed $200?"

That incident always comes back to me when I think about people who have convinced themselves that what they're doing is right and justifiable in some way. I'm over here living in a totally different world of, "What makes you think that Muslims are inherently violent? How can you even get to that place of justifying going to war without understanding why these people hate us. Where did this come from? Could we maybe have done something that caused this? Is there maybe a bigger story here?"

The thing that I often say is that all of this is creating the illusion of safety at the expense of certain people. None of us are actually safe because of these wars. Violence begets violence, and this country puts out so much violence. I think when we talk about national security, people often really think that some of these things are creating safety and security. And I'm like, "They're not. That's not creating safety for anybody." You cannot go to Cumberland, Maryland, and tell me that that's a good, healthy place to live.

Apologies for cursing. I maybe should've asked if that was okay.

Fatema Ahmad is the executive director at Muslim Justice League, where she leads MJL's efforts to dismantle the criminalization and policing of marginalized communities.

HASAN ELAHI

I didn't necessarily seek this out; it kind of found me. And it found me in a very abrupt manner when I was traveling back to the United States from an exhibition in Senegal, in Dakar. I was taken in by an FBI agent at the airport in Detroit. It was the first point of entry into the United States. It was explained to me that there had been a report that an Arab man who had fled on September 12th was hoarding explosives.

And that Arab man would be me. Even though never mind I'm not Arab. Never mind there weren't explosives. Never mind it wasn't the 12th. This was the peak of "If you see something, say something." Even if you only see it in your head and you're making it up. So, the report came into the authorities, and this is what launched the initial investigation.

I think anyone who talks to me for more than a few minutes realizes I'm not exactly a terrorist threat. But the system doesn't trust itself. And because the system doesn't trust itself it needs to go through a verification process, and often that means a much more detailed level of interrogation, and by other people. Because, what if the first guy was wrong? There's this whole thing of like, you're never trusted to do your job, so you have to have another person do it. Then another person do it. And another person do it. The FBI agent that I met in Detroit let me go home to Tampa, Florida. In Tampa, the larger bit of this investigation took place.

If you're accused of being a terrorist, your initial reaction is not, "How can I help you? What can I do for you?" I realized there was something wrong. The FBI agent realized there was something wrong. But neither of us could say, "You know what, this is a waste of everyone's time, let's just move on." We had to go through the whole process.

Because it's about that process. It's the process that delivers the outcome.

This is in retrospect, understanding this. But I did know there was something happening. I knew well enough to know that whatever was happening, was happening outside the law. And I knew that I probably should not get a lawyer, because if I did it could escalate things.

It wasn't ever stated directly, but I realized that at any moment they could take me to Guantanamo and they would not have to explain to anyone what they were doing or why. Realistically, when you're face to face with someone with essentially the power of life and death over you, you revert to very animalistic instincts. In my case, survival meant cooperate. And in that cooperation was this way of actually trying to have this understanding with the FBI agent like, "Look, we both have something to do, let's not escalate this situation worse than it needs to be. I'm completely innocent in this thing, but how do I convince you of that, and how do I convince you that you also know that?" I think bringing legal counsel into this is almost like showing teeth to an animal. And you don't know what the other animal is going to do. So, everything was, How do we deescalate this?

In the end, it was six months long. The very final bit of it was a set of polygraphs, if I remember it correctly, the same questions, repeated nine consecutive times. Very basic, baseline answers. And very complicated, well, not necessarily complicated, because you can only answer yes or no. Things like, "Do you belong to any groups that wish to harm the United States?"

At the end, it was all cleared up. That's when they basically said, "Everything's fine." I was like, "Yeah, that's what I've been trying to tell you all along. Can I get a letter saying everything's fine?"

And, of course, because it's all extra-judicial, also because of the way our legal system works, you could never be not guilty of something you never did. So, you have to be charged with something in order to get a formal document that says that you're clear.

Of course, they couldn't provide the letter. And I was like, "I travel a lot. And all we need is the next guy not to get the next memo and here we go all over again. How do we prevent this? How do we prevent this from happening?"

And that was the moment that the FBI agent gave me some phone numbers and said, "Here's some phone numbers. If you get into trouble, give us a call, we'll take care of it." Ever since then, I would call my FBI agent, tell him where I was going, what I was doing. Not because I had to, but because I chose to. It was a preemptive action. I opted in, for my own safety.

Those phone calls got longer. Then they became emails, and the emails got longer and longer. And then I would write him thousands of words. I would send him pictures of all the places I was hanging out at. I would make websites for him. And he would always say, "Thank you. Be safe."

It was a little bit of an unbalanced relationship. Here I am telling him all of these things about me, thinking that I'm really connecting with him, and he was writing back to me four words.

I felt kind of jilted. It's like, I don't get it, why is this guy so special. So that's when I started communicating openly to not only my FBI agent, but to everybody. I created what these days would, I guess, be called an app. It's kind of funny, but even the word "app" didn't even exist back then. I was using the smartphone, what we called a smartphone back then. But it was one of those Nokias, with like the nine buttons, which actually wasn't a smart phone at all. So, I created this really funky code that basically turned my Nokia 6600 into a tracking device. It would always tell my FBI agent where I was, and send a photo of where I was, and a map that showed how to find me. And, of course, it was also open to everybody else.

In the process of creating this project (which was hardly a project at first, but more of a practicality so I didn't get shipped off to Guantanamo), I started thinking about what else the FBI might know about me. I know I told them every little detail of my life and they probably have my flight records, so I created a list of every flight I've been on since birth. The more recent flights show not only exact flight numbers extracted from my frequent flyer accounts, but also photographs of the meals that I got fed on the flights. I collected all these pieces of information (or evidence of my activities in my particular case) and created a website for the FBI. It was a rather organic process, but eventually it became *Tracking Transience*. There are various databases of images on the site: airports, food that I've eaten at home, food that I've eaten on the road, random hotel beds that I've slept in, various parking lots off of Interstate 80, empty train stations, and some even as specific as tacos eaten in Mexico City between July 5 and July 7, not to mention the toilets that I use. These images are all quite empty, and really could be anywhere, but they're extremely specific to the exact location where they were photographed.

So, in a way I guess that is probably the beginning of this project that is now going nearly twenty years. It's still active, it's still continuing. Except now everybody's doing this.

We're looking at about late 2002. It was at the end of 2002 that I was cleared. So, I started writing that code right around then. It was basically the next year. So, 2003 is probably the beginning of the project.

But it's hard to tell when the project even started. Was it the first phone call? Was it the first email? Was it the first website? Was it the first photo that I showed? I still remember walking into the FBI office in Tampa. I remember bringing my old iBook, the white Mac iBook, and I opened it up to show them my iPhotos library. And I'm showing him I was here, then I went here, then I met these guys for a beer at this place.

I started teaching as an art professor in 1996. So, 2002 is six years after I'd been a professor. The word "surveillance" didn't even exist in my vocabulary as an artist at that moment. But now that I look back to my really, really, really early works, there's a lot of similarity. There's a lot of watching, monitoring, mapping. And then these broader conceptual ideas of citizenship, of migration.

Maybe at that moment I didn't see the connections, but now, looking back at my career over twenty-five, nearly thirty years, even visually the work is incredibly similar now to then.

Probably the biggest difference is prior to that moment the work was very cold and impersonal. The work is still cold, even though it might be super-personal, hyper-personal information. It's presented in such an impersonal manner. It's just the facts, it's just the facts. Even though it is autobiographical. It's autobiographical, and yet it could be anybody.

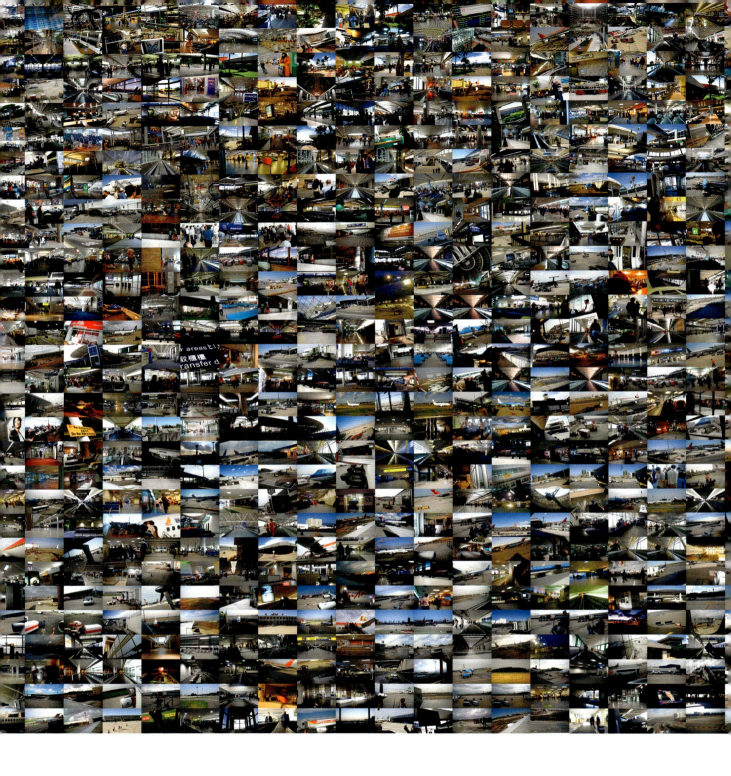

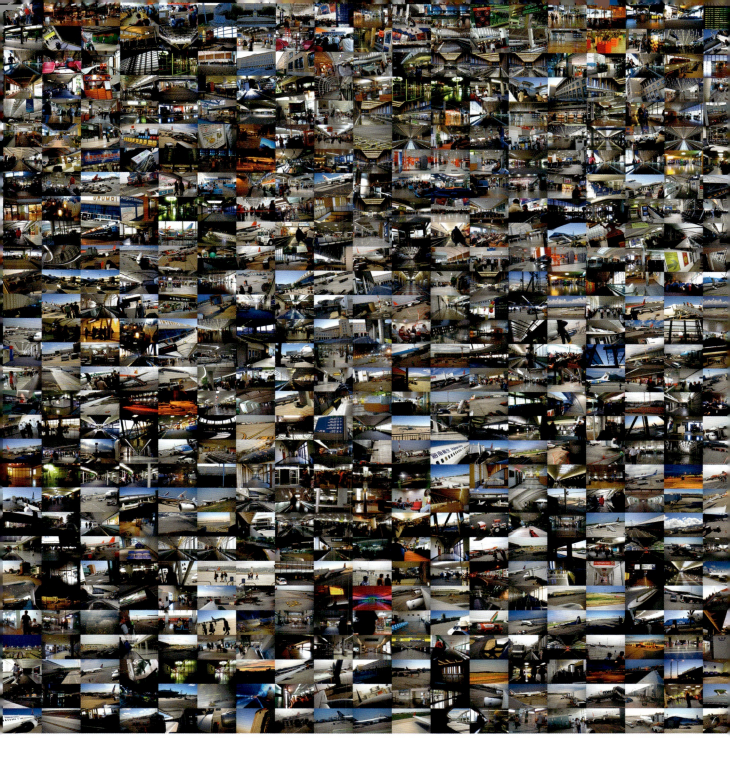

FIGURE 5.5
Transit, 2011, by Hasan Elahi, 30″ × 60″ C-Print. Image
courtesy of the artist.

The FBI, it's a one-way street. They do not provide opinion. They do not provide feedback. Their job is to gather intelligence. And what they do with it, they don't tell you. They don't have to tell you. So, I've actually never gotten a thing from them saying, "Hey, this is what we think of your work."

On the other hand, once my work started getting more and more public, and I was doing these lectures and these conferences, I would get invited to speak to some really interesting groups of people. Many years ago, I spoke at a military institute. I was the opening act for Keith Alexander (former Director of the National Security Agency). I mean, when they invited me, I'm thinking, "Wait, am I being set up as chum for the shark?"

But it's interesting because I think at a certain level, particularly at the managerial level, I think they totally get it. They know what I'm doing. In the past, when we were in an analog system, when we were an analog intelligence system, this idea of flooding the system was feasible, because it was still an analog process that had to filter through all that information.

A really sudden shift that took place recently, across this time that I've been doing this project, is machine learning and AI. The more information you feed it, the more proficient it gets. So, it's kind of gone full circle in a really interesting way.

Conceptually, I've been fascinated with this idea of Magellan. Of circumnavigation. You go far enough to one end you end up in the other.

And it's happened on so many different levels. To the point where I've become so cooperative and so helpful that it's actually defiance. It's defiance through cooperation. Or I think, as a friend of mine likes to say, it's aggressive compliance.

I was this one weirdo doing this. I would pull out my camera and take a picture of my lunch. And people were looking at me like, "What the hell are you doing?" And now it's so commonplace. Everybody does this. What was once considered this weird art project is now so commonplace.

I just love those early paintings of the still lifes of what people were eating and things. That was the pre-early Instagram version of "This is what my lunch looks like."

When I do talks at universities now with students, inevitably there's always someone who's like, "I don't get it. What's the big deal? This looks like my Instagram feed." And then they realize that they're doing this as well.

We generally tend to think of surveillance as a very post-9/11, very twenty-first-century concept. But the concept of surveillance—I mean, God was the original surveillance camera. You behaved because God was watching. Even in scripture, there's something about the eyes of the lord are watching over. I have to look this up. Here it is. Proverbs 15:3: "The eyes of the lord are everywhere, keeping watch on the wicked and the good."

You behaved because God was watching. Except now it may not be rooted in scripture, it may not be rooted in religion. Now we know Amazon is watching. We know that Bezos and Zuckerberg, they're watching. It's not literally them, but it's their algorithms that are watching.

So, it is interesting how we tend to think of this thing as a very post 9/11, very twenty-first-century concept. And yet it's not, it's thousands and thousands of years old.

I live in DC now. We suspect that my neighbor next door is a retired spy. We don't know. We just think he's a retired spy. This is the kind of neighborhood that I live in. The NRA (National

FIGURE 5.6
Hasan Elahi, Queens, New York, 2022.

Rifle Association) is up the road from here. The CIA is out in Langley just a few miles over that way. I drive by the FBI offices all the time. I live between Dulles Airport and National Airport.

Everyone here has benefited from this security industry in one way or another. It's a growth industry, literally. But let's talk a little bit about this thing that we're creating, these new industries. Let's not fool ourselves. Anything in the future economy that can be automated will be automated. For the first time, you have machines taking photos for other machines, for other machines to analyze that no human will ever see.

These security jobs are not going to be permanent jobs, because this will be automated. Or the vast majority of it, because it already is. It's already there.

Once that happens, we don't need them. We don't need them anymore. And, as a matter of fact, humans make mistakes. And the reliability factor is an issue.

Humans make mistakes. It goes back to my initial interaction with the FBI. The human wasn't trusted.

My problem was never getting on a plane. My problem was getting off the plane. It's not that as soon as I came into the United States it was like, "Alert, alert, terrorist alert" on the screen. It's basically like, "Yeah, you're okay. But what if you're not? I don't want to be the guy responsible, so I'm going to hand you over to the next guy." And the next guy is like, "Yeah, I don't see anything, but what if you're not okay?"

And it goes to the next one, and the next one. It goes to the next one, until someone in authority comes and says, "He's okay, leave him alone." Now I show up, it beeps on the machine. The machine says, "You're okay. Okay, fine, go."

It's a little complicated in that way. If the machine says you're okay, you're okay. But if a human says you're okay, then, well, are you really okay, or did the last guy kind of just drop the ball? But this is the system that we're in.

I think it is important for us to acknowledge that anything that can be automated will be automated.

We certainly will not need a massive labor force in an industry that will be automated.

Hasan Elahi is an artist whose work examines issues of surveillance, citizenship, migration, transport, and the challenges of borders and frontiers. He is currently dean of the College of Fine, Performing and Communications Arts (CFPCA) at Wayne State University.

LARRY CUNNINGHAM

I'll invoke Satchel Paige's rendition of aging. How old would you be if you didn't know how old you were? So there it is. You've got to decide what your perspective is.

Let's address the job search perspective for folks who are interested in going into the field in general. My first piece of advice, my first admonition, really, is: don't look at the brochures. Don't look at the Hollywood version. Talk to folks who do it day in and day out. Like anything in life, the reality is sometimes tough. You do a lot of hurry up and wait. Whether you're in the military, in the government, law enforcement—there's a few moments of terror and excitement, but a lot of it's pretty mundane. You've got to decide for yourself is the overall picture, the overall commitment to this kind of work, worth it, or am I just going in to get my lighted hour on the stage?

Let me give an example. When I first started the job, I was in the field running out forged government checks and bonds. And, frankly, it was a lot of mundane admin. Not very exciting. Certainly no real kudos. It wasn't a million-dollar heist. It was a couple of forged checks, and that's how we cut our teeth on learning investigations, learning how to present cases, how to find probable cause, how to create a good case that'll pass muster. Those things can be mundane, particularly if it's not the case of the century.

But I really believe that if you're going to go into a field, whatever it is, even beyond law enforcement, security, fire, whatever, talk to folks who do it day in and day out, and see if you understand the basis of it and can commit to the mission with the good, the bad, and the ugly. That is the key thing. Now, the brochures are great, but chances are you're not going to be running on the side of the president's limo. You might, but probably not. You're going to be doing a lot of mundane stuff. We used call it "counting the pile on the carpet." Ring around the oval. With Reagan, nothing happened. We had these posts. Sure, they were important posts, but eight hours of maybe only two movements in the White House complex. You've got to have a sense of, "Gee, this is for the bigger cause."

Another issue is dealing with boredom. How do you keep yourself focused on that thing that could happen in a couple of seconds or a minute? We'd do a lot of "what if" scenarios. I was involved in the training division for years prior to going to the Secret Service Presidential Protective Division. I was in the field for four, training division for about four, and then Presidential Protection Division for five, and then I finished off as the agent in charge in San Jose, California, seven years. And that was good. It was bittersweet, but I had enough balance where I felt like any other assignments it wouldn't really do a lot for my resumé. But more important, I didn't feel like it would be as fulfilling as maybe biting the bullet and going out on my own. No regrets. I do miss the camaraderie, miss some of the infrastructure, some of the clout, but you have to make decisions like that in life and hope you make the right one.

My grandfather was in the Lafayette Escadrille (in World War I) with Eddie Rickenbacker.[12] He was a Harvard student. About midway through his four years, he decided to go to France as an ambulance driver, and then he became a pilot. And then he went back to school, but that was an inspiration. My dad was in two wars. My mother was in the OSS (US Office of Strategic Services, precursor to CIA). All those things collectively push you. I knew I wanted to serve in some capacity.

I did a lot of pre-med the last few years in college and I got a full academic scholarship. But I had a family early on in my life, and my spouse didn't really want to go look at more school. She probably would've supported me, but it was just one of these things I was trying to reconcile. A job came up right away in the school system in Maryland up here. Vocational evaluator. It was a great job. Couldn't refuse. So I took it, but the interesting thing was the funding ran out, and now there's no job. This job was basically predicated on the idea that you help the folks who aren't academically inclined, help the folks who are struggling to retain their value. My idea was to evaluate folks who weren't academically on the top of the list, find out what their vocational potential was, and try to place them accordingly for a job right out of college. If that had stayed, I'd probably be a clinical psychologist now. Who knows? But the funding ran out. It only lasted a year.

Father-in-law, at the time, was the second guy into Normandy. He was a communicator. Set up all kinds of communications throughout his life. He eventually created the White

House communications systems after the war. I was talking about getting a PhD. He says—typical Des Moines, Midwest perspective—he says, "What do you want to do? Become an educated idiot or do a real job?" His words exactly. I said, "What do you mean?" He said, "I know a lot of idiots who have PhDs. They can't wire a fan. They can't open the door without a problem." And I said, "Yeah, to some degree." He said, "Well, if you're interested, the US Secret Service might be a good career."

I didn't know. There was a uniform division and the agents' side. He thought I was suitable for the uniform division side. I said, "Well, with all due respect, I graduated magna cum laude. If I'm doing this, I'm going to go to the top."

The rest is history. It was a good career, twenty years. I learned a lot. If you're paying attention in the old school, it pushes you beyond your capabilities. And I like that. Twenty years in that, 1974 to 1994, and I've been a consultant, instructor, premises liability expert, citizen ever since.[13]

No regrets. This was a good choice ultimately, but I really struggled with going to medical school. I wanted to go to med school. That was the first thing. I was passionate about that. Took me a long time to get over that, for whatever reasons. In retrospect, they weren't the best reasons. My great uncle at the time was surgeon general of the Navy here at Bethesda Naval Hospital. Grandfather was in and my dad was a colonel in the Army. The unwritten message to us was if you're not a doctor or a lawyer, then you're okay. At age eight or ten, you don't know how to evaluate that statement. You don't have enough experience. I could have done the work. I'm pretty sure about that, but God has a plan and you end up where you are. So here we are.

When you start a job—any government job, actually—you've got to have patience, and you've got to have vision. If you're narrow-minded, narrowly focused, you're going to say, "I'm not doing this anymore. It's too mundane. I'm not even a cog in the wheel. I'm not even the grease. I'm a ball bearing that they cast aside." That's how you feel. But what you've got to do is you've got to look at the big picture. You've got to be visionary and say, "Hey, this is going to be valuable someday." Be optimistic, work hard, and seek out opportunities that might allow you to show your skill set better than the rank and file. You've got to work hard, though. None of this, "Everybody gets a trophy." You have to work hard, and that's what we're losing and missing now. It's a conspicuous void there now.

Millennial attitudes. It's not just millennials. There are some people in the older group. "I want my trophy." This is what it is. If someone tells me, "It's too hard" or "I can't do it," they're talking to the wrong person. I've been in this business forty-five years. Was it all pretty? No. Was it up and down? Yes.

I'll give you an example. I set up security for the 2004 War Memorial dedication on the Mall right in the shadow of the Lincoln Memorial. There's a World War II memorial there. I was involved. I was asked by a former director to set up security to blend Park Police, Metropolitan Police, Arlington Police, Secret Service, and Park Service. All the entities who might be involved in this huge event. Eighty thousand vets were invited. The venue was huge. The biggest thing I've done next to papal security arrangements. It was more of a liaison thing, but it's also tactical. The biggest concern there was the average age of the individual at that event was about seventy-eight, seventy-nine at the time, 2004. So, obviously, one of the critical things was medical response. We set up the aisles and set up the venues so we could have

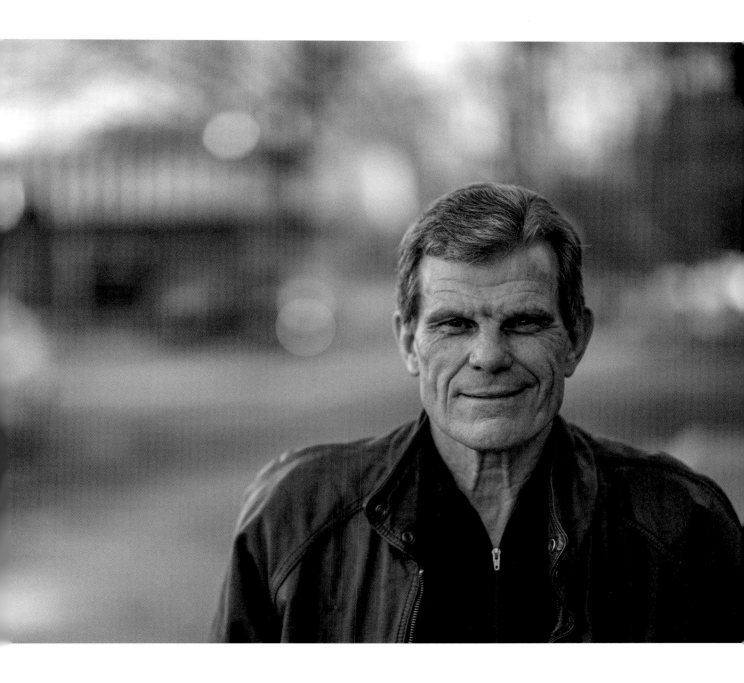

FIGURE 5.7
Larry Cunningham, Reston, Virginia, 2019.

quick response and golf carts for medical interventions. Weather was a big deal. Prayer was a big deal, because the three days leading up was 95 degrees, 95 percent humidity. Disaster for the audience. And so those kinds of things really came to life. Speaking to these people, the war vets, you could tell. They'd do it again, no questions, and I asked a few and my father-in-law as well. I said, "How'd you do this?" "It was very simple," they said. "We just did what we were told. It takes all day, takes all week, go."

I'll give you an example of the contrast. We're doing surveillance with some new agent that we had on the scene. We're doing surveillance, and of course it's Friday. It's always on a weekend or a holiday, and I got a real call, a real call on the radio from one of these guys: "How long is this surveillance going to last? I have plans tonight." I said, "Hold on. I'm going to get out of my car. I'll walk over to the suspect and say, 'Sir, how long are you gonna be involved in this crime' and then I'll get back to you." That was a real question. Are you shitting me? That was a real question.

This is one of the best anecdotes you'll ever know about this, and this is still true today, and, unfortunately, folks don't understand it. This guy was the agent in charge of the Johnson detail, and he was, at the time, I guess it was 1982, 1981, he was in charge of . . . I believe it was the Dallas field office, the Secret Service field office. He comes over to me and says, "I understand you're going to be going to the president's division." I said, "With all due respect, we'll see. I'd be honored, and I'm cautiously optimistic, if I'm so lucky." He said, "Well, let me give you one piece of advice that might help you. My nephew is there right now. It's a great assignment. I gave him the same advice I'm going to give you." And he says, "When they play 'Hail to the Chief,' ruffles and flourishes when the president walks out on stage—da da da da da da, the President of the United States—that's not for you."

A lot of people don't understand that, and let me tell you my point. My mother told me to do it. Everybody should do it once in a while. "Here's my advice, son. Don't get too big for your britches. Don't get too high on your ivory tower, because you'll be knocked down in a second. Eat a piece of humble pie every day. Slowly."

Larry Cunningham is a security strategist and training consultant with forty-nine years of public safety experience. He retired from the US Secret Service as the agent-in-charge in San Jose, California, after a twenty-year career.

6

PORTFOLIO: CONSTRUCTIONS

THESE PHOTOGRAPHS OF clumsily constructed paper models of sites of interest have each been culled from Google Earth Ground View. In some cases, I have reconstructed the sites where interviews and portraits took place but where I had neglected to capture satisfactory environmental photographs. In the case of a site or facility to which I have been denied access, I locate it on Google Earth, then export hundreds of images to be printed and reassembled into three-dimensional models. I then carefully light and re-photograph the sculptural constructions with a $4'' \times 5''$ camera. In some cases, even the virtual proxy for a location is invisible—off-limits even to the eyes of Google Earth due, ostensibly, to its national-security sensitivity. An otherwise innocuous pub in Arlington, Virginia, or the Ritz Carlton in DC, for example, are both locations where we conducted interviews and they are both, coincidentally, essentially invisible in Google Street View. In those cases, the spaces are visualized largely through signs and symbols: the familiar gray checkerboard pattern, for example, of a transparent layer in Adobe Photoshop (which is now a more ubiquitous signifier of empty space than actual empty space) is hand-drawn onto the surface of the model.

FIGURE 6.1
CIA Headquarters (tabletop model), Langley,
Virginia, 2018.

FIGURE 6.2
Richardson, TX (tabletop model), 2019.

FIGURE 6.3
Studio set for *Richardson, TX*, 2019.

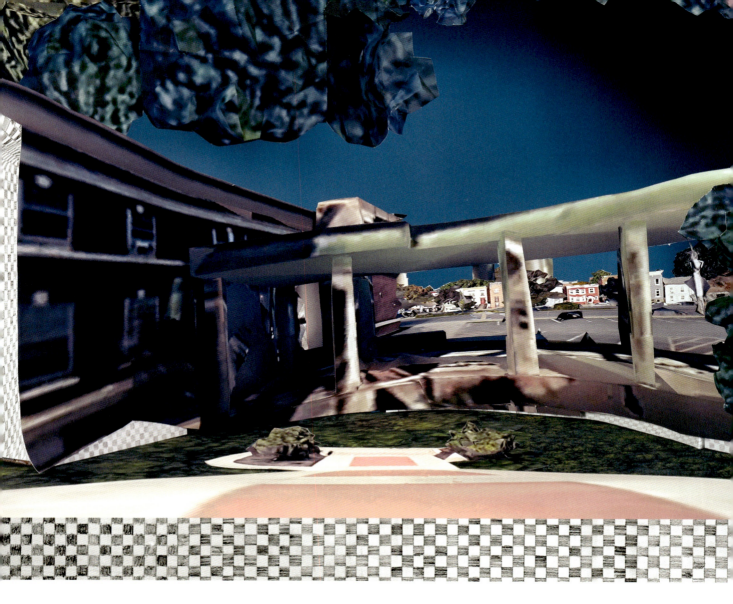

FIGURE 6.4
Draper Hall (tabletop model), University at Albany,
State University of New York, Albany, New York, 2017.

FIGURE 6.5
Studio set for *Tarmac, Reagan International Airport*, 2019.

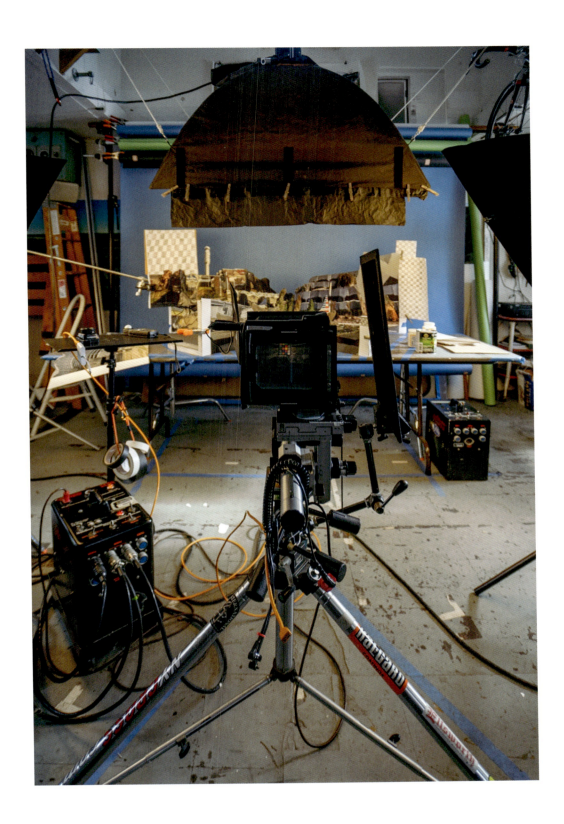

FIGURE 6.6
Tarmac, Reagan International Airport (tabletop model), Washington, DC, 2019.

FIGURE 6.7
Invisible Blackwall Hitch (tabletop model), Arlington,
Virginia, 2016.

FIGURE 6.8
Invisible Ritz-Carlton (tabletop model), Pentagon City,
Virginia, 2016.

FIGURE 6.9
Border of Nogales, Arizona, and Nogales, Sonora
(tabletop model), 2022.

FIGURE 6.10
Studio set for *Border of Nogales, Arizona, and Nogales,
Sonora*, 2022.

FIGURE 6.11
Border of El Paso, TX, and Ciudad Juarez, MX (tabletop model), 2022.

7

EMERGENCY MANAGEMENT

I worked at the National Center for Security and Preparedness (NCSP) for four years. I started off as a paid intern and worked my way up to training and project management section chief. By the time I left, I was managing analysts and subject-matter experts (SMEs) across disciplines to coordinate and develop Homeland Security training for New York State.

I felt like I had such an identity at the NCSP. Everyone knew who I was and what I stood for. I loved that job.

But I'm from Albany; I lived there my whole life with the only departure being in 2009 to take an internship and spend a semester in DC. Following graduate school, I needed something more. I decided to move back to DC and work in emergency management consulting. I joined a DC firm that supported clients across federal, state, and local government. I became a senior analyst supporting training development for a federal government client. I was promoted shortly thereafter. I served as a deputy program manager over a multimillion dollar federal government program. I also spearheaded development of my sector's state and local practice, crafting the strategic vision in collaboration with leadership across the firm, building infrastructure, and fostering partnerships to encourage growth. My focus areas at the company included emergency management, continuity of operations, cyber incident response planning, and active shooter response across planning, training, and exercises.

That's currently what I'm doing and it's unlike my previous professional experiences. It's a different ballgame in DC. If you meet somebody, it's not, "How are you?" It's more, "What do you do?," and "What can you do for me?" is implied. You see people look past you in social settings as if to say, "Oh, it's nice to meet you. I'm sure you're wonderful, but who else is here to talk to?"

At the NCSP, I worked with subject matter experts with impressive careers across law enforcement, fire, emergency medical services, and other disciplines. Many had extensive military experience. Some people have asked if I find it intimidating to collaborate with or manage these SMEs. Thankfully, it isn't; I'd spent five years developing my relationships and working closely with them. You have to have a certain amount of deference and reverence. They've operated in austere environments and have seen things I've never experienced, and you have to honor that.

It is challenging when somebody like me walks into a room full of emergency management SMEs. I don't immediately evoke gravitas; I have an uphill battle. You have to be willing to put in the work if you're a younger person and if you're, say, a female in Homeland Security. I must trust that I know what I'm doing. I have to put in extra effort to gain buy-in, to prove my worth and demonstrate my skills. Some of that is being junior and paying your dues; a lot of that is overcompensating for being a woman.

I didn't come into consulting with a network, in contrast to the NCSP where I built one over time. By the time I left, I had gained the confidence of my boss, my staff, and the SMEs. When I switched jobs, I was surrounded by people for whom I was an unknown quantity. I was constantly thinking, "Don't you know my work ethic? Don't you know that I can do great things for you?" I had to prove in consulting, in a way that I hadn't in years, that I was prepared to get the job done. It felt frustrating to now have the experience in the field but be in a much more junior role relative to my position at the NCSP.

154 | Chapter 7

You stand out as a woman in Homeland Security. You don't want to be flying over the radar for the "wrong" things. People say that if you're uncomfortable, you should stand up for yourself, but it's not always that simple. You've got the military guys, officers, and firefighters—they're going to make some off-color remarks and you have to decide how you're going to deal with that. I am comfortable in a room full of guys and can "take the joke," but I've had to set boundaries that my male colleagues don't even have to think about. At the same time, you have to have a pretty good sense of humor and know that it's an old boys' club and you have to break that mold.

I have been lucky in my career; the extra efforts have paid off. I have forged incredible relationships and friendships and have grown in my positions. This is not everyone's experience, and it certainly isn't fair. I'm glad to see the field is changing to include more women, as well as BIPOC and LGBTQ+ communities. This will create conditions for diverse perspectives as these new voices gain experience and become leaders. Up-and-comers will be able to see themselves more explicitly in the field. Hopefully, one day they will just hustle to show that their capabilities exceed their time in service rather than feel they need to make up for who they are.

The plus side of being a woman in emergency management is that you never have to wait in line for the bathroom. It's pretty awesome. The governor of New York had an emergency preparedness summit in 2013. At the break, the men's bathroom line was out the door. I took a picture of it. I was dying laughing as I just walked into the ladies' room.

In consulting, you can't choose your client; your client chooses you. I need to be adaptable to my clients and give my full effort, regardless of challenges in the client relationship or interest in the project. I like to be 100 percent passionate about my work, and there doesn't seem to be a clear-cut way for me to do that in consulting.

I do enjoy the fast-paced nature of it. I like working on different projects that I would never have been exposed to if I were in one little niche.

It's hard for me to work for someone I don't respect, especially coming from the NCSP where my boss and I had a trusting relationship and I was surrounded by people I admired. In consulting, there are people in positions above me who are not as good at what they do, are not open to feedback, and don't get the emergency management field. But they project a confidence in their approach, and confidence is the opiate of the masses in DC.

With my boss at the NCSP, I could be completely, even brutally, honest. I could approach him and tell him what a terrible decision he was about to make, and he would consider my perspective before moving forward. And when he made decisions that I didn't agree with, he would be open to a serious talk about it. In consulting, you have to be more judicious in picking your battles. You have to be very careful. If you're going to object, you better have people behind you and a crystal-clear position. Without the backup, it isn't worth it to raise the issue.

Recently, I've discovered that targeted relationship building with difficult people can mitigate some of the problems that stem from this disconnect. It is important to try to build bridges where you can. Not everyone will become your best friend, but you can do your part by listening, acknowledging their perspective, and seeking to understand where they're coming from.

What has felt really good in my career? I love building people up. When they sense that you are invested in them, they like you and tend to put their best foot forward. It's gratifying

FIGURE 7.1
Cyndi Mellen, National Cathedral, Washington, DC, 2016.

when someone couldn't do or grasp something and then suddenly you hear them talking to someone else about that very thing and you know they got it. And, in some small part, you helped them get there. That's huge.

I also love cultivating informal relationships, making sure that you're always open to new experiences and inviting to others. You meet the best people that way. When you need something, they're there because you've been in the trenches together on one thing or another.

I'm currently single and I have no children. In DC, it's been hard to find a partner. I was actually out with friends last night talking about this. This one guy, a Marine, said, "Yeah, when I was young and single down here, it was just like picking them off." And then, "Cyndi's making a face." I'm like, "It's just not the same for women." It's really not.

I would like to have a family one day, but I think it will be difficult to balance. In consulting, you're expected to sell your soul. That's how the company makes money, so being available and responsive is huge. I find that I need to set clear boundaries to ensure I'm there for my friends and family.

Sometimes when I'm visiting family, I can take two hours for a work issue and it's not a big deal. But, at some point, you have to draw the line. I have some friends who have missed their high school reunions, who have missed weddings, who have missed a lot of things.

I'm not checking my phone when I'm at my friend's wedding.

Being a motivated professional makes me happy. I want to have a good reputation, but I value my family and friends much more. Sometimes that means you're going to lose out. Someone else will be available when you aren't, and they'll jump in, save the day, and get the kudos. You have to be okay with that. It's the twenty-first century and we can allegedly have it all, but let's acknowledge that there's an opportunity cost. The company is business, and it will always be there in the background drawing you in, so it's important to be intentional with prioritizing the people in your life.

I haven't had a clear line from start to finish in my career. Relationships have driven me forward; they've shaped the job opportunities I've taken and those that I've decided to leave behind. I don't know where I'll be in five to ten years, but I anticipate my next move will be a result of my network and the perspective of the trusted people around me.

Cyndi Mellen is the continuity of operations director at New York City Emergency Management, with a career spanning city, state, and private-sector organizations in Homeland Security and emergency management.

DEEDEE BENNETT GAYLE

My background is in electrical engineering. I went to Georgia Tech. I love computers, I love technology. I've always loved that stuff, and thought I wanted to do something in hardware design. I got a little disaffected with it around the time I was going to graduate, but I ended up working with a design center in Georgia for seven years as their laboratory manager of about $15 million worth of equipment or so, twelve different labs.

I was responsible for teaching people how to use some of the equipment. I was involved with a lot of different research on the periphery. This was just after 9/11. And one of things that people started thinking about was all the communications issues during 9/11. The FCC (Federal Communications Commission) was thinking about using the public safety spectrum band to try to enhance communications among first responders during times of large-scale disasters.

We had analog TVs and then there was this big push for everybody to move to digital TVs, and then everybody didn't know what that was or why we were doing it. But it was part of the FCC's effort to take a portion of the UHF band for this public safety spectrum band and use it to help first responders.[1] That was the idea.

What they wanted was engineers and researchers to look at ways in which we could share that space. A lot of different researchers were working on that in this particular center, and they were showcasing their work and what they were thinking about, because at the time, of course, no one knew how it was going to work.

I kept looking at this, thinking, "There is no way this was going to be operational."

But I was nervous, because I'd only been an engineer. I don't know if you've been in an engineering program, but it was a lot of science and math, and not a lot of essays and reports and things like that. So, I decided to go back and get my master's degree. I did it in public policy to see if I would be able to do the research at that level, so that I could do casework on a large scale. Maybe this was me just being overcautious, but I went back to Georgia Tech and I wanted to do science policy. And when I went there, I met the person who became my mentor, Dr. Helena Mitchell.

She had a background from the FCC. And she was working on the policy side of the public safety spectrum band. And so I was, like, "Oh, this is great. I can learn about it from another angle." And she also was leading, and still is a leader, in looking at the impacts on emergency communications, emergency management, for people with disabilities. She was looking at the public safety spectrum band and trying to figure out how that was going to impact individuals with disabilities in our country.

I worked in her center for some time, and learned a lot about this area that I didn't know anything about. I ended up writing a master's thesis, because I wanted to see if I had the chops to do that. And I learned all about emergency management. I ended up publishing a paper at my master's level, and had to present that paper at a conference to people at FEMA (Federal Emergency Management Agency), and one of the things that my paper was looking at was how inclusive state emergency management plans were when it came to people with disabilities. I was looking at their plans and trying to figure out: How are they including people with disabilities? How are they thinking about them from all the different levels? Not just communications, but all the way to sheltering, and things like that.

This is dated, but at the time, it wasn't really good. One state didn't even want to give me a public response plan. They didn't want to share it with anybody. I guess they were embarrassed, or didn't have it, or whatever. But they didn't want to share it. They didn't have it on their website at the time. And I think that really alarmed FEMA. They were, like, "What? They didn't even show it to you? That's weird, because it's public. It's public information."

When I did that presentation, one person who was in the audience was a leader, another leader, in looking at social vulnerability for disasters. And that was Dr. Brenda Phillips. She listened to my presentation, then sat with me at the round table, and apparently she and

Helena had known each other. And she says, "Hey, have you ever thought about doing a PhD in emergency management? I think with your background and your interests and the things that you've already learned, you'd be really great for this." And I was like, "No, I'm thinking about going to law school."

She was like, "Well, are you sure you don't want to do this?" And then Helena said, "Yeah, we need more people of color, you know. We need more women going into research period, and getting PhDs." She was also saying this field is just so new. It's old but it's new, in terms of the way people have been researching it.

They talked me into thinking about the PhD. I never even took the LSAT, believe it or not. I decided, "Okay, well, let me just take the GRE and see what happens." And then, Brenda gave me her card and said, "I'm at Oklahoma State. You can work with me." And I was like, "I'm in Atlanta. I don't want to go to Oklahoma." She said, "No, we have a really good program."

I ended up going to Oklahoma.

That's the way I ended up getting a PhD in emergency management. I'm definitely one of the first Black women to get that degree. I know I am the first for Oklahoma State. I'm not sure nationwide. But if I'm not one, I'm number two.

I'm named after Lieutenant Colonel Dee Bennett Jr. Most of my family is military. All of my cousins—not all of them, I think there's two, three of us who have not been in the military. But everybody else has either been Air Force or Army or Marines.

After he retired from the military, one of my Marine cousins started doing a lot of work in Las Vegas. He did a lot of active shooter training, and he actually does this thing where he goes around the country and teaches people about active shooter training, so he's in the Homeland Security field. And my aunt used to work for IBM, but after retirement, and after I got my PhD, she started working for FEMA, helping them with case management after disasters and things like that.

It was like all of us, all of the sudden, were connected to Homeland Security and emergency management. But it wasn't like we were being led by any of it. We just all fell into it depending on where we were in our lives.

I guess 9/11 was the seminal disaster that led me into it.

I was in Atlanta at Georgia Tech. I was just about to graduate. I was in a class, and I had—I'm trying to remember if it was a pager or a phone—but it just kept beeping in class the whole time. And you know, professors frown on that, but it just kept going off and I was, like, "Okay, this has to be something." I stepped outside and everybody was crying on the phone, saying, "Look at the news, look at the news."

I went to the student center and saw the second building go down. I was, like, "Oh my gosh." I've been in the World Trade Center. I went to Windows of the World to eat. And I remember seeing helicopters go really close, and you could wave to them from the window.

I got a friend of mine, and met up with my mom, who'd also moved to Georgia, and we discussed what we saw, and talked about it and got out all our tears, and then tried to reach out to family members. But the service wasn't working. Pretty much everybody you called at that time, it was just a busy signal. You couldn't really get through.

My stepmom was a flight attendant for United and was flying at the time and was diverted to Canada. She knew people, personal friends, who were on the flights that went down. I had family members at the Pentagon, I had family members in the air at the time. Everybody was all over. And I'm originally from New York. I was just, like, I can't believe it.

In junior high or high school, I realized that there was not a lot of subjectivity in the math classes or the science classes. I did really well in all my schooling, but I realized it was a lot easier in math and science. You got things right, you got things wrong. I was, like, "Okay, well, at least I can do and show my work, and it does not have to be about who I am. Or about anybody's bias against me."

I felt like I had to prove myself a little bit more when things were subjective, in terms of writing about something. I could write something well, but it may not be an A to some folks. It might be a B-plus. I think that also led me down this path of doing engineering. Even though I scored well for engineering, and got into Georgia Tech, my guidance counselor had cautioned me not to apply, because they had never had a person from my high school get into Georgia Tech, and they just thought, that's probably going to be too hard or too whatever.

I think that also pushed me to do it anyway, because I'm a rebel, in terms of that.

I went into Georgia Tech thinking, "Okay, this is going to be great. Just do the math, do the science." It was super hard. I'm not going to lie. The first classes for me were physics and calculus and Java. And those classes were hard, because I didn't have calculus in high school. I was learning from the start. And it was one of six calculus classes I had to take. So it was just the bottom-level calculus, and I was, like, "Oh my God, there's more of this?"

After getting through the sophomore level, you start to get a little bit more focused into your engineering program. A lot of times, I might be the only woman, or I might be the only minority in the class. And that would come up in different ways. If we had a group project, people didn't pick me to be in their group. And if I was in their group, they didn't really include me on all the discussions. They'd have a lot of side discussions and they'd just give me a task and be, like, "Okay, do what you can on it."

In class, if we were doing something and it happened to be either for women or for minorities or for some underrepresented group, everybody just turned and looked at me, like this is something I'm supposed to be interested in. Little things like that, I just felt like, that's so crazy. I don't really like it.

Some professors didn't really make it hidden that they were not too pleased. They didn't have high expectations from me. And there was also this, "Oh, you just got in because you're Black, or you're a woman." Like, they just had to let somebody in and that was that.

After I got my degree and I started working as a lab manager, one of the things that they asked me to do was to help with fund raising and I would give the lab tours to anybody who was interested in financing or partnering with the development of anything. These would be big-time companies. Usually they sent in the person who's over the money, which would be a manager, who doesn't have an engineering background, and they always paired them with an engineer who knew what the heck was going on.

I also was responsible for going to conferences, sometimes going to meetings outside the United States. So, I'd been to Germany, and Paris, and all these different places, just to highlight the lab, because I knew so much about everybody's work. I'm more of a social butterfly than a lot of the engineers were. I was able to articulate it in a way that would capture the attention of the manager, satisfy the engineer at least on the base level about what we are doing, and entice them enough for them to want to come back and see our lab and then talk and have real detailed conversations with engineers. In some ways, I was the first line of defense for them, in terms of getting money.

One time I was doing one of these tours for a company; I don't remember the name of the company. It was a white guy and he had a white engineer with him. He was clearly the manager. I met them at the front door, did the whole song and dance, and I'm showing them to the labs. And the guy's like, "Well, where is this person?" Like, he's looking for doctor so and so, and I said, "I'm the person who does these tours, because I'm the one who can articulate it for both groups. When you're ready to get to that conversation."

And he says, "Oh, well, they must not think we're important if they've sent you."

I was like, "Wow, okay," so, I just kept giving the tour. I gave the tour, and the engineer guy kept cringing, right? Because he understood everything I was saying. I was doing a fantastic job. And it was clear I knew what I was talking about. But the manager guy kept making these comments. Comments like, "Are you sure this is right?" And he'd look at the engineer, and the guy is like, "It's fine, everything is fine, right?"

After I gave the tour, he says, "Okay, is there anybody else I can talk to who would know a little bit more?" And I realized where this was going. And I said, "Okay, let me find somebody that you might be comfortable with." I found one of my friends. He was a post-doc. And I asked him if he would just talk with this guy for a little bit to put him at ease about what it is that we do. And he was not from the United States, and this is his first introduction. He'd heard about this thing. He gets it. But he didn't understand it. So, he was, like, "This is what you do." I said, "Yeah, but, that's not what this is about. Just talk to this guy," and so he says "Okay, fine."

So he sits there and he's talking to the guy, and the guy starts asking a lot of questions, and he says, "I'm sure DeeDee went over this, right? This is what she does." The guy says, "Well, I just want to know from an engineer." And he says, "She's an engineer. And she went to Tech. I didn't go to any school in Georgia. I'm from Lebanon. I don't know anything about this."

I remember feeling that was a good quintessential story to showcase the issues. You can do the work, you can be doing it well, but if people have a problem, you're not going to pass that barrier. And I just didn't want to deal with that.

And then I ended up in emergency management, and guess what? It's very similar. I keep picking out careers and places where it's a predominantly white male profession. So sometimes I still get comments like that. Very less so now, because it's in the media more. But, yeah, I've had comments. Nothing real—I mean, I can't say not real damaging, because it does hurt you in a way, and it kind of steers you out of a profession. But, once I realized, "Okay, this is also happening here," then I had to have a come-to-Jesus meeting with myself on what I was going to do. Because you can't just keep running from one career to the next, because of racism or discrimination or whatever it is.

And I can never really tell if it's because I'm a woman, or if it's because I'm Black, because people aren't that direct anymore. You don't really know what their issue is.

It's always slight and subtle. Or not so subtle. It's the questioning and it's the type of questions. It's not like they're saying epithets or anything like that to you, or something that you can clearly say, "Oh, yeah, you got a problem." It's more like the lack of confidence in anything you have to say, just because you walked in the door.

Usually, I have students whose family members were either a first responder of some sort, or they have some aspiration to be in emergency management because of a disaster, or

FIGURE 7.2
DeeDee Bennett Gayle, University at Albany, State
University of New York, Albany, New York, 2023.

something they've been through, and they kind of got a taste of it then. Or they're interested in working for one of the three-letter agencies or something like that.

So there are students who are driven to us for some reason, but there are also a lot of students repelled just because of the name "emergency management" and they're like, "I don't know what that is. I just keep hearing about it in a negative light."

But then I start talking to students, and they're listening to "Hey, what do you remember about Hurricane Sandy? Let's talk about the people who were impacted and affected and then let's look at some proportionality."

I think now, because of the pandemic, it gets a lot easier. Because this is global. It's in everybody's face right now. It's in the news over and over again about indigenous populations' issues. Black folks' issues. Hispanic Latino issues and Asian issues. And all these things, layer upon layer, and they're like, "Why is this a problem? What is it that the virus is doing?" And I'm, like, "That's not a virus. That's a social issue."

And so we're trying to talk about that. And then when they hear some of the research I'm doing, I think that attracts students a lot more than saying anything about emergency management. The disasters. The fact that you're coordinating or organizing all this stuff. Like, that kind of just goes past their head, because all they see in a lot of news post-disasters is all the problems that happen.

And then if they're tying it to Homeland Security, they're tying it to all the Homeland Security issues. When you think about border control, border safety, kids at the border. All these issues. Then they're layering that on top of what emergency managers are into. And just feeling like, "I don't want to have anything to do with that." So that's a barrier, that's a problem already.

There's also a problem with attracting the people you probably need to have in the field. Because if it's repelling some folks, it's also attracting some folks. Probably the wrong folks. I have come across that a couple of times, where students are attracted to emergency management for all the wrong reasons. They like the guns, they want to have guns, they think it's a power struggle, a power thing over people. That's not a reason, hopefully, to go into any field, but definitely not a field where you're supposed to be a public servant or a servant of some kind.

I did an introductory course last semester where I just came in and spoke about who I was and what I do. Right now, I'm looking at a lot of the ways technology has either empowered certain individuals or has presented a barrier for certain individuals during the pandemic. And one of the reasons is because, as our response to the pandemic, we said, "Hey, everyone, stay at home unless you're essential. Work from home. Educate from home. Daily activities at home. That's going to stop the spread of the virus."

This is 2022. That was 2020. Nearly two years later. What has happened? Was everybody able to do that successfully? Is that a good response that we want to give individuals? What I'm noticing is things like digital divide issues come up. Outside of digital divide, let's say you have access to broadband wireless, you have the right devices to do your homework or your work, but you live in a 500-square-foot space with three other people. Low-income populations, and racial ethnic minorities who maybe live multi-generationally have different issues and concerns.

We're starting to see layers upon layers of issues. And then women? Not only is this the great resignation. Apparently, it's also a resignation of women in droves during the pandemic. Why? Because you're balancing life and work and home and all the cultural and societal things. You're told that you're supposed to be the person taking care of the kids and the family. And now you have a job. One of those things has to go, because you have to do all of that in the same spaces. It's not tenable for a lot of people, right?

I'm starting to look at things around that. I'm on the Engaged Researchers for the Minority Health Disparities Group that looked at the pandemic here at UAlbany. We're also doing a book that I'm editing. I got a small grant looking at technological innovations during COVID from the Natural Hazards Center. I've been doing that with Professor Jenny Yuan in my department, and she looks at human-computer interactions. You start really getting involved with all these different layers when you start adding in stressful situations like disasters.

We've been finding a lot. And with some of her connections, we've put together another book looking at technological innovations during COVID in the United States and in China. And looking at this specifically from a vulnerable population's perspective. There are things with older adults. There are things with children. There are things with different racial and ethnic minorities. People with disabilities.

I'm working on another grant that's looking at the contact tracing apps and vaccination apps. What the heck are these? Are people using them? Do they even care? Are there any privacy or security concerns with using these things? And then I am recently on a large-scale NSF (National Science Foundation) grant that's out of Rutgers, and we're looking at decision making due to climate change in terms of sea-level rise along the coast in New York City, New Jersey, and Philadelphia. With that project, I want to look at racial and ethnic minority–led households to see if they understand what's happening with climate change, how it's impacting them, whether it's financial or whether there's some cultural concerns involved.

The EPA (Environmental Protection Agency) just recently released a report that said for every two degrees of temperature increase, we will see racial and ethnic minorities in the minority communities impacted the most in terms of mortality, connected to asthma, to finances, to employment. That's just their broad number. I want to know what's happening at the local level. That's probably the only thing I'm doing that doesn't have a technology spin on it. But I'm pretty sure I'll learn something.

Once students hear about my work, they're like, "Oh, wait, that sounds interesting. These things sound very compelling." And they can relate to it. It doesn't sound so esoteric.

Numbers are kind of bleak for women professors in terms of having a family. Not that I realized it when I first went into it. I thought, "Oh, yeah, professors have it great, because they have the time off; they also seem like they can come and go as they please. So, if I have children, that should be okay."

But it's challenging. I only recently got married, and I just had a baby. So, I'm doing everything late, and just happy to be able to do it. My husband is supportive of my job. I have to ask him how much he understands what I have done, what I do, because he's coming from the same standpoint that I had when I was looking at my professors. Like, Well, you guys have all this time. I don't understand. But now, he's on the other side of it, and he says, "You're always working. You're always doing something. Don't you want to stop?"

So, that's one concern. I think the other is, having a baby is different. It is a lot more challenging to schedule my time the way I did before, because the baby is on his schedule, and you have to conform to it. I don't write when the spirit hits me anymore. Now I have to schedule time to figure out how to write. Trying to also be there for his important milestones. And trying to figure out what that looks like going forward.

I have no idea.

I don't know when the next disaster is going to come. I have a one-year-old. He's not even walking. He's still in diapers Trying to walk. I mean, he takes two steps, and then he realizes it, and then plops down, like, "Nope, nope." Can't bring him. My husband works in the hospital. It's a whole different dynamic here on what opportunities to take. One thing I will say, at least having someone supportive makes it a lot easier.

I study disasters. I still don't know when the next disaster is going to hit and what it's going to look like. The pandemic, huge. But I was doing a whole lot of work. I mean, I published an insane amount while being pregnant, and then having a baby, and going through all of that, people are like, "How did you do that?" And I'm like, "It was just the opportunity was here for me to study exactly what I needed to study." And if I didn't do it then, it's not like I can go back to do it later, right?

I don't really want to say no. I don't want to say no to the wrong things. And I don't want to hold anybody else back from reaching their goals either. It's all very interesting, and, honestly, I love what I do, so that's also another issue. That becomes like a gift and a curse.

Even if you're an engineer, and I've worked with some engineers, from all angles of emergency management, and studying disasters, you have to get to know a little bit about community engagement.

I think you don't necessarily have to know that in every other field, but, in this one, you're looking at infrastructure and you're going to have to know how this impacts a community. You're going to have to get involved with a community. You're going to have to have some chops in talking to people, understanding what's happening with them, and caring a little bit more about it. Not doing everything from your office and not being so distant from what's happening.

I think everyone in this field needs to be sensitive to cultural competency, in whatever form that takes as it shifts and evolves over time. That is going be an issue. Someone said once that we are only as resilient as our most vulnerable. And that's the truth, right? But we make our plans for our least vulnerable. We have to start making our plans with the most vulnerable involved. We need to start thinking about our research with the most vulnerable involved.

Our designs, our new technologies. It comes up in so many different areas that, "Hey, you didn't think about these individuals; why not?"

Someone said that in 2020 and 2021 there were several disasters and all of them were in the billion-dollar range of damages. Billion, right? Where do those damages most occur? Along our coasts. Low-income communities. Underserved communities. Areas of blight, that we didn't even look at. Places where we didn't do anything with our infrastructure.

All of this is coming to a head. It's a financial issue at some point. So, even if you're not going to study that directly, it's going to come up. It's going sneak its way in there, so you should probably be aware of it.

DeeDee Bennett Gayle, PhD, is an associate professor in the College of Emergency Preparedness, Homeland Security and Cybersecurity (CEHC) at the University at Albany, State University of New York.

JOHN DELANEY

I love my job because I don't think that there's anybody else in the country who is doing what I'm doing. I think I have a unique job, and—this is going to sound corny, but—I think what we're doing right now is going to lead to substantive change in the fire service, and in emergency response altogether, which is really exciting for me. I love going to work.

I dream about this stuff. I live and breathe it.

My dad was a workers' comp lawyer, my uncle was a lawyer, and I did a couple of summer internships with them, from 1988 to 1992, and I was like, "I hate sitting behind a desk."

So I did some volunteering at James Madison University where I went to college, and I said, "Well, I hated sitting behind a desk. What are some options where I don't have to sit behind a desk?" And I thought, "Well, there is the fire service, and there's law enforcement." I didn't know which one I wanted to do, but I applied after college to become a wildland firefighter.[2] I took the first job that was offered, and I became a wildland firefighter in Worland, Wyoming, for the Bureau of Land Management.

I did wildland firefighting one summer, and I lived on a farm, surrounded by snowcapped mountains, and I realized I liked firefighting, but I realized more I didn't want to sit behind a desk. So I came back and applied to fire and police departments.

I was going through a small town—I think it might have been Herndon Police Department—and I was getting interviewed by a detective. He's like, "Why do you want to be a cop?" And I'm like, "I don't know." He goes, "You have a great shift in the fire service, and everybody likes you." And I'm like, "Okay, I'll go become a firefighter."

So I focused my efforts, and got hired in Prince William County, and stayed there for two years, and then left, and went to Arlington, and I've been with Arlington for . . . I start my twenty-fourth year in July.

I manage a program called our High Threat Response Program. It's a new program that looks at integrating police and fire, and other agencies. It looks at integrating police and fire capabilities to respond to nontraditional, atypical events. And we classify those as active shooter events, fires a weapon, explosives, weapons of mass destruction, and civil disturbance. The basic idea is that these terrible events are happening time and time again, both nationally and internationally, and it requires, in our opinion, an integrated police and fire capability to effectively and efficiently manage those incidents. We see time and time again the red lights and the blue lights show up, but they're messing up. They're not doing it right. You're seeing failures in Parkland, in Orlando.[3]

There was a study where they evaluated the autopsies from the Pulse nightclub. And what it showed is that there were sixteen folks who had survivable injuries who could have been saved had they intervened. The Orlando fire chief had ballistic equipment, medical equipment, that was at the fire training academy. They didn't have unified command established in this place.

The sheriff for Broward County, where the Parkland school shooting occurred, was just relieved from duty. And you know what the governor's excuse was? A failure of leadership. How can that be? I mean, these incidents are occurring in every community. You know, the fact that we're not addressing them, and preparing for them, and training for them, and doing all of this stuff, is just beyond me, and it's extremely frustrating.

Some are very unique circumstances, and I'll give you an example. Go back to 1999 in Columbine, okay?[4] The cops responded to that event the way they were trained and supposed to. What the end result was, was that it wasn't right. It wasn't the correct way of doing business. It was right at the time. Now, theoretically, you're supposed to engage immediately. They want to stop the killing. You stop the killing, then you stop the dying. And it was a game changer for law enforcement.

What we see time and time again, it takes a huge loss of life for the fire service and law enforcement to change the way they do business. Our whole purpose in our program is to not wait for that tragedy to happen. It's to get ahead of the game. But we've seen the fire service has changed over the years. Before the 1960s, the fire service just largely fought fire. But in the '70s and the '80s, emergency medical services were started, and the guys went kicking and screaming. They didn't want to change back then. They didn't want to run medical calls, but they did. And then in the '80s it was HAZMAT. The guys didn't want to do HAZMAT, but it became a necessity. In the '90s, it was technical rescue, in the 2000s it was WMD (weapons of mass destruction). This is the next iteration. And what we're seeing is that departments are going kicking and screaming. There are a lot of departments that aren't prepared like they need to be for these high-threat, new world threats that we're dealing with. And shame on them.

I started a nonprofit called the High Threat Institute. We have international first responders who are involved in this. We've got academic-natured, focused, smart people who are in this group. And the whole idea is to take this group, and answer the tough, challenging gaps, problems, questions related to high-threat incidents. And the reason why we started it is because if we wait for the feds to give us the answers, we're never going to get them.

We had an event recently in California, where a guy went in and shot up the dance club. He used smoke grenades there. We're not going to get an after-action report[5] from that event, we're not going to know the details of that event, until much later. That's problematic because new tactics, new techniques are being utilized, and we don't learn about them until years later, and even then, they're watered down, they're redacted.

And so we started this High Threat Institute, number one, to answer challenging questions and issues; number two, to respond immediately to these events in an informal way, to try to get lessons learned as quickly as possible.

I was a firefighter, and I'm going through recruit school, and one of our old captains managed the Metropolitan Medical Strike Team. He told us about this team. It was a weapons of

FIGURE 7.3
John Delaney, Loudoun, Virginia, 2019.

mass destruction response team that was established, managed by Arlington County. It was a regional group of firefighters, police officers, that was stood up as a result of the Aum Shinrikyo sarin attack in Tokyo back in '95.[6]

When I got out of recruit school and got restationed, one of those WMD response vehicles was at the station I was at. And it just sat there, and sat there, and sat there. And one day I finally started looking through it, and it's a mess. I mean, shit's everywhere, and I'm like, "What the hell is this? This is ridiculous. This is an important capability that we should have." And so I started to clean it up, and fix it up on my own initiative.

It was like a brand new, white-painted Coke truck, with the rollup doors all along each side, and shelves' worth of supplies and materials inside it. No rhyme or reason. I started to take interest in this, and I started to clean it up, and I loved the idea, the concept of it. And I started getting more and more involved, and next thing you know, I was the only one in the department that was doing anything with it, and that became my second job. I would work fifty-six hours a week on that, and on my days off I'd go and I'd work on this team. And I built it back up to be a fairly robust, efficient response asset for the national capital region. We had 150 to 200 doctors, nurses, HAZMAT folks, police, fire, from every jurisdiction around the national capital region, almost every law enforcement agency.

All before 9/11. And I'm not making this up. I was not surprised 9/11 happened. I was surprised it happened in Arlington. I was not surprised that it happened. I'm getting chills right now just thinking about it. And I knew something was coming. And I was not surprised.

You want me to tell the story of this?

I want people to hear this story, because, you know, it was a shitty day.

I was working that day. I had gotten off the night before, and they needed somebody to work what we called a partial, couple hours, on a unit, until somebody got in to work later that day. I was driving a medic unit. I remember we had just picked up this cranky old lady. Nothing was wrong with her. She was just whiny. And we dropped her off at Arlington Hospital.

So, we're in the hospital, and we see what's going on on one of the screens after we drop this lady off. I had left my portable radio inside the medic unit. And we're watching this, and the medic is doing the paperwork, and kind of paying attention, and he has his radio. He comes banging on the door where I was, and was like, "Plane just hit the Pentagon, let's roll." I'm like, "All right, let's do it."

We ran out to the medic unit, and we're listening to the chatter, we're driving down 66 to 110, and we get on 110. And you see this huge column of smoke coming up from the Pentagon. We drive and the whole way down, the medic, who was in my recruit class, he's punching the dashboard. He's like, "These motherfuckers, I'm going to fucking kill these motherfuckers." He's pissed as shit, and I'm just like, "Dude, you've got to chill."

We get into the parking lot, and we see this huge column of smoke, and, obviously, the Pentagon's huge. We stop to try to get our bearings, because we know we want to locate where they're going to bring all the casualties. We know that we're going to have to deal with medically compromised patients. And so we get out, and I look over to the left where the national airport is, and I see this plane banking. And I'm like, "Fuck me." I'm just hoping that this plane's not coming for us, because we know that there's multiple planes out there, and there's nothing we can do. Fortunately, obviously, it wasn't coming for us, but that was our concern right away. Then we come across this guy, a military guy who was in fatigues. The whole half of his head was bleeding, but he was walking and talking, and we're like, "We're not taking you, brother. You can come with us, but we're picking up more people." We know that there are a lot of people who are in trouble.

We lose that guy. He's like, "I'm out of here."

We reposition to a different area of the parking lot. We get our bearings again, and there's a ton of radio traffic, and we're trying to figure out where to go. We reposition again on Washington Boulevard, just north of the impact area at the Pentagon. There's a bunch of folks over there. We pull up, and we take this large, Black lady. I'll never forget this. She had this long dress on, and she was burned from the top of her head to her ankles, all on the back side. Her dress was on, on the front, but not on the back, because it had just been burnt completely off. And we loaded her into the back of the medic unit.

The next thing I know I get this tap on my shoulder, and a Park Police helicopter had just landed behind us. I didn't even know that they were there. They're like, "We're here to take the worst ones." I say, "You gotta take her." We pull her off of the medic unit, and wheel her down, and load her onto the helicopter. I jump into the helicopter. I tried to give her words of encouragement, and I said, "Sing 'You Are My Sunshine.'" To try to have her think something positive. That's our family song. Then they're loading up another military guy in the helicopter. I'll never forget his eyes, because he's sitting up in the stretcher, and I look at him, and his eyes are yellow, like they had been completely burnt. I don't know why they were yellow, but I say, "Hang in there, buddy. We're going to get you out." And I hop out, and they take off.

Find out a day or two later that that lady died. I don't know the status of the gentleman we put on the helicopter.

I run back to the medic unit. Some other medic units were there, and they had already taken some people and moved on. We put another person in, and we got a report of more planes inbound, and so we decided that we're going to load and go. We threw a couple of people in and we raced off to Arlington Hospital, dumped the patients off, got a bunch of supplies, and we went back to the Pentagon. We thought there would be more patients, but there really weren't that many more.

That day ended, I had multiple other responsibilities, and did a lot of different things that day. But I always tell this story, because I think it's important.

My defining memory of the Pentagon is an ankle. That's what I think of. That's my first thought when I think of the Pentagon and 9/11. An ankle.

The Pentagon is five stories, five rings, and five sides, obviously. And it goes E ring, D ring, C ring. In between the C and the B, there's a road that goes all the way around the Pentagon. When the plane hit, it plows through the E, D, and C ring, and burns the living shit out of it. It punches a hole that looks like the nose of the airplane between the C and B rings. It punches all these bricks and stuff against the outside B wall on that road.

We're there the second or third day, I can't remember, doing secondary searches for victims. And in that pile of bricks is an ankle. For whatever reason, that has stuck with me forever. It's amazing the devastation that was done. But there were people literally burned at their desks. There were people who were literally still in their uniforms who had nothing, no signs, no symptoms, but I'm sure it was the concussive effect of the explosion. I still remember a Navy guy, lying on his side with a swipe card still in his hand. Still in uniform, still dressed, no signs and symptoms, just dead. Right there. Crazy. And I think it's important to tell those stories, because the bad guys did some real damage, you know, and we can't forget that.

The PTSD thing, you know—I think everybody's different and deals with it differently, but one of the things that they told us when all this shit happened, was you need to talk about it, so I've never not talked about it.

I don't tell my family everything. I can tell my wife anything; I choose not to, but if I wanted to, I could. What it is for me is motivation to do my job. I don't want this shit to happen again. I'm secure with who I am professionally, academically, and as a person in general. I'm going to call a spade a spade, and fuck you if you don't like it, because I do my due diligence beforehand. I know the issues, and I'm not afraid to voice my concerns as needed or necessary.

I got two tattoos. I got 343 on one arm, and I got my family crest on the other—343 firefighters lost their lives in New York.

Captain II John B. Delaney Jr. is the high threat program manager at Arlington County Fire Department, Arlington, Virginia.

CHAUNCIA WILLIS

I'm from St. Petersburg, Florida, so I'm from these hurricane-prone states anyway. I can remember as a child we had a storm called Hurricane Elena, and I remember just the feeling of exhilaration when they told me we were in the eye of the storm.

I ran and got my bicycle, and my mom's like, "Wait. Where are you going?" And I started running, riding my bicycle down the street so I could see everything happening. I remember looking at the gray sky and the movement of the clouds and breathing in the air, and I could smell the rain, and I just loved it. It was almost like a primal response. And my mom's like, "Come back!"

I went to college at Loyola University in New Orleans. I think it was 1997, before Katrina. There was a huge hurricane that was coming in, and the city flooded at the drop of a dime anyway. When that storm was forecast, I was prepared to leave, as we do in Florida, like with Hurricane Andrew. Everyone leaves if you're in a flood-prone area.

I noticed that people in Louisiana and New Orleans, they didn't leave. A lot of people didn't have transportation. They couldn't leave. I lived next to a cemetery, and I had heard the stories that when it floods there the bodies come out of the graves. And I said, "I'm not staying here to see that."

So after my last class, I asked my friends if they wanted to go with me to Dallas. By the time I was walking back to my apartment, the flooding had already begun. The water was up to my chest, almost up to my neck. I waded through the water for about six blocks to get to my apartment.

I can remember the sheer terror because I was afraid, for some reason, of alligators. I probably should've been afraid of snakes, but I was thinking of alligators for some reason. I kept walking through, and I saw the other kids just doing the same thing. My friend, Lacy, fell through a manhole and had to be rescued. But I finally got to the apartment, and my friends arrived. To leave New Orleans and get to Baton Rouge would normally take about an hour or two, but that day it took six hours.

In 1999 I was a graduate student at Georgia State University's Andrew Young School of Policy Studies. One of my professors had just finished another book on disaster response and recovery. And he was talking about someone being deployed to Hawaii. I said, "Wait a minute, you mean there's a job where you can be deployed to Hawaii?"

He said, "Yeah, are you interested?"

And I said, "Uh-huh."

And he said, "Well, that would be interesting, because no one is ever interested in disaster management, so you'd be my only mentee."

I said, "Great."

And then he said, "Well, I know you're working full-time and going to school full-time, but would you like to intern with the Atlanta Fulton County Emergency Management Agency (AFCEMA)?"

And so I went in as a Black woman, and I already had an undergrad degree, but I was working on my graduate degree in public administration, focusing on policy and things like that. I actually went into an environment where the acting director was another Black woman, and her name was Pansy Ricks.

And she set her sights on making sure I was a part of everything they were doing. They wanted me to become a part of the emergency management field and I wanted the same thing. After about six weeks I asked if I could compete for an open position. They said absolutely, and hired me.

I started doing everything that everyone was kind of reluctant to do, like writing the plans and meeting with all of the different municipalities. I think I even started a new division for the geographic information system division, to incorporate mapping into disaster response.

I was able to actually go in there and innovate. And that was how I got my start.

I expected to put my head down and work. Growing up, I saw my mom work three jobs, and I just figured I'd be working for someone, and that was going to be it. When I started working fulltime for AFCEMA, they really encouraged me.

They said, "We've never seen anyone come in and actually be able to write a plan from scratch. We've never seen anyone who has a heart for the community." Because I was already thinking of programs to help the community. And I was just very passionate about the work.

One thing that stifled me a little bit was that they said, "You really don't belong in this field because you're an academic. You're coming in with all these degrees, you have extra degrees, you don't need all that to be working in emergency management." And then the other emergency managers I met were white males, and they were former police officers or former firemen, or former military personnel.

I just didn't fit in. My boss at the time, she would tell me to go to the meetings and not say anything. She was like, "Sit in the back and stay quiet. We don't need any issues. We don't need any problems. Because you're Atlanta, and we have a lot of counties to deal with, and we are the only one that looks like you. So keep quiet."

In the beginning that's what I did, until I realized that these other guys didn't know emergency management. They weren't studying this stuff. They didn't want to innovate and do new things. They didn't want to have everyone at the table.

We had a flood in Vine City, which is one of the more vulnerable communities in Atlanta, and it was predominantly African American, very, very low income, very poor. And the director came to me and said, "Put together the response, the individual assistance plan, but first before you do that, go meet with the mayor."

I said, "What? Go meet with the mayor? You mean Mayor Shirley Franklin?"

And she said, "Yeah. She's asking for somebody from our office to go there, and we're sending you."

I said, "Oh god."

So I went to meet the mayor and I said, "Hi, I'm Chauncia. I'm . . ."

"Sit down," she said.

I sat down.

And she said "You have two days. Two days to get checks to those people in Vine City."

I said, "That's not how—"

"Two days."

I said, "Yes, ma'am."

I got up and left, and I said to my boss, "They said we have two days."

She said, "Okay, well, go ahead and call the state. Tell them we need money and that Atlanta says give us the money."

With that whole process, I saw the political side. You don't set up a recovery site that quickly.[7] But we did. This was my first opportunity to actually lead a response, and I hadn't even graduated from school yet.

We ended up giving out, I think, $1.7 million in relief checks to renters. The experience was phenomenal for a number of reasons. It was my first time seeing a low-income community in a situation where their concerns were my concerns.

Seeing the people come in . . . I remember in particular a young lady came in and she was very embarrassed. She didn't have her documentation, she just had her license, and she looked like a different person. And I said, to myself, "This is fraud, this isn't her." So, I said to my boss, "I think this lady is using somebody else's ID."

And he looked at the ID and he thought the same thing. He said, "Ma'am, is this you?" And she picked up her head, and she said, "Uh, yeah." And she looked so embarrassed, and immediately I recognized that indeed this is the same woman who's on the license. She's just aged. She's missing teeth, she's probably on drugs. Just the shame she felt at having to verify to me—in my buttoned-up uniform—and, you know, the shame she felt at being a part of this disaster.

It made me ashamed of my behavior for judging her. And so I have never forgotten that. There is a level of shame that is thrust upon the victims, the people who are surviving disasters because they have to ask for help from strangers.

And most people don't acknowledge that, especially when they come into a situation looking down on people because they don't identify with them. I've heard people say, post-Katrina, "If it was me, I wouldn't give them another dime. All they're going to do is buy a forty-ounce with it." Those are the people who are coming in to assist, and they're coming in with so much bias and disregard for the survivors.

That was a monumental change for me, because I've never forgotten her face, and I've never forgotten that I was basically behaving in a very biased way. I didn't see her perspective and what she must be experiencing, going through the worst days of her life.

It changed me. Now I tell people who are coming into the field to make sure you leave your bias at the door, but pick up your compassion, and approach it that way. Because you're going to see things that they don't prepare you to see. You're going to see things, and when you deploy, you're going to see things, you're going to hear things, you're going to smell things. Leave your bias at the door. And just be as useful as possible.

My friends tell me that if anything is going to happen that deals with racism, or bias or gender bias or discrimination, I'm going to be the one to see it and experience it. A lot happened along the way.

I spent maybe three or four years with Atlanta Fulton County Emergency Management. While I was there we had the largest ice storm. I think we went through the Super Bowl. And I was able to see an EOC (Emergency Operations Center) stand up outside of a disaster. We had Y2K, I ran the EOC for that. We had 9/11, I ran the AFCEMA EOC for that.[8] So, before I left, I had gotten to see quite a lot. And that was a city-county emergency management agency—City of Atlanta and Fulton County—so I had two bosses, the county administrator and the mayor. The politics and navigating the politics of that is significant, because the two bosses never agreed and you had to be able to appease both while seeing the value of having both. You need a city EOC, you need a county EOC.

Then I moved on to the state of Georgia, Georgia Emergency Management, and when I arrived they told me, "Hey, we heard of you."

I thought that was the neatest thing, and then I understood why. It was because I was coming from Atlanta, and they always had to make sure that Atlanta was okay. So all of my plans—they read them and they understood Atlanta the best because we had the most resources.

I had never realized how much racism was involved in every aspect of emergency management. At Georgia Emergency Management, I became the statewide planner and trainer, disaster planning.

And I realized that only white people were deploying for these disasters. When you're deployed, you get extra money. You get deployment money. And so I had a problem with that, so I talked to the director—I probably was totally out of line. I asked him if he could start some kind of program like Donuts with the Director. And they started that program, and in that meeting I said I think that it's not fair that everyone doesn't have the opportunity to deploy, because that would be great for everyone to experience.

They said, "Okay, you're right. We usually just use the same people, but we think if you'd like to go . . ."

So the next day they had a hurricane that hit North Carolina, and they said, "You have twelve hours to get there." I was like, "I am so ready, I've been ready." So sure enough I deployed to North Carolina, to Raleigh, and they sent me out into the communities.

And I noticed, again, some issues, because they weren't going into the Black communities. They were literally going to the beach communities, the more affluent communities. And so I said, "Now, this is interesting. They haven't sent anyone to Prince William, they aren't going into Black communities." So I decided that's where I was going to survey damage, to provide community assistance, and to speak to the people. And that's what I did my entire time there.

But when I arrived in New Bern to meet the FEMA team, the guy there from Boston said, "Oh, they sent the colored girl."

I said, "Yeah, I guess they did."

And you're supposed to bond and ride around with that team, and of course, that wasn't going to happen. They didn't want me in their car. Luckily, I had my own rental car. I went to the resource center and got what I needed and went on my own throughout the state of North Carolina to the different cities that I'd been assigned to.

I went to the churches and to the African American communities, and I looked for anyone who was nonwhite, any nonwhite community to be of help and assistance, and provide information and explain the process. And, at some point, a lady flagged me down. She was like, "Can you come into our house?" And you're not really supposed to do that, but I said, "What's the problem?"

And she said, "Well, we're having a problem with my mother." I said, "What's the issue?" And she said, "Come in." So I came into the house and there were a bunch of people there. I said, "Hello, everyone. How are you doing? I'm Chauncia. I'm here on behalf of FEMA. I'm here to help. What's going on?" And they said their mother had been going back to the house every day, but the house was gone, there was only an empty slab, there was no toilet, no nothing. I looked at the mom, she looked to be about maybe seventy or seventy-five. And I knew she was having issues with a psychological break. A fugue. I said, "Okay, well, she probably needs to get some help. You're going to have to get her to the hospital so they can check and see what's going on."

And that was another thing I realized. These traumas keep happening to Black communities but they aren't deploying mental health assets. Those need to be deployable assets. I shouldn't be here trying to handle a psychological break. And the family has already lost their home and all these other things, and now their mother is having a psychological decline, and I don't know if it's permanent or temporary.

It was things like that, all over the state.

After that, I decided I didn't want to work for Georgia anymore. But I was stuck. In that time, a lot of things that happened. I realized that the people being promoted around me had less education, less experience, less training. I didn't like that. But it was in Georgia, so it was one of those things.

Then, one day, I got a call out of the blue from a young lady with a company called EG&G based in Crystal City, Virginia. And she said, "We have heard of you, and we'd like to hire you."

At the time I was getting paid $36,000, and she said, "You tell us how much you want to be paid."

They hired me to become the program manager for EG&G, a division of URS.[9]

I was assigned to the public health contract doing anthrax response with the CDC (Centers for Disease Control and Prevention). And I was assigned to manage public health contracts in Georgia, Massachusetts, South Carolina, Tennessee, and Florida.

That's what I did for a year, and then I went to work for SAIC (Science Applications International Corporation)[10] and I was assigned to the Centers for Disease Control. And then from there I got a call from Tampa, Florida, and they said, "Hey, we hear you're from St. Petersburg. Would you like to come home?" And I was like, "Sure."

At the time I was dealing with husband issues. I can remember sitting in my cubicle crying, and I got a call, and it was the fire chief from Tampa. He said, "We need a decision." I said, "Okay, well, I need time to think about it," because I knew if I left I was going to be getting divorced. I was having so many issues with being away from home. My ex-husband was blaming me for not being there, for being on the road all the time.

Because I was gone. I was gone like three weeks out of every month. I was on the road. I had so many states and they kept piling on states, and giving me more and more responsibilities. And it was overwhelming, but I didn't know how to say no. I didn't say no to too much. As a consequence, though, I did lose my marriage.

My ex-husband was Colombian, and he was a graduate of Tulane University playing football. He wanted a traditional wife. Even after I came home from work, whether I was working in Georgia or somewhere else, there was an expectation that the clothes were clean, the house was clean, the food was cooked, and everything else. In Atlanta it could take three hours to get home, depending on traffic that day, but even if I came home after him, well after him, I still had to go in and cook. And I'll be honest, I didn't have a significant issue with that. Sometimes when you are productive, your reward is that you get more assignments. And as a woman, and as women do, we find it hard to say no sometimes, and so keeping a balance was very hard for me.

I couldn't make it balance. I don't blame myself for the divorce, because there are plenty of women who work and—you know. And you can't blame it on me having a job that had a lot of requirements for travel. I don't attribute it to emergency management. I think it was more just a flaw in his personality. Perhaps I should've considered not chasing the money and just taken a job as something different. I don't know.

As I approached the age of forty, I really wanted to have a child. And I realized that in the city of Tampa, because we didn't have a large department, all of my movements were tracked. Other people could take off for a week and be gone, but if I wanted to take off for a week, I had to get it approved, tell them where I was going, how long I would be there, and how I could be accessed while I was there. I told my boyfriend, who became my fiancé, I said, "You know, I don't know how long I can do this. This is so stressful for me. It's hard for me to do anything."

And I really wanted to have a family. And I was having a difficult time with that. It was hard. I had to sleep near two phones: the mayor didn't have an issue calling me at three in the morning, no one had an issue calling me at three in the morning. And, you know, there was the political side, the work side, the employees you manage, and then there's so much else going on.

I said, "Let's go ahead and build our family, and not worry about it." So we decided to go ahead and get married and have a baby. Well, unfortunately, or fortunately, the baby came before the marriage, and by the time the baby came and all that, we were like, we probably should never get married. But having a mayor who was Irish Catholic, he was personally offended that the emergency manager would dare to have a baby out of wedlock.

I became like a target. I received word that I'd better not take more than six weeks off for maternity leave. In fact, I never took time off before I had the baby. I was getting dressed for work and my water broke. I never had time to rest.

There was an incident where we had a major flood and I was eight and a half months' pregnant. It was on a Saturday. I got a call from the chief of staff. He said, "We've been calling you."

I said, "Yeah, I'm resting."

"Well, we want someone in the EOC."

And I said, "Well, it's raining outside. It's flooding. What are we putting people in the EOC for? Is something happening? Because I get all the alerts, so I would let you know if something was happening."

He said, "We just want to have a presence in the EOC."

They had me, eight and a half months' pregnant, get up and drive through the flood waters to the EOC.

And I told my immediate boss that I knew they wouldn't do this to any other woman.

And he said, "I don't believe they would, Chauncia." And so I sat there in the EOC, while it rained, and I didn't know why. But they wanted me to go in and turn the lights on and sit there.

What else did they do? They said, "Well, Chauncia doesn't need a vehicle." And they took away my vehicle. And the janitor and everyone else kept their vehicles. And the mayor was like, "Why does she need one?"

If anyone knew the level of discrimination and bias that women in emergency management have to go through, especially if you're taking a nontraditional route . . . That's only one or two things. There was so much on a daily basis. That's the reality of it when you're already outside the norm. Me being a Black female and relatively young, I was already outside the norm, not what they expected. But, you know, very pleased with my work. Always very pleased with what I was able to do, and I received awards and all that stuff. But at the same time there was always a desire to control me.

I don't know where it comes from, because I'm not a male, but any guy who was in that position of authority over me wanted to control me. And when I say me, I mean every aspect of my life.

But that's the reality of it.

In Tampa, I finally said I'm going to actually complain. I went to HR and I filed a complaint. I did a discrimination complaint. I said I'm being mistreated, yadda, yadda, yadda. And six weeks later I came in and they said, "Your services at the city are no longer needed." And I said, "You are doing this because I filed that discrimination complaint." And they said, "We don't have to give you a reason."

But I had already gone to an attorney, and she said, "Chauncia, if you file a discrimination complaint they're going to fire you." And I said, "Well, I have an idea about an organization that I'd like to start, just for people who are different. And I want to do that anyway."

And she said, "Well, guess what. The moment that you complain, they are going to fire you. So you need to have your organization ready." And I said, "I have it ready. It's in my heart, and I'm ready to go." And I did, and I went to HR, and HR of course gave me the runaround and said, "Well, you know, perhaps it wasn't him, perhaps it was this, perhaps it was that." And I said, "Okay. Whatever you say." And when I came into work, they said, "After fifteen years all of a sudden we don't have to have a reason to terminate you."

Then, of course, everyone was like, "Go to the EEOC" (US Equal Employment Opportunity Commission). I went to the EEOC, I told them everything, and they were like, "OMG,

you should've come to us long ago because this is extraordinary." And I had the documentation and all that stuff. It was pretty fantastical. But in my heart, I knew everything happened for me to create I-DIEM (Institute for Diversity and Inclusion in Emergency Management). Because, you know, I-DIEM will help someone else.

September 2019. It was my son's birthday when I was fired. And on September 21st I had a meeting with Columbia University in New York to talk about diversity, equity, and inclusion. And I was going to cancel it, but I went. And the rest is history.

Throughout 2020, I worked to build I-DIEM. And then COVID happened. And the day that the COVID transition came to FEMA I was with the FEMA administrator explaining that we need to be focused on underserved communities and communities of color so that this response would be equitable.

Unfortunately, because of the Trump administration and their desire to not focus on racial equity in disaster response, they made the response very political. We saw more African Americans, more Native Americans, more people of color die. And I always say to myself if they had allowed us to participate in the response and allowed us to work with them on diversity, equity, and inclusion, fewer people would have died.

Because of politics we never got an opportunity to do that. But now, with the new administration, President Biden has made equity his priority, and required all federal organizations to do an equity assessment, which is what we do. And the new FEMA administrator, she's already said that diversity, equity, and inclusion are her priorities.

I-DIEM will help increase representation within the field of emergency management. So there are more women in positions of leadership, so there are more women, people of color, LGBTQ, more people with different abilities, more diversity in general. That's what's needed. That's why I went through so much, because there wasn't enough diversity.

And so now I push diversity. I push diversity, and where there is diversity, you can produce equity. And equity is addressing the needs of the community. But if you don't have anyone from all of these diverse communities being represented in the decisions being made, in the funding of these things, then you're producing inequity, and promoting additional harm. We need more inclusion.

I-DIEM is an organization that hopes to increase representation, increase diversity within the field of emergency management, and we're an organization that's focused on producing equity in plans, programs, practice, and policy. We believe in inclusive resilience. We use data. We demonstrate the inequities using data. And we work with different organizations as well as the federal government to create change. Change in policy, change in practice, change in funding decisions. In essence, we are an interrupter. We're trying to interrupt the cycle and create equity through that interruption and infusion of diversity.

I hear my son crying. Are there any more questions?

Chauncia Willis is a disaster equity expert, author, emergency manager, and cofounder of the Institute for Diversity and Inclusion in Emergency Management (I-DIEM).

AFTERWORD

Below, I consider several of the major takeaways of cases in this book: how they illuminate discussions about labor; what they invoke for critical security studies and the encroaching security society; how they underscore growing trends of technology and surveillance; what are the crucial underpinnings of gender, masculinity, racialization, and transnationalism; what are impacts on individuals, family life, and communities; and what they suggest for strategies of resistance.

A FOCUS ON LABOR

The book is organized in four sections that reflect several broad categories of security, including Homeland Security and military jobs; running and working in Border Patrol; intelligence work of the FBI, CIA, and Secret Service; and emergency management. This goes far in exposing the range of jobs that can be captured under the umbrella of security.

Looking at formal job titles alone, one might not be able to appreciate the expansive breadth of these jobs. The Bureau of Labor Statistics, which generates a formal list of occupations catalogued by the US Department of Labor, has identified some job titles that include the word security—things like "security guards" and "information security analysts."[1] But as indicated in the foreword, this book brings to light many more kinds of jobs that fall under the broad category of security. My own research outlines how the work of the security state is being diffused broadly throughout the labor force, even into jobs that seemingly have nothing to do with it—like flight attendants, call center workers, and travel agents.[2]

We might think of security jobs as being fixed or static. However, in reading the interviews, one gets a sense of how much fluidity they can involve. For one thing, workers are quite mobile between departments, divisions, and occupations. Few of these workers stay in the same position their whole career. Rather, they often move from one to another, like from the military to border patrol (in the case of Adrian Aizpuru). Workers also move out of it as easily as they move in: most of the interviewees, in fact, worked in security for certain periods and then transitioned to other related careers in education, teaching, and the private sector.

Second, this book reveals how jobs themselves change over time. One interviewee recounts how a job in "engineering" switches to "cybersecurity" (Terri Merz). I especially enjoyed a passage about how emergency service work has shifted (John Delaney)—from protecting against fires alone, to dealing with medical crises, weapons of mass destruction, chemical attacks, and then guns—fundamentally changing in each period as the conception of the "threat" was revised. This says a lot about historical transformations of what security means, and how it is being integrated into activities where it didn't exist before. We also see the way that jobs become more surveillance-oriented with time. For another interviewee, border patrol through time becomes less about watching over peoples' homes (and picking up their newspapers!), and more like law enforcement and monitoring (Adrian Aizpuru).

Workers in this book are largely anchored in government sector organizations, although there are touchpoints of contact with the private sector (such as the tech industry). This is a significant part of the story of security labor. The US state has had a central role in constructing, shaping, and proliferating these jobs. Its heavy influence creates both opportunity and trouble for workers, though. A more uplifting takeaway of the book is how these jobs have provided stable employment during a time of declining full-time work and increasing labor market precarity. This is especially true for people with working-class roots. In so many instances here, workers use security jobs as a stepping-stone into the middle class and upper-level jobs with pensions (which are so rare these days) (Adrian Aizpuru). That's not a small thing.

However, we also see the failures of the state vis-à-vis workers. The state doesn't always follow through on its promises. An example is in Edward Schwarzschild's opening statement, where we see the Veterans Administration losing his father's records for military service. Perhaps a more esoteric failure of the state is on a moral level. Working for the state in security means submitting to its foreign and domestic policy agendas, including militarism, incarceration, and surveillance—whether or not those agendas conform to your own system of ethics, as discussed more below.

DOING SECURITY

What do security workers do? A Secret Service professional explains how the job can be quite dull much of the time—like "counting the pile on the carpet" (Larry Cunningham). At the same time, it can be quite horrific, as in managing the dead after the 9/11 attacks. While some tasks are overtly militaristic, like "door-kicking" (Dan Izzo) and building a detention center, others involve direct service, like distributing checks after a disaster (DeeDee Bennett Gayle). This variation signals importance differences in whose security is being maintained—the labor of protecting the state versus the public.

Why do workers go into it? It was interesting to me that many people didn't end up in security on purpose. Some workers had only a tenuous connection to the field, and ended up in it out of happenstance and convenience—because a recruiter was on campus, or a counselor suggested it. For others, it seemed inevitable, as they were following a family tree of generations doing security.

Significantly, the book considers not only what security says about labor, but what these stories of labor say about the meaning of security in US society. We learn about many pivotal moments of security in these vignettes. Highly controversial and infamous flashpoints of US domestic and foreign policy are recounted by individuals who were there, who witnessed them, who participated in them—and even by those who were in charge. This includes Abu Ghraib Detention Centers in the Iraq War, the separation of families and detention of immigrant children (i.e., "kids in cages") policy starting in 2018, and the ongoing search and apprehension of crossers at the US-Mexican border. We also learn, at the same time, about incidents of national pride, like the role that the Border Patrol played in desegregating Mississippi schools in the Civil Rights movements of the mid-century (Adrian Aizpuru). These accounts are reminders that the US state is a not a monolith, but in fact works in contradictory ways: sometimes aiding and protecting, and in other cases, targeting and abusing people inside and outside its borders.

Accordingly, how workers feel about such events varies quite a bit, and their accounts represent of a full spectrum of viewpoints. We hear from those who are "for" and "against" security,[3] as well as those at many stages in between. Interviewees are at times staunch nationalists, and other times quite vocal critics. How they make sense of their jobs may reflect narratives of government service, military honor, community protection, saving lives, and disaster response. Alternatively, some are just doing their jobs, honing a particular technical skill, or earning for their families.

INTERSECTIONALITIES: GENDER, RACE, NATION

Security labor is shaped by major systems of inequality. Cases here illustrate the power dynamics of gender, masculinity, racialization, and transnationalism that are endemic to security work.

To start with, we learn a great deal in this book about how security activities are tied to masculinity. Male workers explain how notions of aggression, violence, and bravado are associated with the job for them. A Navy SEAL recounts how some of his colleagues were motivated by "revenge" and "unsettled scores." Some were disgruntled that their assignments did not include enough battle (Dan Izzo). Another casually tosses out phrases with misogynistic and homophobic undertones.

Such narratives and practices are part of what scholars in the field call "military masculinities."[4] These principles of male dominance are embedded in the institutions themselves. Even if not present in formal policy, they may be diffused throughout the work culture and validated informally. This book extends the concept of military masculinities to a new domain of security. It reveals how "security masculinities" might apply in noncombat settings, and how they invoke unique sets of masculine qualities that are associated with technology, surveillance, and similar domains.

An important feature of this concept is its multiplicity. Rather than a single of way of behaving, individuals often display many versions of idealized manhood. These masculinities represent different levels of power in a hierarchy, however, and may come into conflict.

Some security workers, for instance, may adopt "hegemonic" masculinities (as in the examples above), which often carry more authority. Workers representing alternative or "subordinate" masculinities may reject those principles. One of the interviewees explains how he was singled out among the other men in his unit as a non-athlete and avid reader of Jane Austen, while surrounded by captains of the football team (James Vizzard). Another explains how he didn't agree with the formidable infrastructures of security that he was building overseas. Not all men enact and experience the privileges of masculinity in the same way. Moreover, there may be harmful consequences for landing on the wrong side of hegemonic masculinity.

We learn more about these masculinities through the perspectives of female interviewees. Working in hypermasculine environments can be very difficult for women in security. It is true that some patterns of discrimination can be subtle. Women may face lowered expectations and a general lack of confidence in their skills (DeeDee Bennett Gayle). However at other times, the patterns are more overt. Some report harassment by male colleagues (Diana Bolsinger). Feminist scholars remind us that this can extend to the home as well. Security personnel may carry this harassment off the job site. Male police officers, for instance, exhibit alarming rates of violence against intimate partners in their households—higher rates than civilians.[5] And because of the extensive training they receive from law enforcement institutions, the impact can be much more dangerous.

We also learn much about women's agency in this climate of masculinity. This book presents many cases of women navigating these kinds of conditions and excelling despite them. Several end up supervising those male-dominated departments and teams. Having women mentors is reported to be instrumental for such promotions (DeeDee Bennett Gayle). In more than one case, women's careers in security extend for two generations, as mothers and aunts pass the torch to daughters and nieces (Carla Provost, DeeDee Bennett Gayle). Such career success for women in security has been a curiosity in my own research—how women have been able to rise through the ranks of security professions in ways that they haven't been able to do as well in tech occupations.[6]

Of course, there are variations within these security jobs, and some fields are reported to be better for women than others. For instance, in one women's view, the CIA is more conducive to women than the state department (Diana Bolsinger). And we hear about the drawbacks of women's career mobility: feelings of guilt about rising up while so many women are stuck at bottom, and feelings of regret about sacrificing marriage for career (Diana Bolsinger).

It's not a coincidence that we learn of the underside of security mostly from workers of color. Scholars have been documenting how security systems are often targeted at marginalized racial-ethnic communities. In this book, we hear about this first-hand. An Arab Christian was detained and interrogated by FBI when in transit at the Detroit airport (Hasan Elahi). A Latinx worker describes how his mother faced raids by the border patrol at her workplace (Adrian Aizpuru). A Muslim experiences Islamophobia and psychological effects of the security state (Fatema Ahmad). These individuals uncover the racialization and xenophobia of security. They provide insight into how the weight and energy of monitoring itself is applied differentially by the US state.[7]

This signals the intersectional implications of security labor. Intersectionality refers to the way systems like gender, race, class, sexuality, and nation operate together—not merely as add-ons—to make qualitatively more severe experiences for women of color.[8] Black women, as recipients of compounded race and gender hierarchies, are in a unique position to see and report on discrimination throughout the entirety of their security careers (Chauncia Willis).

Intersectionality as a concept also emphasizes the contradictions generated as these hierarchies are crossed. In other words, lower positions on one hierarchy (like gender, and being female), do not preclude enacting privilege from higher status on other hierarchies (such as being white, and thus participating in the oppression of racial-ethnic minorities). Indeed, scholars have reflected on the role that white women have played in security regimes for the US state.[9] We see examples of that in this book too, as white women participate in "writing about the risks of these foreign Arab fighters, and tracking them" (Diana Bolsinger).

I was inspired by many stories, however, of Black women who navigate these roadblocks to craft successful careers in security. Some describe seeing fields of math and science as a refuge from the racism they face in other settings (DeeDee Bennett Gayle). We also see many "firsts" here—like one of the first Black women PhDs in emergency management. These are examples of Black excellence in security.

TECHNOLOGIES OF SURVEILLANCE

Datafication, technical systems, and surveillance are all having greater roles in security work. This book provides rich material on that process, as well as the historical transformations motivating them. In one case, we see how computers are first introduced in a defense-related workplace. One worker calls her job "computer whisperer," even though there was no formal job title related to computers at that time. She describes how these shifting technologies lead to odd combinations of tasks—like computer troubleshooting, while bartering for logistics parts (Terri Merz). We find out that, in some instances, datafication is not even prompted from supervisors above, but by the workers themselves. Interviewees report pushing their organizations to develop more technology *for workers* (Carla Provost).

Surveillance tasks are endemic to many of the jobs in this book. An interviewee explains how his job was the "desert tracking of aliens" (Adrian Aizpuru). In a pre-digital throwback, this task did not involve high-tech devices, though, but rather the use of animals. His canine unit deploys dogs for finding and chasing a wide range of targets, from people to drugs to bombs.

On this point about surveillance, Goodwin's construction artwork is so revealing. His installations uncover the complexity of who gets monitored and who doesn't. Many of the locations for their interviews, or places where they were denied entry because of clearance restrictions, are not visible on Google Street View. These include a pub in Arlington, Virginia, and the Ritz-Carlton in Pentagon City. Goodwin recreated them as tabletop constructions so they can be visible to us, while simultaneously underscoring their hiddenness on platform search tools like Google.

Some of the contributors here actually generate their own surveillance tools, which truly shocked me. Before there were apps, one interviewee created a website for self-tracking, and then a code on his phone conveying his locations with a photo and a map. As a penultimate representation of self-monitoring, this apparatus was meant to deter suspicion from an FBI officer who had been tracking him (Hasan Elahi). This shows how self-surveillance *enacted by citizens* may be used as a survival strategy—or as generation of nuisance data and thus resistance—against surveillance *enacted by agents of the state*.

IMPACTS: SECRECY, FAMILY DYSFUNCTION, NECROPOLITICS, RESISTANCE

Among the memorable takeaways of this book are the impacts of security work on individuals, families, and communities. The personal costs to workers, whether physical, ethical, or both, are high. Families pay the price too. One interviewee noted that his entire deployment team ended up divorced.

Another unique cost of security work for the job-holders and their families is secrecy. Having to withhold events of one's workday vis-à-vis one's family is a big ask, and something that most of us don't have to do on a routine basis. Several of the interviewees talk about the strains this puts on family relationships—in the form of tensions and barriers vis-à-vis intimate partners, spouses, and children. Families are often the buffers of multiple strains in security labor.

Impacts are described for communities as well, in terms of both spatial arrangements and social relations. We see a culture of securitization in the daily lives of these workers. This happens directly in their jobs and in their nonworking lives as well. The places where these workers live are profoundly affected by location of state administration offices and the activities of security industries.

Workers in this book paint a picture of how their residential and metropolitan neighborhoods are full of security personnel, architectures, and markers. One interviewee reports delivering newspapers to border patrol agents as a kid, and regularly encountering agents in the act of migrant capture when traveling in local spaces: "You'd go downtown and they would always be out there driving around, chasing people" (Adrian Aizpuru). Astounding to me is that more than one worker in the book reports living nearby (and even next-door) to people they suspect of being spies. A male interviewee passes this off nonchalantly as a descriptive feature of the area (Hasan Elahi), while a female raises concerns about her safety and the fact that they would be able to follow her home (Fatema Ahmad). In addition to this, spies are suspected to be infiltrating their everyday spaces—like their mosques.

We find this in more than one region of the country. Some of the workers, like those in El Paso, Texas, describe proliferating checkpoints in border regions and how they become barriers in the daily lives of residents (Adrian Aizpuru). This is something that authors of a special issue of *Information and Culture* on "Digitizing Borders, Cities, and Landscapes" outline in detail.[10] Surveillance regimes reshape and extend the space of the border inward. Rather than limited to the physical line between two nations, checkpoints now pervade *internal* spaces of cities and thus block major arteries going in and out.

Goodwin's photography of the landscape at the border reinforces the social implications of these security infrastructures. Images of the border wall in Tijuana give us a visual sense of how it divides spaces and portrays contradictions. The Mexico side is a lively, thriving social space; the US side is barren.

Interviewees living in the Washington, DC, region point out how geographies create class distinctions in security worlds. One worker remarks that only wealthy security professionals can afford to live close to the centers of power, where the military headquarters are located. The working class of security, in contrast, lives further out—like in Appalachia. Where you live has a bearing on what types of security jobs you have access to. When a local prison is the major employer in your community, it becomes a feeder into security guard positions for the young generation (Fatema Ahmad).

For me, the most upsetting impact of security as an industry and as a profession is for communities of color. We see how security infrastructures are expressions of power with "the capacity to decide the fate of who lives and who dies," as reflective of the scholarly term "necropolitics."[11] This is made all too apparent in Goodwin's images of cemeteries in border towns. In this location, where one interviewee requested to be photographed, we see the back area where there are gravestones of unidentified migrants. Death is a feature of border politics, and what Sayak Valencia refers to as "gore capitalism."[12]

Inspiring, however, are the stories of rising above the moral and ethical problems of security, and how workers turn them around. One worker notices how emergency management funds are deployed to white, affluent communities first. In turn, she takes the initiative to seek out low-income communities and people of color, to hear and address their particular problems (Chauncia Willis). Other workers are advocating for tech rights of marginalized communities. They seek to lessen the digital divide and improve access to broadband for people of color (DeeDee Bennett Gayle). These workers are also rethinking security in terms of resilience and from the point of view of the most vulnerable.

Some security workers even become critics and professional activists, and leaders of nonprofit advocacy organizations. This is another important "impact" of security—turning agents of security into agents of change. More than one interviewee has left their job to become a voice in opposition to wider systems of global security.

CONCLUSION

Eyal Press, in his interview, summarizes well the broader aims of this book and the novel way it helps us reflect on the world: "security is a great lens through which to look at where we are as a society and to look at our failures and how broken things are."

Understandings of those failures—and how to redress them—are sprinkled throughout this text, and I urge readers to look for them carefully. Francisco Cantú, for instance, frames security work in a clever metaphor—as an exercise in putting out a fire that we created in the first place:

> to feel proud of rescue work as a Border Patrol agent is like being a firefighter and feeling proud about putting out a blaze, but it turns out that blaze was actually started by the fire chief. That's kind of what it comes down to. These people are there to avoid your presence. They were out there to avoid my presence. So even when I show up and I'm bandaging somebody's blisters or giving them an IV, bringing them back from a dehydrated state, it's like, in a very real way, I—or any agent out there—is the reason that that person ended up in that state in the first place.

Another interviewee suggests that our goal of safety might be achieved in a more efficient and equitable way. Echoing Harvey Molotch's conceptual framework,[13] Fatema Ahmad talks about the illusion of security created by these jobs and institutions: "all of this is creating the illusion of safety at the expense of certain people. None of us are actually safe because of these wars. Violence begets violence, and this country puts out so much violence. . . . When we talk about national security, people often really think that some of these things are creating safety and security. And I'm like, 'They're not. That's not creating safety for anybody.'"

What this book does, perhaps best of all, is bring people back to the labor of security. When we were in the process of editing, I suggested to the authors that we place job titles next to interviewees' names at the front of each chapter. As a labor scholar, it didn't even occur to me to separate them from each other. But the authors resisted this, and made the case for humanizing these individuals. Thank you Danny and Ed for pointing this out to us. Workers are not their jobs, they are their own people. Maybe that's the first step to thinking critically about security labor as a system while we also focus crucial attention on the individuals carrying it out.

Winifred R. Poster

ACKNOWLEDGMENTS

This book has been a deeply collaborative effort from the very beginning and we are indebted to many, many people for their help, inspiration, and trust.

We first met Rick Mathews at the College of Emergency Preparedness, Homeland Security and Cybersecurity (CEHC) at the University at Albany, State University of New York. He agreed to take a meeting with us and he believed in this project from the moment we began describing it to him. Nothing was more essential to our progress than his decision to help us move forward. In addition, the unwavering support and encouragement we've received throughout this long process from Robert Griffin, dean of CEHC, has been crucial in ways too numerous to mention.

Several other UAlbany colleagues offered vital advice and guidance. Thomas Bass generously wrote and talked about our work-in-progress with clarity and passion, indelibly shaping how we moved forward. Stephen Coulthart expanded our vision of this project, connecting us with individuals who made this book far richer and more complex.

UAlbany—and the College of Arts and Sciences in particular—has provided us both with a nourishing, vibrant, scholarly and creative community for over two decades. We've received critical financial support over the years from UAlbany's Faculty Research Awards Program. And we've been blessed with remarkable colleagues in our home departments (English and Art/Art History).

Meighan Gale carefully read version after version of our book proposal and patiently taught us how to strengthen it. Without her, we might have never reached this point.

The MIT Press has been an absolutely ideal home, and we are incredibly fortunate that Katie Helke agreed to take on this project. We are indebted to Winifred Poster for including our book in the Labor and Technology series and for contributing both the foreword and afterword. Both Katie's and Winnie's insights vastly improved the book. Indeed, the two of them—along with the anonymous peer reviewers, and the entire MIT Press team—made every single page of this book better. The mistakes that remain are all our own.

It's simply not possible to fully express our gratitude to the people who have taken the time to share the stories of their lives with us, but we still want to try. Again and again, we were overwhelmed by the honesty and grace we encountered throughout the interview process. Clearly, this book wouldn't exist without the openness and generosity of everyone we interviewed. It has been an honor and a privilege to sit with, talk with, and learn from so many hard-working, insightful, dedicated men and women.

Finally, our most fundamental sense of security—and love—comes from our families. We are forever grateful to them. To our parents, our siblings, our wives, and children—thank you for making everything possible.

NOTES

BEGINNINGS

1. James Agee and Walker Evans, *Let Us Now Praise Famous Men* (Boston: Houghton Mifflin, 1941), x. A few paragraphs from this introduction originally appeared in different form in Edward Schwarzschild, "Anxiety at the Gates," *Hazlitt*, June 15, 2017, https://hazlitt.net/longreads /anxiety-gates.
2. "Governor Cuomo Applauds First Academic Year of CEHC," University at Albany, https://www .albany.edu/news/69797.php.
3. Studs Terkel, *Working: People Talk about What They Do All Day and How They Feel about What They Do* (New York: Pantheon/Random House, 1974), xx–xxi.
4. "About DHS," US Department of Homeland Security, https://www.dhs.gov/about-dhs.
5. Patrick Radden Keefe, "The Surreal Case of a C.I.A. Hacker's Revenge," *New Yorker*, June 6, 2022, https://www.newyorker.com/magazine /2022/06/13/the-surreal-case-of-a-cia-hackers -revenge.
6. Sarah Schulman. *Conflict Is Not Abuse* (Vancouver: Arsenal Pulp Press, 2016), 280.
7. "The 1973 Fire, National Personnel Records Center," US National Archives, https://www .archives.gov/personnel-records-center/fire-1973.

LEARNING TO SEE SECURITY

1. *CIA Museum*, Danny Goodwin, https://www .dannygoodwin.com/central-intelligence-museum.
2. *Aerial Countersurveillance*, Danny Goodwin, https://www.dannygoodwin.com/aas-aerial-auto -surveillance.
3. *Decoys, Duds, and Dummies*, Danny Goodwin, https://www.dannygoodwin.com/decoys.
4. *Inert*, Danny Goodwin, https://www.danny goodwin.com/inert.
5. Yasha Levine, "Google's Earth: How the Tech Giant Is Helping the State Spy on Us," *The Guardian*, December 20, 2018, https://www .theguardian.com/news/2018/dec/20/googles -earth-how-the-tech-giant-is-helping-the-state -spy-on-us.

CHAPTER 1

1. The Navy's Sea, Air, and Land Forces—commonly known as SEALs—are expertly trained to deliver highly specialized, intensely challenging warfare capabilities that are beyond the means of standard military forces. SEALs are an elite part of the US Special Operations Command (SOCOM), which also includes Air Force, Army, Marine, and Joint Special Operations forces. "US Naval Special Warfare Command," United States Navy, https://www.nsw.navy.mil/.
2. Basic Underwater Demolition/SEALS—the training required to become a SEAL. "BUD/S," Navy Seals, https://navyseals.com/buds/.
3. The Armed Services Vocational Aptitude Battery (ASVAB) is an aptitude test that measures developed abilities and helps predict future academic and occupational success. "ASVAB Enlistment Testing Program," Armed Services Vocational Aptitude Battery, https://www .officialasvab.com/.
4. In 2006, the number of American military deaths in Iraq since the beginning of the March 2003 invasion reached 3,000. Lizette Alvarez and Andrew Lehren, "3,000 Deaths in Iraq, Countless Tears at Home," *New York Times*, January 1, 2007, https://www.nytimes.com/2007/01/01/us/01deaths .html See also "Interactive Timeline of the Iraq War," *New York Times*, https://archive.nytimes .com/www.nytimes.com/interactive/2010/08/31 /world/middleeast/20100831-Iraq-Timeline .html#/#time111_3279.
5. Nonoperational sea-duty billets are naval assignments that include maintenance duties and training/pre-commissioning duties. "Permanent Change of Station Fact Sheet," US Department of Defense, https://media.defense.gov/2020/Jun /17/2002317607/-1/-1/1/PCS%20RESTART%20 FACT%20SHEET.PDF.
6. The First Intifada was a sustained series of Palestinian protests and violent riots in the West Bank, Gaza Strip, and within Israel, aimed at ending Israel's occupation of those territories and creating an independent Palestinian state. "The First Intifada," Britannica, https://www .britannica.com/topic/intifada.

7. Eyal Press, *Beautiful Souls: Saying No, Breaking Ranks, and Heeding the Voice of Conscience in Dark Times* (New York: Farrar, Straus and Giroux, 2012).

8. Eyal Press, *Dirty Work: Essential Jobs and the Hidden Toll of Inequality in America* (New York: Farrar, Strauss and Giroux, 2021).

9. Everett C. Hughes, "Good People and Dirty Work," *Social Problems* 10, no. 1 (1962): 3–11, https://doi.org/10.2307/799402. Press is referring to this passage: "The minor prison guard, in boastful justification of some of his more questionable practices says, in effect: 'If those reformers and those big shots upstairs had to live with these birds as I do, they would soon change their fool notions about running a prison'" (8).

10. Eyal Press, *Absolute Convictions: My Father, a City, and the Conflict That Divided America* (New York: Henry Holt and Co., 2006).

11. Force Reconnaissance (FORECON) is one of the United States Marine Corps' special operations capable (SOC) forces that supplies military intelligence to the command element of the Marine Air-Ground Task Force (MAGTF). Wikipedia, https://en.wikipedia.org/wiki/United _States_Marine_Corps_Force_Reconnaissance.

12. On October 23, 1983, 220 Marines, 18 US Navy sailors, and 3 US Army soldiers lost their lives in the Marine Barracks at the Beirut Airport. "Marine Barracks Bombing at Beirut, Lebanon," US Marine Corps, https://www.marines.mil /News/Marines-TV/videoid/634642/dvpTag/Beirut/.

13. The infantry reconnaissance platoon is a specialty platoon comprised of infantry soldiers. Unlike traditional infantry platoons whose primary mission is to kill the enemy, the reconnaissance platoon's primary mission is to provide the battalion commander information about the enemy. "Infantry Reconnaissance Platoon," Global Security, https://www.globalsecurity.org /military/library/policy/army/fm/7-92/fm792_2.htm.

14. *Field stripping* is firearms terminology for the act of disassembling a firearm to the greatest possible extent without the use of tools.

15. The Boeing Vertol CH-46 Sea Knight is a tandem-rotor transport helicopter produced between 1960 and 2014. "CH-46 Sea Knight Historical Snapshot," Boeing, https://www.boeing.com /history/products/c-46-sea-knight.page.

16. The Lockheed C-130 Hercules is a four-engine military transport aircraft designed and built by Lockheed Martin. "C-130J Super Hercules," Lockheed Martin, https://www.lockheedmartin .com/en-us/products/c130.html.

17. A litter is a foldable canvas stretcher used for emergency evacuations via helicopter.

18. A bomb appraisal officer (BAO) is an employee of the Transportation Security Administration (TSA) skilled in the identification and safe disposal of explosive devices. TSA/DHS now refers to this position as transportation security specialist—explosives (TSS-E). AviationPros, https://www.aviationpros.com/home/news /10390606/tsa-to-add-bomb-experts-at-100-airports.

19. Archived site from the Federation of American Scientists, https://irp.fas.org/nsa/rainbow.htm.

20. The Beechcraft C-12 Huron is the military designation for a series of twin-engine turboprop aircraft based on the Beechcraft Super King Air and Beechcraft 1900. Wikipedia, https://en .wikipedia.org/wiki/Beechcraft_C-12_Huron.

21. The Lockheed C-141 Starlifter is a retired military strategic airlifter that served with the Military Air Transport Service (MATS), its successor organization the Military Airlift Command (MAC), and finally the Air Mobility Command (AMC) of the US Air Force. Wikipedia, https:// en.wikipedia.org/wiki/Lockheed_C-141_Starlifter.

22. Information assurance is defined as measures "that protect and defend information and information systems by ensuring their availability, integrity, authentication, confidentiality, and non-repudiation. These measures include providing for restoration of information systems by incorporating protection, detection, and reaction capabilities." "Information Assurance," Computer Security Resource Center, National Institute of Standards and Technology, US Department of Commerce, https://csrc.nist.gov /glossary/term/information_assurance.

23. A zero-day is a computer-software vulnerability previously unknown to those who should be interested in its mitigation, like the vendor of the target software. Until the vulnerability is mitigated, hackers can exploit it to adversely affect programs, data, additional computers, or a network. "Zero-Day Computing," Wikipedia, https://en.wikipedia.org/wiki/Zero-day _(computing).

24. Deep reinforcement learning (deep RL) is a subfield of machine learning that combines reinforcement learning (RL) and deep learning. RL considers the problem of a computational agent learning to make decisions by trial and error. Deep RL incorporates deep learning into the solution, allowing agents to make decisions from unstructured input data without manual engineering of the state space. "Deep Reinforcement Learning," Wikipedia, https:// en.wikipedia.org/wiki/Deep_reinforcement _learning.

25. The S-3, or operations officer, is in charge of operational planning and training at the battalion and brigade level.

26. A legislative liaison is an individual appointed by a department to communicate to legislators and others the positions of the department.
27. A forward operating base (FOB) is any secured forward operational-level military position, commonly a military base, that is used to support strategic goals and tactical objectives. Wikipedia, https://en.wikipedia.org/wiki/Forward_operating_base.
28. Combat Outpost (COP) Keating was a small American military outpost in Afghanistan. Eight members of Team Keating died following an assault by 300 Taliban fighters on October 3, 2009. "Fallen Heroes," US Army, https://www.army.mil/medalofhonor/carter/fallenheroes.html.
29. An explosively formed penetrator (EFP) is a device that forms "slugs" at detonation that maintain their shape over distances of over 100 yards or more, traveling at speeds of nearly a mile per second. John Ismay, "The Most Lethal Weapon Americans Faced in Iraq," *New York Times*, October 18, 2013, https://archive.nytimes.com/atwar.blogs.nytimes.com/2013/10/18/the-most-lethal-weapon-americans-faced-in-iraq/.
30. See *Henry V*, Act 4, scene 1, lines 182–183: "Every subject's duty is the King's, but every subject's soul is his own."
31. Values Education Teams deliver the character development curriculum at the military academy at West Point. "Character Program," United States Military Academy at West Point, https://www.westpoint.edu/character-program.
32. The seven Army values are loyalty, duty, respect, selfless service, honor, integrity, and personal courage.
33. A division is a large military unit or formation, usually consisting of between 10,000 and 16,000 soldiers. A battalion commander rank is typically that of lieutenant colonel (O-5), who is responsible for a unit of 300 to 1,000 personnel. The duties of a commander depend on the officer's pay grade and area of expertise. "US Army Ranks," US Army, https://www.army.mil/ranks/.

CHAPTER 2

1. Grace Ashford, "The School Shooting Is Fake. Can It Prepare an Officer for a Real One?," *New York Times*, September 24, 2022, https://www.nytimes.com/2022/09/24/nyregion/gunman-shooter-training-schools.html.

CHAPTER 3

1. Flight line refers to the area of an airfield, specifically the parking area and the maintenance hangars, where aircraft are onloaded, offloaded, and serviced. "Flight Line," *American Heritage Dictionary*, https://ahdictionary.com/word/search.html?q=flight+line.
2. Customs and Border Patrol (CBP) officers (as opposed to agents) at GS-12 grade are also referred to as "journeymen."
3. The CBP Canine program is headquartered in El Paso, Texas. The primary goal of the CBP Canine Program is terrorist detection and apprehension. The Program's secondary goal is detection and seizure of controlled substances and other contraband, often used to finance terrorist and/or criminal drug trafficking organizations. Additionally, CBP canine teams assist local law enforcement agencies when requested. "Canine Program," US Customs and Border Protection, https://www.cbp.gov/border-security/canine-program.
4. The General Schedule (GS) payscale is the federal government payscale used to determine the salaries of over 1.5 million federal civilian employees. An employee's base pay depends on two factors—the GS pay grade of their job, and the pay grade step (or line) they have achieved (depending on seniority or performance). The GS pay scale ranges from GS-1 to GS-15. "Policy, Data, Oversight," US Office of Personnel Management, https://www.opm.gov/policy-data-oversight/pay-leave/pay-systems/general-schedule/.
5. CBP canine units rely on their dog's signals, or alerts, that they've discovered something of interest. Narcotics units will often utilize aggressive alerts, such as scratching or pawing at the spot where they've found something of interest. In the case of explosive ordnance detection, aggressive alerts can be catastrophic. Handlers train their dogs for this type of work to relay passive alerts, such as merely sitting beside the luggage or cargo to indicate they've discovered something. "Canine Program," US Customs and Border Patrol, https://www.cbp.gov/border-security/canine-program.
6. The higher the grade level, the higher the pay. The General Schedule (GS) pay schedule is the most common pay schedule, but there are others, including the wage scale and special rates. "What Is a Series or Grade?," USA Jobs Help Center, https://www.usajobs.gov.
7. Francisco Cantú, *The Line Becomes a River: Dispatches from the Border* (New York: Riverhead Books/Penguin, 2018).

8. Francisco Cantú, "7-Year-Old Jakelin Caal Maquin Died at the Border. What Happened to Her Is Not an Aberration," *Los Angeles Times*, December 18, 2018, https://www.latimes.com/opinion/op-ed /la-oe-cantu-border-patrol-cruelty-20181218 -story.html.

9. Following the introduction of the US Border Patrol's Prevention through Deterrence (PTD) program of the 1990s, which deliberately funnels migrants through the most treacherous stretches of the Sonoran Desert and other entry corridors by simultaneously increasing the number of agents at fortified official checkpoints, the Border Patrol has been the fastest-growing federal enforcement agency in the United States. Since 9/11, the Border Patrol has seen a nine-fold increase in personnel. Jason De Leon, *The Land of Open Graves: Living and Dying on the Migrant Trail* (Oakland: University of California Press, 2015), 317.

10. Sensitive compartmented information (SCI) is information about certain intelligence sources and methods and can include information pertaining to sensitive collection systems, analytical processing, and targeting, or which is derived from it. "Sensitive Compartmented Information (SCI) Program," US Department of Commerce, https://www.commerce.gov/osy/programs /information-security/sensitive-compartmented -information-sci-program.

11. Temporary duty travel (TDY) refers to a US Armed Forces service member's—or civilian Department of Defense employee's—travel or another assignment at a location other than the traveler's permanent duty station as authorized by the Joint Travel Regulations. "The Joint Travel Regulations (JTR)," US Department of Defense, https://www.defensetravel.dod.mil/Docs/perdiem /JTR.pdf.

CHAPTER 5

1. "Since the mid 1980s, the black and gray arms markets have emerged as major forces in the arms trade. Though they are much smaller than the orthodox trade, covert transfers are of great importance, providing the weapons most likely to actually be used in conflict. The totally illegal black market arises in reaction to embargoes. It is antipolicy, the mirror image of official intentions. The state-sponsored gray market, although it receives less attention, is much larger and more destabilizing." Aaron Karp, "The Rise of Black and Gray Markets," *Annals of the American Academy of Political and Social Science* 535 (1994): 175–189, 175.

2. James E. Steiner, *Homeland Security Intelligence* (Washington, DC: CQ Press, 2014).

3. The Directorate of Operations (DO) handles the collection of intelligence acquired by human sources (human intelligence or HUMINT). When necessary, and under unique circumstances, they conduct covert action as directed by the president. "Organization," CIA, https://www .cia.gov/about/organization/#directorate-of -operations.

4. Senior intelligence service (SIS) is one of a set of ranks on the civil service scale. Normal ranks go from GS-1 through GS-15, for most of the federal government. Above GS-15 is senior executive service (SES), which has different rules (e.g., for promotion) and much higher salaries. In the intelligence community, the SIS is the counterpart, with a few details tailored to the different demands of the intelligence community. US Office of Personnel Management, https:// www.opm.gov/policy-data-oversight/senior -executive-service/scientific-senior-level-positions/.

5. In 1999, Ahmed Ressam attempted to bomb Los Angeles International Airport during millennium celebrations. Ressam had attended al Qaeda training camps in Afghanistan and was part of a terrorist cell in Canada. "History," FBI, https:// www.fbi.gov/history/famous-cases/millennium -plot-ahmed-ressam.

6. J. Cofer Black served as directorate of operations at the Central Intelligence Agency. Prior to joining the State Department, Ambassador Black was the director of the CIA Counterterrorist Center. In this capacity he served as the CIA Director's special assistant for counterterrorism as well as the national intelligence officer for counterterrorism. Black was sworn in on December 3, 2002, as the State Department coordinator for counterterrorism with the rank of ambassador at large. "Archive," US Department of State, https://2001-2009.state.gov/outofdate /bios/b/15367.htm.

7. Lynndie Rana England is a former US Army Reserve soldier who was prosecuted for mistreating detainees during the Abu Ghraib torture and prisoner abuse that occurred at the Abu Ghraib prison in Baghdad during the Iraq War. "Lynndie England," Wikipedia, https:// en.wikipedia.org/wiki/Lynndie_England.

8. *(T)error* is a documentary directed by Lyric R. Cabral and David Felix Sutcliffe: https://www .pbs.org/independentlens/documentaries /terror/; *Watched* is a documentary directed by Katie Mitchell: https://www.collectiveeye.org /products/watched.

9. Matt Ford, "The Case of the Fitness Instructor Who Spied on California Muslims—Then Helped Them Sue the FBI," *New Republic*, November 8, 2021, https://newrepublic.com/article/164295/fbi-fazaga-supreme-court-muslim-surveillance.

10. *Ramy* (2019–present) is a Hulu TV series created by Ari Katcher, Ryan Welch, and Ramy Youssef: https://www.imdb.com/title/tt7649694/.

11. Sylvester A. Johnson, "The FBI and the Moorish Science Temple of America, 1926–1960," in *The FBI and Religion: Faith and National Security Before and After 9/11*, ed. Sylvester A. Johnson and Steven Weitzman (Oakland: University of California Press, 2017), 58. See also Edward E. Curtis IV, "The Black Muslim Scare of the Twentieth Century: The History of State Islamophobia and Its Post-9/11 Variations," in *Islamophobia in America: The Anatomy of Intolerance*, ed. Carl W. Ernst (New York: Palgrave Macmillan, 2013), 75–106.

12. Edward Vernon ("Eddie") Rickenbacker was an American fighter pilot in World War I and a Medal of Honor recipient. With twenty-six aerial victories, he was the most successful and most decorated United States flying ace of the war. "Eddie Rickenbacker," Wikipedia, https://en.wikipedia.org/wiki/Eddie_Rickenbacker.

13. Expert witnesses in premises liability can consult, prepare reports, and testify in litigation to determine if a property owner is legally liable, and damages owed, for accidents and/or injuries that have happened on their land or within their facility. "Premises Liability Expert Witnesses," ALM Experts, https://www.almexperts.com/expert-witness/premises-liability.

CHAPTER 7

1. Public safety spectrum serves the mission-critical communications needs of first responders charged with the protection of life and property, such as police, firefighters, and emergency medical services (EMS) providers. Public safety spectrum also serves the public safety–related telecommunications needs of state and local governments generally. "Public Safety Spectrum," Federal Communications Commission, https://www.fcc.gov/public-safety/public-safety-and-homeland-security/policy-and-licensing-division/public-safety-spectrum.

2. The US Forest Service and other federal agencies hire wildland firefighters at different times of the year, depending on the location. "Wildlife Fire Careers," Forest Service, US Department of Agriculture, https://www.fs.usda.gov/managing-land/fire/careers.

3. Delaney is referring to the school shooting at Stoneland Douglas High School on February 14, 2018, and the Pulse nightclub shooting on June 12, 2016, respectively.

4. The Columbine High School shooting occurred on April 20, 1999.

5. An after-action report is a "document intended to capture observations of an exercise and make recommendations for post-exercise improvements. The final AAR and Improvement Plan (IP) are printed and distributed jointly as a single AAR/IP following an exercise." "Glossary," Federal Emergency Management Agency, https://training.fema.gov/programs/emischool/el361toolkit/glossary.htm.

6. This was an act of domestic terrorism in Tokyo, Japan, on March 20, 1995.

7. FEMA (Federal Emergency Management Agency) describes its recovery centers as "accessible facilities and mobile offices set up after a disaster . . . in an area that offers equal access and resources to everyone." Disaster Assistance, https://www.disasterassistance.gov/get-assistance/forms-of-assistance/4627.

8. The emergency operations center (EOC) is responsible for the strategic overview, or big picture, of any disaster or incident. "Emergency Operations Center," Fulton County Government Services, https://www.fultoncountyga.gov/inside-fulton-county/fulton-county-departments/atlanta-fulton-emergency-management-agency/emergency-operations-center.

9. "EG&G, formally known as Edgerton, Germeshausen, and Grier, Inc., was a United States national defense contractor and provider of management and technical services." Wikipedia, https://en.wikipedia.org/wiki/EG%26G.

10. "Mission Support," SAIC, https://www.saic.com/what-we-do/mission-support.

AFTERWORD

1. US Bureau of Labor Statistics, *Employment Projections 2008–18* (News Release: US Department of Labor, Washington, DC, 2009); US Bureau of Labor Statistics, *Fastest Growing Occupations 2021 and Projected 2031* (Office of Statistics and Employment Projections, Washington, DC: https://www.bls.gov/emp/tables/fastest-growing-occupations.htm, 2022).

2. Winifred R. Poster, "Managing Digital Bodies at the Border: Women's Techno-Affective Labor for the State" (unpublished manuscript, 2022).

3. H. L. Molotch, *Against Security* (Princeton, NJ: Princeton University Press, 2014).

4. A. Chisholm, "Marketing the Gurkha Security Package: Colonial Histories and Neoliberal Economies of Private Security," *Security Dialogue* 45, no. 4 (2014): 349–372, https://doi .org/10.1177/0967010614535832; J. Hearn, "Men /Masculinities: War/Militarism—Searching (for) the Obvious Connections," in *Making Gender, Making War: Violence, Military, and Peacekeeping Practices*, ed. A. Kronsell and E. Svedberg (London: Routledge, 2011), 35–48; P. Higate, "In the Business of (In)Security? Mavericks, Mercenaries and Masculinities in the Private Security Company," in *Making Gender, Making War: Violence, Military, and Peacekeeping Practices*, ed. A. Kronsell and E. Svedberg (London: Routledge, 2011), 182–196; P. Higate and J. Hopton, "War, Militarism, and Masculinities," in *Handbook of Studies on Men and Masculinities*, ed. M. S. Kimmel, J. Hearn, and R. W. Connell (Thousand Oaks, CA: Sage, 2005), 432–447.

5. L. Goodmark, "Hands Up at Home: Militarized Masculinity and Police Officers Who Commit Intimate Partner Abuse," *Brigham Young University Law Review* 5 (November 2015): 1183–1246.

6. W. R. Poster, "Cybersecurity Needs Women," *Nature* 555 (March 29, 2018), 577–580.

7. S. Browne, *Dark Matters: On the Surveillance of Blackness* (Durham, NC: Duke University Press, 2015).

8. P. H. Collins, *Black Feminist Thought: Knowledge, Consciousness, and the Politics of Empowerment*, 2nd ed. (New York: Routledge, 2000); K. Crenshaw, "Demarginalizing the Intersection of Race and Sex: A Black Feminist Critique of Antidiscrimination Doctrine, Feminist Theory, and Antiracist Politics," *University of Chicago Legal Forum* 140 (1989): 139–167.

9. I. Grewal, *Saving the Security State: Exceptional Citizens in Twenty-First-Century America* (Durham, NC: Duke University Press, 2017).

10. W. R. Poster, ed., special issue, "Digitizing Borders, Cities, and Landscapes," *Information & Culture* 57, no. 2 (2022).

11. A. Mbembe, "Necropolitics," *Public Culture* 15 (Winter 2003): 11–40; S. Threadcraft, "Embodiment," in *The Oxford Handbook of Feminist Theory*, ed. L. Disch and M. Hawkesworth (New York: Oxford University Press, 2016), 207–226, https://doi.org/10.1300 /J108v05n03.

12. M. W. Wright, *Disposable Women and Other Myths of Global Capitalism* (New York: Routledge, 2006); S. Valencia, *Gore Capitalism* (Cambridge, MA: MIT Press, 2018).

13. Molotch, *Against Security*.

FIGURES

All images by Danny Goodwin unless otherwise specified.